Reclaiming Culture

reclaim', v.t. & i, & n. Win back or away from vice or error or savagery ... civilize (COD until 1990)

Reclaiming Culture

Indigenous People and Self-Representation

Joy Hendry

palgrave
macmillan

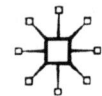

RECLAIMING CULTURE
© Joy Hendry, 2005.

All rights reserved. No part of this book may be used or reproduced in any manner whatsoever without written permission except in the case of brief quotations embodied in critical articles or reviews.

First published in 2005 by
PALGRAVE MACMILLAN™
175 Fifth Avenue, New York, N.Y. 10010 and
Houndmills, Basingstoke, Hampshire, England RG21 6XS
Companies and representatives throughout the world.

PALGRAVE MACMILLAN is the global academic imprint of the Palgrave Macmillan division of St. Martin's Press, LLC and of Palgrave Macmillan Ltd. Macmillan® is a registered trademark in the United States, United Kingdom and other countries. Palgrave is a registered trademark in the European Union and other countries.

ISBN 1–4039–7018–1
ISBN 1–4039–7071–8

Library of Congress Cataloging-in-Publication Data

Hendry, Joy.
  Reclaiming culture : indigenous people and self representation / Joy Hendry.
    p. cm.
  Includes bibliographical references and index.
  ISBN 1–4039–7018–1 (alk. paper)
  ISBN 1–4039–7071–8 (pbk.: alk. paper)
  1. Indigenous peoples—Ethnic identity. 2. Indigenous peoples—Ecology. 3. Indigenous peoples—Education. 4. Racism in museum exhibits. 5. Cultural property—Protection. 6. Cultural property—Repatriation. 7. Culture and tourism. I. Title.

GN495.6.H46 2005
305.8—dc22   2005049182

A catalogue record for this book is available from the British Library.

Design by Newgen Imaging Systems (P) Ltd., Chennai, India.

First edition: October 2005

10 9 8 7 6 5 4 3 2 1

Printed in the United States of America.

For Keith and Phyllis, with thanks

Contents

List of Figures   viii
Note on Spelling and Terminology   ix
Prologue   x

Introduction   1
1. Museums are Transformed   28
2. Aboriginal Tourism and that Elusive Authenticity   56
3. Indigenous or Alter-Native Forms of Cultural Display   81
4. Language and Formal Cultural Education   105
5. Arts, Architecture, and Native Creativity   131
6. Land Claims, Archaeology, and New Communities   156
7. International Links, Cultural Exchange, and Personal Identity   178
8. Conclusions: What We Can Learn   200

Epilogue   218
Index   221

List of Figures

(Photographs by Joy Hendry, except 1.1)

1.1	Model of Baldwyn Spencer in Bunjilaka (reproduced courtesy of Museum Victoria, photograph by John Broomfield).	39
1.2	*Gus-wen-tah*, the two-row wampum, in the Woodland Cultural Centre.	41
1.3	Iroquoian ironworkers display at the Woodland Cultural Centre.	42
2.1	Leonard George in the offices of Historical Xperiences.	72
2.2	Greeting for visitors at the Maori Arts and Crafts Institute.	73
2.3	Men's Fancy dance at the Grand River Powwow, Ohsweken, Ontario.	76
3.1	The Woodland Cultural Centre, formerly the Mohawk Institute.	88
3.2	Keith Jamieson in the Library at the Woodland Cultural Centre.	88
4.1	The First Nations University of Canada building, Regina, Saskatchewan.	122
4.2	Students of the Aang Serian School in Arusha, Tanzania.	124
4.3	Bernadette Wabie talks to a Grade 3 class.	126
5.1	The Jean-Marie Tjibaou Cultural Centre, Noumea, New Caledonia.	134
5.2	The Dänojà Zho Cultural Centre in Dawson City, Yukon.	140
5.3	The Emily C. General School, Ohsweken, Ontario.	142
5.4	"The Great Tree" carving by Stan Hill.	154
6.1	Iqaluit cathedral, Nunavut Territory, Canada.	165

Note on Spelling and Terminology

I mulled for sometime over the question of whether to write appellations such as Aboriginal, First Nations, Indigenous, and Native with capital letters or not, and, indeed, how and when to use the terms in this book. Some of the people who are referred to by such terms find the very words unacceptable, others like a capital letter to be used in reference to themselves. My own first inclination was not to use capitals because the peoples I am describing are clearly all of these things in their own contexts; indeed it is by defining them as such that I chose my subject matter. The people I worked with all claim first status in the lands where they live, and I respect their claims. However, in the end, I decided for two reasons to use the capital letters. First, because it seemed that it would be more offensive to people who like their use not to use them than it would be to my sense of English grammar to use them. Second, it provides a way of emphasizing the shared context within which all the peoples I talk about exist. If, to some people, the use of the terms themselves is offensive, then I apologize unreservedly. Part of the very movement I am describing is that people around the world are regaining pride in their Aboriginal/Native status, and I use the terms always in that context, rather than in any derogatory sense they have acquired in the past.

Another concern was whether I should use capital letters for places of spiritual importance, notably the "longhouse," and I decided to use the capital for its use in that context, but not when it describes a place of residence (as in the past), or learning, as at the University of British Columbia.

As for the spelling of tribal names, this is also difficult, because sometimes several different conventions have been adopted. Here I have as far as possible used the spelling preferred by the people with whom I have worked.

Prologue

> Our Culture was not lost, only silenced for a while . . . but not any more.
>
> Nika Collison, Haida, "Communicating Who We Are"

In the summer of 1971, when traveling around Japan, I visited a place in Hokkaido described as an Ainu village. It contained a couple of rows of houses, built in a fashion that was said to be traditionally Ainu, and a bear was tethered in the middle of the street. In some of these houses, accoutrements of daily and ceremonial life had been arranged for the visitor to examine, and in others, craftspeople were to be found carving wooden bears, very often holding a salmon in their mouths. Those working in the village were wearing garments that one assumed to be Ainu, but when asked if they were actually Ainu people, they shook their heads and explained that they were students from Tokyo engaged in summer employment. One of them went on to tell me that the Ainu people had died out, or become assimilated into mainstream Japanese society, but that if I went with him I might meet the last remaining Ainu man. The person in question was also carving, but he was clearly very old, with a long white beard, and I felt privileged to have met him, though deeply saddened by the situation he portrayed.

Some years later I attended an anthropological conference and heard a middle-aged man, who described himself as Ainu, addressing the audience. He was speaking in Japanese, the language of the assembly, but to my astonishment, he spoke with a strange accent, almost foreign-sounding. Could it be that this man's first language had actually been Ainu, the language that was supposed to have died out with its people? As I listened to his talk, I became aware that there were other Ainu speakers remaining, and some had agreed to offer classes and even to speak on the radio in a special early morning slot that would not—he explained somewhat ruefully—interfere with the regular Japanese language broadcasting. A move was clearly afoot to revive at least the Ainu language.

My next 'Ainu experience' took place in England, when I was asked to help entertain a group of Ainu dancers who were coming to Oxford to perform. They knew little English, but it was assumed that they would know Japanese, and indeed we were able to communicate quite well. They had presented themselves as Ainu, so I asked them if they also considered themselves to be Japanese. They answered without hesitation, "We are the first Japanese." There is a collection of Ainu objects in the Pitt Rivers Museum, and I suggested that we make a tour and see what was in the display. I was unprepared again, particularly for their laughter, and I felt embarrassed to discover that an item used by the Ainu in a sacred ceremony for the soul of a slaughtered bear was displayed upside-down. I'm not sure how they felt about the sometimes quite old and decrepit representations of their culture that were on display, but at least I was able to arrange for the poor bear's skull to be set up the right way.

About ten years later, and over thirty years after my first visit, I made another trip to Hokkaido. This time I encountered a splendid culture center run entirely by Ainu people, including Masahiro Nomoto whom I had inadvertently entertained in Oxford. There I observed carefully produced representations of Ainu activities, past *and* present, and I learned much about Japan's "first peoples," all against the backdrop of the beautiful northern scenery that characterizes their homeland. I also visited two well-stocked museums, one that had been put together by the man I had heard talking at the conference, none other than Shigeru Kayano, who has written some 80 books about his people. I stayed in a hostelry run by an Ainu family, headed by a local Ainu councillor, and I talked to a large number of other people who were happy, once I had described my intentions to their satisfaction, to talk about themselves and their situations as Ainu people.

What then has taken place during this 30-year period? How could a people described by university students as virtually extinct be flourishing again? Where were the people I met on my recent trip 30 years ago? They were certainly not all descended from the one old man I met. For one thing, he lived in a different, distant part of Hokkaido, and in any case, many of them were well over thirty years of age. No, these people have *been there* all along. Presumably, they have *been Ainu* all along. How can it be, then, that university students, wearing Ainu clothes and working in a village set up to represent an Ainu way of life, were describing them as extinct? And what, mercifully, has changed? This book is dedicated to answering questions such as these.

Reference

Collison, Nika, 2002, "Communicating Who We Are: The Qay'llnagaay Heritage Centre Preliminary Content Development Report, Phase 1," Qay'llnagaay Heritage Centre Society.

INTRODUCTION

> For the longest time I didn't know what to say when someone asked if I was "really Indian."
>
> Deborah Doxtator, "The Home of Indian Culture and Other Stories"

This book, and the study on which it is based, were inspired by the transformation described in the Prologue. It is not specifically about the Ainu people—there are Ainu working on their own representation now, and there are growing sources of information in various media. But the Ainu are not the only contemporary people who were almost obliterated from the consciousness of the wider public, and I was further guided into devising the project by the words of an Ainu woman who sought to account for the growth in her people's confidence. She explained, with an expression of some content,

> We discovered that there are other peoples in the world who had been largely erased from their country's memories. We are in touch with each other now, and we are all learning to feel pride in our ancestry again.

This book, which builds on several years of research, recounts a whole range of exciting ways in which people in different parts of the world are doing that learning. It focuses on the reclaiming of cultural identity, and at the same time sets out to explain the importance to the world at large of the movement they are engaged in. My intention here is not to speak *for* these people. Like the Ainu, they are happily there to put their various views for themselves. My job, as I see it, is to create as fine and textured a picture as I can of the extraordinary diversity that was almost obliterated, to demonstrate the breadth and depth of its vibrancy, and to explain why this should matter in a world that had almost forgotten that real people made the objects they admire in museums. My book may also guide readers to visit for themselves some of the many interesting new public outlets that have sprung up around the world as part of this movement of resilience and renewal.

I also want to deal with the embarrassing question of how I and many other members of the 'educated' world were duped into believing that whole groups of our fellow human beings had been wiped out—perhaps even exterminated—or had at least completely lost their cultural heritage. Political and economic explanations abound, and readers in all kinds of circumstances will recognize local factors as they crop up. A larger aim here is to uncover some of the less obvious factors, however, big global factors that have influenced the broad views of the world that many of us learn, and some of us disseminate. Despite opening the book in Japan, my initial context is actually the amorphous, but almost ubiquitous 'Western' world. This is not only because of the frightening power its members have exercised (and still exercise) in appropriating any number of other people's ideas, but also because, perhaps paradoxically, I believe it is this same context that has made possible the cultural renewal that I describe.

The book suggests that many of those involved in the 'wiping' actually had intentions that were quite benevolent. Often enough, they believed they were preserving cultural heritage on behalf of the people whom they thought had lost it. Museum curators, novelists, filmmakers—ethnographers like myself—who became fascinated by the cultural forms of other peoples, created splendid images of those peoples that impressed our audiences. We believed (and some of us still believe) that we were 'educating' those who consumed our work. Indeed, those consumers who take their children to museums, who make a point of keeping up with educational films, and who study anthropology in university, undoubtedly think they are being educated. In practice, I am going to try and show how our very representations have been part of the imprisonment at a point in their past of the people whose cultural features we were trying to 'save'.

An important aim of the book, then, is to reverse the idea that anthropologists, museum curators, and ethnographic filmmakers, among others, work to 'salvage the past', or to record 'disappearing worlds'. Instead, our work on the understanding of diverse peoples, with varying ideas and ways of thought, is a highly relevant contemporary issue. It is also vitally important if we are to prevent the world of knowledge from being swamped by another branch of the same aggressive Western hegemony that presently threatens the economic and ecological makeup of our globe. The diversity we work with is far from disappearing; it continues, and it grows, and it is more complex than scholars in many other disciplines have ever realized. Numerous peoples who had been relegated to the past are alive, quite well, and fostering individuals who speak forcibly for themselves. It could be the anthropologists, curators, and ethnographic filmmakers who are threatened now, but only if we keep excluding the people we work with from our larger discourses.

For years social scientists in various disciplines predicted the disappearance of cultural difference. They were sometimes called convergence theorists. They expected that the spread of systems that their own societies had invented would obliterate all other systems, and they devised theory to bolster that view. They talked of 'modernization' as if this were a phenomenon that would displace cultural and social variety at the same time as spreading knowledge about technological achievements. They looked to philosophical ideas formed during a period in eighteenth-century Europe, that became known as the Enlightenment, literally to enlighten all people everywhere about the advantages of the social systems they saw as superior. They tried to demonstrate the rationality of the 'sciences' that were developed at the time to lead others in their 'progress' toward that same 'development'. A powerful reinforcement came in the nineteenth century when ideas about the evolution of societies toward the model they felt their own exemplified were bolstered by biological ideas about the evolution of all species of life.

Social scientists even reported this trend they had predicted, noting the increasing similarity in commercial outlets throughout the world, the spread of familiar brand names, and the seemingly unstoppable tide of capitalist endeavor. They thought that people would become more and more alike in their thinking, along with their consumerism, and the first large body of material that became known as 'globalization theory' put this case. It was followed by any number of other studies that emphasized instead examples of local difference, phenomena sometimes described as 'glocalization', though some saw this as a temporary matter too, perhaps again to be salvaged as the world became more 'Westernized' or Americanized. Japan was often described as a 'late developer', for example, when it seemed to hang on to clear differences in ways of behaving despite astonishing technological accomplishments (Dore 1973). Others responded to the inaccuracy clearly evident in their first sociological predictions by devising whole new bodies of theory they called 'postmodern', which included something they described as 'fragmentation'.

This book documents a totally conflicting movement, already well recognized by Indigenous people in widely separate parts of the world (see, e.g., Tuhiwai Smith 1999). These are the people who are concerned with recording and displaying their cultural difference, not as a salvage exercise, but as a blueprint for the future of their descendants. They are people actively involved in dismissing and dismantling the way they have been portrayed as extinct, or peoples of the past, perhaps merely offering historical and archaeological color to the nation that exhibits them. Instead, they are building constructions of their own cultural identity as part of the ongoing education of their children. This book portrays the results of some of their efforts, and examines them in relation to past depictions. It explores the rationale for, and the meaning of, these new displays, both for the contemporary people involved, and for the wider public that has for too long been misinformed about the rich diversity that our world has to offer. It also tries to communicate some of the fascinating complexity that has been sorely missing.

My use of the word 'culture' here is taken directly from the presentations that I have been looking at, in 'culture centers', for example, and from the discourses about the need for its reclamation and its healing power. There have been many discussions among social scientists about this notion of 'culture', and one sociology textbook offers five different definitions (Bocock 1992: 231–34), but the differences outlined there largely express changes in its use in the European intellectual context outlined above. In American anthropological debates, the plethora of publications addressing the subject of 'culture' often belittle its value to those who are reestablishing an identity for themselves by 'reclaiming' it, so although I plan to address these questions elsewhere, I would like meanwhile to refer a reader wishing to gain an insight into my own leanings to an excellent article by Marshall Sahlins (1999).

The public places that form the first focus are precisely of the kind described in the Prologue—museums, 'villages', culture centers, even gardens—all manner of sites that offer the 'display' of peoples, their 'artifacts', and their various 'cultural forms'. This kind of display is primary in defining the identity of a group, and as we have seen, it can in fact do this whether the people themselves are there or not. The issue is one of identification, and this book charts a strong demand by people all over the world to identify themselves. It describes a range of displays that have been modified to accommodate these demands, demonstrates how it has become less and less acceptable for groups of people to be entirely represented by others, and it discusses in detail some of the problems that have arisen in places that tried to ignore this trend. It then goes on to examine various ways in which people have sought to represent their own existence, first to themselves, and then to others with whom they interact.

An important part of the focus is on the power these displays can confer—or remove. A recent manifestation of this truism is to be found in the fashion for brand-design. No enterprise worth its salt lacks an image these days, and this image, once designed, is displayed mercilessly in building signs, name cards, notepaper headings, web sites, T-shirts, and tiepins. Through this image, the public recognizes the organization and can locate it and its outlets for all practical purposes. Once an image is known, the use of it confers a tremendous power of identification, and for this reason alone companies and other organizations will pay huge sums to secure a professional job (Matsunaga 2004). Indeed, a band of designers has sprung up and grown rich simply responding to this realization. The misappropriation of a design, on the other hand, is cause for legal action, and if intentional reproduction can be proved, it spells big and expensive trouble for the miscreant—if the owners of the design are deemed to exist, and are in a position to make that claim, that is.

A case we consider again in chapter 1 illustrates just this point. It concerns the way a museum in Canada chose and modified, for an exhibition logo, a design that had been a sacred symbol for a particular Native people who still live in various parts of Canada. The original was taken from an object carried home to Italy by an early-nineteenth-century explorer, but returned to the museum in Canada—not to the people—for an international exhibition, in 1988. Moreover, the 'logo' was modified to incorporate elements of design from other Native peoples whose objects were to be displayed in the exhibition, and its colors were altered, largely for marketing purposes (Phillips 1990: 17–18). The exhibition did cause trouble for the museum, as we shall see, and the good news is that the trouble was eventually instrumental in bringing about a greater cooperation and consultation between museums and the peoples whose objects they display, but, as far as I know, there was no identified group to sue for the use of their design.

Museums actually exemplify an older and more comprehensive example of the power of cultural display in the way they formed a crucial part of nation-building projects. States around the world have invested enormous sums of money in the erection of imposing buildings and monuments, the designing of flags, stamps, and uniforms, the composing of anthems, and in the building and stocking of splendid museums. Within these museums, displays generally illustrate the geography and geology of the nation in question, demonstrate its technological achievements, regale its monarchy and/or political leaders, and recount its history. This last, notably in Europe, depicts evidence of exploration and colonization around the world; in the colonies that were founded—even though they may no longer be colonies—it depicts tales of the arrival and settlement of the personages of such heroic activity. They also usually boast triumph in conquests during wars among neighbors, and include all manner of other explanations and justifications for whatever the contemporary national situation might be.

These national displays also usually include some depiction of the cultural forms of the people who live in the country: their clothing, their housing, their treasured possessions, their lifestyle, and their customs. In times of imperial expansion, it became a measure of power and achievement to display evidence of the 'other' peoples a nation had dominated, and European countries vied with one another to build up collections of artifacts just as they vied with one another for land to dominate. During the nineteenth century, they even also began to bring back samples of the peoples and their 'artifacts' to display at the Great Exhibitions that were all the rage during the time of early industrial and technological development. Japan was for a while among the exotic peoples displayed, but the Japanese worked hard in various ways to create a status comparable with that of the great European powers. In 1910, as part of this process, they brought to the Great Britain–Japan Exhibition in London a group of Ainu people to put on display (Hendry 2000, Street 1992).

I have previously used the concept of 'wrapping' to define all these elements of cultural form. The notion came from Japan, where the wrapping of gifts is a highly elaborate art form, but the principles work quite well everywhere. 'Bodily wrapping' may refer to clothes, jewelry, make-up, tattoos, 'piercing', and other decorations, for example, and buildings, monuments, museums, and all manner of interior décor may be described as the 'wrapping of space'. Formations of human beings, for example in a parade, a dance, or even organized office seating, may be described as 'people wrapping people', and the way they organize the proceedings, the movements, or their meetings may be described as the wrapping of time. Languages devise ways of communicating that wrap messages in elaborations according to the occasion and the people involved, and they may invoke material symbolism as well as words and grammar. Indeed, in Japan, the wrapping of gifts is an important part of this communication, and in unwritten languages all manner of mnemonic devices have been used to prompt oral transmission through generations.

I also argued that the display of these forms of wrapping exhibits their power. Buildings are an obvious example, and no state, province, town, or city lacks a government building to impress its citizens. Most have many more, to show off the establishments that are important to them and their founding history. Most states also organize parades from time to time to illustrate the particular hierarchies they administer, suitably attired in appropriate garments and adorned with hats, badges, and regalia of office and achievement. At the same time, a significant part of the retinue may include all manner of weapons and machinery to demonstrate their readiness to defend the system they have created. The Great Exhibitions, and the World Fairs that followed in America and other parts of the 'New World', were excellent venues for the temporary display of the trappings and wrappings of power, and the national pavilions that were constructed became mobile versions of the museums being built back in the homelands.

The display of peoples and/or their forms of cultural wrapping grew alongside the ideas of social evolution that allowed imperial powers, and their offspring such as the United States, to justify extraordinary interference in the lives of the Natives of the countries where they settled. The 'scientific' explanation of their evolutionary superiority was used as part of the displays, sometimes even as a way of ordering particular peoples at various stages of so-called development. These ideas were then used to rationalize government policies, again supposedly benevolent, to 'help' the peoples that had been dominated to 'develop'. This posture underpinned all sorts of schemes to eliminate the people's own cultural practices, including their languages, as we discuss in some detail in chapter 4. It also systematically destroyed perfectly successful but 'inferior' ways of making a living off the land, which governments then appropriated and reallocated for supposedly 'superior' practices of which the peoples had no knowledge or experience. To this day, members of many succeeding governments and the societies they govern wonder why their Native people are so poor and demoralized.

More subtly, individuals operating within their big material manifestations of power learn to manipulate linguistic and other smaller symbolic forms of wrapping in dealing with each other, and in negotiating with representatives of other systems with whom they may engage—for trade, for example, and for alliance and diplomacy. I argued too that those most skilled at these arts are able to understand different forms of wrapping, use them to their own advantage, and neatly switch between them. In periods of worldly exploration, initial encounters between people who did not share a spoken language made much use of gifts and other material objects in their communication, and subsequent negotiations included objects of the mnemonic kind that had for long been used by nonliterate people as historical records. How much shared understanding ensued at the time is a subject for historians, but objects such as these form another important focus in this book, for some of them became valued parts of museum collections and are now sought for return by their original owners.

The fate of these objects provides one example of what happens when peoples have important parts of their cultural wrapping appropriated by another group. In the ensuing chapters, we consider many others. In an obvious way, this is what happens when nations go to war. They destroy each other's buildings, occupy each other's land, and take over the lives of ordinary citizens living in the war zone. Much less obvious, but perhaps even more insidious, is what happens when people 'explored', 'discovered', and claimed for themselves vast areas of occupied land that they classified as 'empty' (*terra nullis*) because the 'inferior' people living there had very different ideas about their relationship with that land. The images the new nations built up as they formed their museums and monuments included the cultural wrappings of the people they had subsumed into their new territories, and on whom they practiced policies of assimilation. They also sent home examples of the 'wrappings' of the culture of these peoples as evidence to those back home of their powers around the world.

In this way, the cultural 'wrapping' or 'clothing' of colonized peoples was disseminated throughout the world and within the new nations that were formed around them. Stereotypical false images took root in the minds of the wider public, and they were perpetuated over the ensuing years. An exciting part of the process of cultural reclamation, which we discuss in more detail in chapter 2, was an exhibition entitled *Fluffs and Feathers*, which took on the task of examining just this subject. Held at the Woodland Cultural Centre in Brantford, Ontario, and curated entirely by First Nations people, the exhibition displayed all kinds of material manifestations of what the museum director described as "these absurd and inaccurate impressions of our culture" (Hill T.V. 1992: 6). It responded to "the dire need to educate the non-Native public to the reality of the historical and contemporary culture of our people and the pervasiveness of stereotypes" (ibid.) and invited the "the quiet questioning of good people; people who will reject the false and seek the true understanding of those neighbors who are of the First Nations of this Continent" (Bedard 1992: 5).

This Woodland Cultural Centre is the place where I did my most detailed research for this project and I chose it for several reasons. One of these was the comprehensive way in which it covers most of the aspects of cultural renewal that are discussed in this book, and material I learned there appears in almost all the chapters. Another very practical reason was the international reputation that this center has built up, so that I heard of its work before I left my desk in England, and applied for a grant specifically to spend time there. Probably the most important reason, however, is the long experience it has had, for its period of activity spans the whole 30 years covered in the transformation of the Ainu situation described in the preface, and reading the documents pertaining to its work provides an excellent case history of the practice of cultural renewal by a group of First Nations living in the woodland region of the area of the world now known as Canada.

To get a more in-depth feel for the experience of Native people who had been portrayed so falsely, I also spent several months staying on the reserve of the Six Nations of the Grand River, home of the Haudenosaunee people who took the side of the British in the American revolution and thus ended up living on the Canadian side of a border they still don't fully recognize. The family that put me up (for further details, see the acknowledgments in the next section) included Keith Lickers, the man who wrote the original feasibility study for the Woodland Cultural Centre, now an employee of the Ontario Ministry of Education, and his wife, Phyllis, whose grown children filled many important positions in the community and in wider networks of First Nations people. It was a great opportunity to get to know some of the real people who had been portrayed so falsely, and to learn first hand how it feels to live in a community where tourists stop while driving by to ask Native people washing their cars, or mowing the grass in front of their houses, "where are the Indians then?"

It was also in Canada, at EXPO 67, that an important reversal was initiated in the way that peoples were portrayed at the magnificent Exhibitions and World Fairs that have punctuated international trade and cultural exchange since the mid-nineteenth century. In 1967, at the 'universal exhibition' held in Montreal, nations from all over the world, as had become customary, built pavilions to display their wares and accomplishments. Canada, as host, had several of its own pavilions, and agreed that First Nations people should put one together too. They had still to choose that name—First Nations—but the pavilion told the story of the peoples who were living on the site of the exhibition when it was 'discovered' by Europeans in a most poignant and powerful way. I happened to visit this pavilion, and I can still recall some of images that were depicted there, so I was delighted to meet, during this research, two of the individuals who had been involved. One of them was Tom Hill, the museum director of the Woodland Cultural Centre, quoted above, whose name will pop up again in different chapters for he has spent his life working relentlessly toward the reclamation of the culture of his and other First Nations. The other was the Chef de Mission, Andrew de Lisle, and we meet him in chapter 2.

The late 1960s was a turning point for many people in the new world that was created by the children born after the devastation of World War II, or the Pacific War as it is known by those who were not involved in the war described, with the usual European bias, as World War I. Students demonstrated almost simultaneously in capital cities of at least three continents—notably in Paris, Mexico, and Tokyo—and they were forcibly subdued. So, eventually, were the Native people of America who occupied the island of Alcatraz, site of the former prison in San Francisco Bay, and sought to claim back the country they had lost. But the movement for change—and a new freedom—was unstoppable, and it frames nicely the movement for cultural renewal that I have chosen as the focus of this book.

This study tracks broadly some of the many things that have happened during the period of 30 years covered by the tale told in the Prologue then. It seeks not only to explain *how* cultural forms were imprisoned in the past, but what has now made it possible for a people described by university students as virtually extinct to be flourishing again. It tries to explain why people who may have tried to pass as members of the wider public and deny their Native past have now rekindled a pride in their ancestry. It is a complicated story, which has been built up in many different parts of the world, and it unfolds gradually throughout the chapters of the book, though details of the actual sites of research may be found in the acknowledgments and methodology section that follows this one. It is also in some ways the story of what has become known as globalization, but from the point of view of people who were at first swept away in the tracks of too much theorization.

The theory here is quite simple. It proposes that before people can engage in any kind of action—for example the legal action that might be taken when a logo, or vast tracts of land, are stolen—they need to have an identity. Only then can they go on to engage acceptably and successfully in the political activities necessary to retrieve them. In other words, the expression of cultural form, which defines a people, or a 'nation', call it what you will, is an essential part of cultural revival when people and their very existence as an entity has been presented as eliminated, or at the very least under severe threat. Thus the culture centers I describe are not found so readily in areas where people still speak their own languages, live on land they regard as their own, and go about lives close to the ones they learned from their ancestors, whatever their allegiance with regard to nationhood.

It is rather in areas where First Peoples were subjected to programs of deliberate assimilation, intentional or unintentional genocide, or simply systematically represented to the world at large as having become extinct—their lands being deemed *terra nullis*—that their revival is required if they are to act as an entity. Only then, when they have recreated an identity that can be named and recognized, can they engage in political activities such as claims to their ancestral lands and demands for a system of self-governance. These political activities are well covered elsewhere and are not discussed in great detail here, though some cases will be raised toward the end of the book, where the interesting situation is considered of Aboriginal peoples turning the tables on being represented, and instead employing non-Aboriginal experts in various fields to help with their representation. Chapters in the book also address deeper expressions of renewal such as the revival of languages and cultural knowledge, the proliferation of Aboriginal art and architecture as examples of tremendous Aboriginal creativity, and the reclamation of ancestral remains and stolen regalia.

Many of the people I have been working with are *having* to revive their languages and cultures because they and their parents and grandparents were told that their ways of speaking and of making a living were 'bad', 'backward', even 'demonic', and that at the very least they were hindering their 'progress' in the 'developing' world. Many of these people were subjected to 'assimilation programs', punished severely for speaking their own languages, and forced to attend schools that undermined their self-confidence for generations to come. Fortunately, these programs eventually failed, and quite a number of the First Peoples they were aimed at have survived to tell the tale, and to work to renew their cultural wealth. This book retells their story, and I argue at the end of the book that if enough of us take the trouble to listen to them and their powerful messages, we might even be able to rescue our world from some of the forces of physical destruction that currently form a major threat to our globe.

The reasons that people were depicted as 'dying out', or even extinct, are various, and they often reflect the wider plans of the governments of countries where they are found. Even these were still sometimes quite 'benevolent' in intention, but in many parts of the world the effects have been devastating. In the end all those stories could have been self-fulfilling, and there are those involved in their telling, or the support of it, who were aware and encouraging of that possibility. But something called 'culture' is a powerful tool, and self-identity a strong personal need, both now used as a form of 'healing'. This book shows how, and it brings the good news that many peoples around the world, like the Ainu, think of themselves as having survived the efforts of the mainstream societies to wipe them out. They have survived, and unsurprisingly, they now want to do their own representation. The book examines how we, the wider public, can continue to value our fascination with cultural form without letting it devalue any of the forms we value.

Acknowledgments and Methodology

I set out to examine this subject in a most unconventional way by usual anthropological standards, indeed by any academic standards, and I have built up the knowledge I have acquired to write this book more than ever through the kind cooperation of a large number of people. A (Western) scholar would normally expect to read all the books and other materials about the people with whom he or she intended to work, but I have visited so many different peoples that I could not have read all the books had I spent several lifetimes devoted entirely to the task. I have not even read a few books about many of the people I have visited, some of whom are anyway quite scathing about a lot of the things that have been written about them. Instead, I have traveled around the world scrutinizing museums, culture centers, and other forms of material display that purport to represent people, and I have relied on friends and other anthropologists to introduce me to members of those 'people' themselves to help me interpret the displays. This way I have been able to evaluate the extent to which they present an accurate picture of the contemporary social or cultural groups to which those people claim allegiance, and see how far they are involved in their own representation.

In anthropological terminology, this could be, perhaps, called global fieldwork, and my acknowledgments of assistance have in practice become part of the explanation of the methodology I have used for the study. Anthropologists do not usually mention all the people they have consulted in their fieldwork, and I suspect that this is one of the reasons why the people they worked with have begun to resent their work. For an (old-hand) anthropologist to travel to places about which they know almost nothing is a humbling experience, and it certainly made clear to me the value of individuals I met locally who could even just guide me about, let alone help to interpret the materials I was examining. There will be some of those 'guides' whose names I didn't note down—some were even just 'doing their job' as drivers of taxis or various forms of public transport—but I want to thank those too, for without the helpful ones, I could not have even got beyond the tourist zones. The whole project has also been a learning experience in how to do this kind of work, and with time I have grown more accomplished at keeping a proper record of those who have helped me.

A list of names is boring to the reader who knows few of those mentioned, and because I relied so heavily on the people I am going to thank, I would like to take you, the reader, virtually to meet some of those people and learn a little about them. For this reason, the section headed 'acknowledgments' in this book is longer than most, and I have added the other term 'methodology' to the title to explain this length. Other names mentioned here appear again in the text of the book, and you learn more of them there. I hope, by this means to give readers a clear idea of how the material was gathered, and allow you to assess for yourselves the nature of the work. I am of course responsible for the writing of the book, and the way I have interpreted the information I collected, though I have also tried as far as possible to send portions of my writing back to the people whose words I am using for verification. However, I may have mistaken or misrepresented some of the intentions of those who spoke to me, so if you disagree with anything you read here, I recommend that you shoot the messenger in this case, not those I have quoted.

The next problem is to decide where to start, for the project has been many years in the making, and I have found myself drawing on ideas that entered my head as many as 35 years before the time of writing. However, I have published work along the way, and in each volume, I have tried to thank those who helped me, so I have decided to refer first to the two major pieces of research that have led me to the thinking that informs this one. In the introduction, I have explained some of my ideas about culture as a form of wrapping, and the book *Wrapping Culture* lists the many people who contributed in one way or another to the ideas laid out there (Hendry 1993: vii–ix). The other volume that leads almost seamlessly into this one—though focusing on a part of the world less well covered here—is *The Orient Strikes Back* and there I thanked many people who helped with that (Hendry 2000: xi–xiii).

For the start of this particular part of the project, I am particularly indebted to friends and colleagues at the Pitt Rivers Museum—for their advice, and for introductions to some of their seminar speakers who gave me invaluable support when I visited them elsewhere. Laura Peers is the star here, for giving me much information about the North American part of my journey, for allowing me to audit her class on 'Museums and Source Communities', and for inviting the people I mention shortly to give seminars. Chantal Knowles, now in the Royal Scottish Museum, along with Chris Gosden, advised me about where to visit in the South Pacific, who to meet when I got there, and how to acquaint myself with some of the issues particularly important in that part of the world before I left.

My first journey was a round-the-world trip, largely to get a feeling for the subject I had decided to pursue, though as I have discussed already elsewhere in a longer paper about the methodology of this project (Hendry 2003), I did not yet have a clear idea what exactly that subject was! I know, however, that it was in part inspired by a talk given at the Pitt Rivers by Nokomis Paiz, an Ojibwe woman who expressed movingly an opposition between abhorring to the point of physical sickness the preservation of human remains and sacred objects in the Museum, and a simultaneous appreciation that there would be no material record of the past of her people if such collections had not been made. Nokomis told us that her mother, Jody Beaulieu, had been setting up a record of the cultural foundations of her people in a Tribal Information Center, located at the site of her home in Red Lake Nation, North Minnesota. After the talk, Nokomis was most encouraging when I asked if I could visit Red Lake, and Marcia Anderson, from the Minnesota Historical Society, who had brought Nokomis to Oxford, and who is responsible for the care of many objects originating there, also welcomed me warmly when I visited the History Center in St. Paul.

As for Jody, herself, when I met her at a feast she invited me to attend in response to my e-mail of inquiry, she could not have made a stronger impression had she tried. She introduced me directly to the plight of a people who have had their cultural clothing appropriated; she bluntly criticized members of my profession who have helped in that stripping process; and she demonstrated clearly some of the ways that her people are reviving their strength and their regalia. Her welcome was nonetheless warm and I am indebted to her for opening my eyes. We meet her again in chapter 3.

Next I must introduce a long-standing friend who greatly facilitated my visit to Red Lake and several later research locations by driving me to them and by providing a wealth of local background knowledge. Mary Louise Bracho and I shared accommodation many years ago in Mexico City; she now lives in Chanhassen, Minnesota, and her occupation as a historical novelist allows her to be mistress of her own time. She and her parents have also taken an interest in Native American people and their forms of cultural display for much of their own lifetimes, and together they could give me an insight, which would have been difficult otherwise to locate, about where I might find places to visit, and about how these have changed during the 30 years I have chosen to make my focus. A couple of years after this first visit, Mary and I drove 3,997 miles together visiting museums and cultural centers all across the Plains of the United States and back through the Canadian Prairies. Much of the value of chapter 1 of this book would be diminished had I not had access to her old-hand visitor's knowledge and her fine powers of observation.

Back to my first trip, then, which I have to admit was largely organized around the advice of friends and contacts in far-flung places, though my next destination—Mexico City—was chosen because I had worked there in the past, and already had the language and considerable local knowledge. Here I was lucky enough to be invited to stay with Patti Brewster, a Mexican friend who had spent time in Oxford, and she provided a first haven in a city that seems a lot more dangerous now than when I lived there some 30 years ago. Her friend German Perez, of the Facultad Latinoamericana de Ciencias Sociales, not only introduced me to several people who helped me in the week that followed, but also dispatched me in a car to the crucial first couple of appointments. Patti and German advised me to visit Oaxaca, rather than Chiapas, which was my first intention, and here Teresa Morales, of the local branch of the *Instituto Nacional de Antropología e Historia* (INAH), kindly drove me out to the Zapotec community at Santa Ana del Valle, which we visit in chapters 1 and 3. I would like to thank all these people, as well as Virginia García Acosta, Jaime Bailón Corres, Sergio Saramiento, and Carlos Varo Berra for advice along the way, and the people of Santa Ana del Valle who spent time with me during my visit whose names I sadly neglected properly to record.

My next big thank you must go to Peter Surman, father of my former student Bronwen, who on the basis of that relationship alone drove the sometimes quite treacherous road from Suva to Nandi to make me welcome in Fiji, put me up, introduced me to many of his friends and acquaintances, and even lent me his car so that I could visit various cultural centers there while he was at work. He and his family also provided me with much background material about Fiji, and gave me an insight into the lives of long-term ex-pat compatriots who work on in the postcolonial world they have helped to build. For a native

Fijian perspective, I would particularly like to thank Peter's helper, Dorothy, Sangali Buadromo and Tarisi Sorovi of the National Museum, and Leone Yaragamudu in the Pacific Harbour Cultural Centre.

I traveled from Fiji to Vanuatu, and there, thanks again to Peter, I was made welcome by Tony Somers Vine, who took me along to a gathering at the University of the South Pacific which was a good opportunity informally to meet ni-Vanuatu people such as Ralph Regenvanu, who will appear in later chapters of this book, and another Fijian, Epeli Hau'ofa, whose Oceania Centre for Arts and Culture we visit in chapter 5. Mary Patterson, of the University of Melbourne, was an invaluable source of advice in my preparations to visit Vanuatu, and locally, Joy Wu, proprietor of the Kaiviti Hotel, was a mine of information. I must thank Ralph Regenvanu for the time he found for this totally ignorant visitor (me) in his busy life, and in New Caledonia, I would like to thank Emmanuel Kasarhérou for the same courtesy.

On this, my first visit to New Zealand, I was made to feel welcome by a fellow Japan-specialist, Ken Henshall and his family, who met me in Auckland, offered me excellent hospitality in Hamilton, and drove me to Rotorua to visit the museum and cultural centers there. Ken invited me to give a talk at Waikato University, and there I benefited greatly from meeting the late Hirini Melbourne in Maori Studies, Mike Goldsmith and colleagues in the Anthropology Department, and Mike Roberts in Japanese Studies. On my second visit to New Zealand, a couple of years later, Sally Simpson in Wellington and Crispin and Fiona Shore in Auckland were kind enough to put me up, and to share with me their links with Maoridom, which again helped the progress of this project. This time, thanks go especially to Erenora Puketapu-Hetet and Patsy Puketapu in Lower Hutt, and Ann Sullivan and Maureen Landers at the University of Auckland. Fuli Pereira, curator of the Pacific collection at the Auckland Museum, was also extremely helpful.

I visited Malaysia on that first round-the-world journey, where A.B. Shamsul, professor of the University Kebangsaan Malaysia, invited me to make a presentation, arranged wonderful accommodation for me in Selangor, and introduced me to his student, Athi Sivan, who was an excellent guide. Athi took me to visit many places, both those I had myself identified in advance, and others that he thought might be useful for my study, and I learned a huge amount. I haven't made much reference to Malaysia in this book because the material I gathered there does not really fit the remit, but the overall experience of that visit made an important contribution to my thinking at the time, and I am grateful to them both.

A year after that first trip, I had the opportunity to attend a conference in Tanzania and I applied for a grant to spend the rest of the spring vacation pursuing some of the ideas I had been gathering in this African context. My experience of traveling to many places in a short period of time had made me aware of the amount of local help I would need, and I was careful this time to make detailed plans in advance. These worked out extraordinarily well, and I would like first to thank Pat Caplan for putting me in touch with Tony Janes, who is a local travel agent to beat all local travel agents. First, he arranged for me to take part in some examples of cultural tourism, which formed an interesting and very African part of the project itself, which is discussed in chapter 2. Secondly, he arranged for me to be met by reliable and interesting local driver-guides at all points of arrival so that I lost none of my precious short-time consulting maps and timetables. All my African guides spoke excellent English, as well as Kiswahili and their own tribal languages, and they provided much local cultural information as well as being good companions for the sometimes quite long journeys. Again, I regret that I did not properly record all their names. Tony also organized for me to meet and spend time with the artist Robino N'tila, whose international reputation, knowledge, and networks sadly only became clear to me too late for a proper appreciation at the time, and I would like to thank him now for all his help and introductions. His help is made clear in chapter 5. I must also thank the Nuffield Foundation for the small grant that supported this part of the research.

For excellent information before and during the conference I would like to thank the director of the National Museum of Kenya, George Abungu, whose lecture is discussed in chapter 1, and his colleague Hassan Wario Arero, whose e-mails were helpful before I even arrived. Hassan introduced me to John Rigano, of the Ethnography Department, who later gave me a great tour of the museum in Nairobi and several outlying locations, and was a fund of information about his own Rendille tribal circumstances. During the conference, Liv Haram introduced me to Tom Ole-Sikar, a very dynamic Maasai man who had been running the local program of cultural tourism, and was very informative and helpful. Last, but certainly not least, I must thank Gemma Burford and her fiancé, now husband, Lesikar Ole Ngila (see figure 4.2), for arranging a wonderful visit to a local Maasai community, and for providing much ongoing information about the educational work they are both engaged in, which is discussed in chapter 4.

Collecting information in this piecemeal manner was all very well, and it was vital to my overall understanding of this project, but I felt that I needed to look at one place in detail to gain a more in-depth knowledge of what I was doing. By far the longest and most productive part of this research, then, was carried out in Canada during a period of two terms' leave from my usual duties, made possible by the T.H.B. Symons Fellowship in Commonwealth Studies and a Leverhulme Study Abroad Fellowship. I am immensely grateful to both these bodies for this period of almost uninterrupted research, and I thank Matt Cooper and his colleagues at the Department of Anthropology at McMaster University for allowing me to hold the tenure of these awards there, and particularly Trudy Nicks, one of the people I met through the Pitt Rivers, who was my chief mentor during this time. She introduced me to the Department, to the Woodland Cultural Centre, and to the family with whom I lodged for a large part of the time. She and her husband John Nicks also made me welcome in their home when I first stepped off the plane and offered me an immeasurable amount of good advice on a great range of topics.

The postgraduate students at "Mac" at the time were also wonderfully friendly and full of good ideas and advice, and I only don't name them all here because I am afraid I may hurtfully forget one, so mobile were they. One of them, Linda Scarangella, is mentioned below, but collectively, I thank them all for their welcome. Members of the faculty were also good to be among, and I would like particularly to thank Harvey Feit, Eva Mackey, Andrew Martindale, Wayne Warry, and Matt Cooper for sharing their local knowledge and listening to my undoubtedly naive enthusiasm as a newcomer in their midst. Ravi de Costa, a postdoctoral fellow working on "Globalization" at the time, was also a stimulating person to share ideas with, and Dawn Martin-Hill, head of the Indigenous Studies Programme, was a patient, if somewhat reluctant source of good advice about my stay on the Reserve, which is also her home. Sonja Green, a student of Indigenous Studies at the time, was unreservedly helpful and welcoming, and I am particularly grateful for her insights. Last, but of course not least, I thank Rosita Jordan, Janis Weir, and Rabia Awan for practical support in the Anthropology Office, and Gerald Bierling for technical help with e-mail and other computing problems.

Phyllis Lickers, with whom I lodged for several months on the Six Nations Reserve, made me more than welcome in her lovely home from the moment I finally arrived—after losing my way for several hours. I am also immeasurably grateful to her husband, Keith, for his patience in explaining basic elements of the relationship between his Native people and the Canadian government, which are probably well known to most people who have been brought up there. He and

Phyllis knew most of the people with whom I came into contact during the local research, and they were always willing to help me to work out complications, and to fill in details I might otherwise have missed. Phyllis's two children with Keith, and six by her former marriage to the late Robert Jamieson, all live within the community, and together with their own many offspring, and burgeoning offspring of offspring, they made me deeply aware of the value of strong family ties. These 'children', and several of their spouses, actually hold important positions in the wider Aboriginal world, and I would like to thank them all for sharing aspects of their lives with the curious foreigner in their midst.

The story of two consecutive days in May will serve to illustrate the point. They were a Sunday and Monday, the latter set aside in Canada to celebrate the birthday of Queen Victoria. On the Six Nations Reserve, the holiday Monday is known as Bread and Cheese Day because everyone who lives there is given a sizeable chunk of bread and cheese to celebrate the way Queen Victoria annually remembered their loyalty to the British by doing just the same. Fireworks are let off the evening before, and the whole family gathered at the home of Roberta, the current chief of the elected Band Council, to sit around a bonfire and watch the show. In the afternoon, Phyllis's eldest daughter Mary, an influential Aboriginal consultant, offered me a computer at her house for some work I had to complete. Once it was done, she invited me to share the delicious dinner being prepared by her younger sister Connie, specialist in Aboriginal tourism, with another sister Kathy, a land claims lawyer, plus her brother David, her daughter Erica, and their respective partners and children.

The next day there was a parade, and the family gathered again to watch it pass at a corner in the center of the village where they used to live many years ago. Here I met Phyllis's eldest son, Ronnie, who looks after Aboriginal customers at the Bank of Montreal, and his wife Rebecca, who helps local young people to find and fund their post-secondary education. Another son, Mark, is a builder and he introduced me to his boss Brian Porter, the architect who designed the school buildings that are discussed in chapter 5. His wife, Linda, had set up the gift shop at the Woodland Cultural Centre. The last remaining son is Keith Jamieson (figure 3.2), to whom I am particularly indebted for he is a local historian and exhibitor who was taking care of the Library and Resource Centre at the Woodland Cultural Centre, and was (and is) most generous with his time and vital information. His wife, Cathy, was a senior teacher in another school (discussed in chapter 4) and I was delighted when the two of them came to visit me in the United Kingdom.

At the Woodland Cultural Centre, many other people generously gave time to help with this project. Tom Hill was the first person I contacted, as head of the museum, and partner with Trudy Nicks in the Task Force I discuss in chapter 1. He gave me a great introduction to the place, and was always welcoming when he found me wandering around there. I didn't meet Amos Key until later, but he was executive director at the time, and was also most welcoming, especially at various meetings of the Sweetgrass First Nations Language Council, whose work is discussed in detail in chapter 4. Angie Monture and Joan Greenbird must also be thanked here for much practical help as well as useful information for the research. Amos resigned his post to devote his time to developing a performing arts center that is described in chapter 5, and before I left a new director was appointed, a young woman named Janis Monture. It seemed I already knew Janis quite well, for an exhibition she mounted had been in place when I arrived and she had allowed me to tag along on various tours she led around the museum when she was working as an assistant to Tara Fromen, the education officer. Tara is a trained anthropologist as well as a Native member of the Six Nations, and she was always happy to turn over ideas, as well as to give me her views on a variety of subjects. For information on educational outreach, and some more tagging along, I would also like to thank Bernadette Wabie (see figure 4.3) who was another great person to discuss things with. In the gift shop and reception area, Darlene Hill and Jessica Hill during the week, and Sonja Green at weekends, were always friendly faces and founts of information. [Jessica soon moved to work as Tom Hill's secretary, and she was always helpful later when I sent back parts of my writing for review.] Other members of the center will appear in chapters of this book, and I would like to express my gratitude to all of them for their support.

During my stay in Canada, I also tried to visit a sample of other museums and First Nations on both sides of the present border with the United States, and many people were generous with their time. Some of their names crop up in later chapters, but let me mention a few of them here as I draw you into another whistle-stop tour. My first trip away from the Reserve was to see an old friend, Gill Wogin, in Ottawa, who met me at the airport, put me up, and helped me to orientate myself in visits around the city. I made contact with several government departments, including Canadian Heritage, and the Treasury, where Gill works, and I visited the Canadian Museum of Civilisations, where Andrea Laforet invited me to a splendid lunch and provided me with much useful information. I was also made welcome at the busy head office of the First Nations Confederation of Cultural Education Centres (FNCCEC), where national coordinator Claudette Commanda, filled me in on much of what they do. She later arranged for me to attend their annual conference, which is discussed in chapter 3, and I thank her and Gilbert Whiteduck, president at the time, for allowing me to be there, and to share the experience of Hurricane Juan, which hit the town of Halifax while we were there!

I made a longish trip to the West Coast of Canada, where I built up many obligations. First, in Vancouver, Jill Baird gave me some of her precious time at the Museum of Anthropology at the University of British Columbia, and I was delighted to meet Michael Ames, who was acting as interim director, although officially retired. Later, I had a wonderful tour of the museum with Xai:sla student, Frances ("Fran") Bolton, and later still, with the new director, Anthony Shelton. I would like to thank Linda Scarangella for sharing her research on the Hiwus Feast House on Grouse Mountain (which is presented in chapter 2) and Bob Baker for making me welcome during that first visit, and for meeting me again in 2004 and giving me a tour of Squamish territory. He appears again in chapter 7. During both my visits to Vancouver for this research, Naomi Brown, a former student of the Department of Anthropology in Oxford, offered me good local advice, and on the second occasion, very pleasant accommodation. She and her husband, Alan, also gave me a welcome glimpse into the Chinese community in Vancouver.

On my first visit to the West Coast, I flew directly from Vancouver to the Haida Gwaii, islands that are mentioned in several chapters of this book, and I must thank Anita Herle, of the Museum of Archaeology and Anthropology in Cambridge, who encouraged me to go there in the first place. At the Haida Gwaii Museum in Skidegate, director Nathalie MacFarlane, and Nika Collison, prime mover behind the new Qay'llnagaay project that we hear about in chapter 3, made me welcome and offered me much local information. I thank them, and Vince Collison, who came back to work well after five to answer my queries in Old Massett—again, details in chapter 3. Gracie, at my hotel "Gracie's Place," was also very helpful, as was her daughter, Kate-lyn, who was home from university for the summer, and was working at the museum.

The crossing from Skidegate to Prince Rupert was a little rough (notorious, I later discovered), and the timing of the less frequent boats and planes in the area meant that I arrived on and could stay only for a weekend, but Susan Marsden, director of the Museum of Northern British Columbia there, and Lindsey Martin, a graduate of the Canadian Museum of Civilisations Aboriginal training course, about whom I had heard in Ottawa, were kind enough to come out to lunch with me. The conversations we had were very interesting and I thank them both. Prince Rupert also offered a couple of surprises. First, it was the weekend of the Sea Fest, which had a great parade, including two or three flamboyant groups of the local First Nations, and second, I met a young Nisga'a man named Chris Nelson. Chris had recently graduated from an Aboriginal Tourism Management Programme at a First Nations Training and Development Centre, and he was full of enthusiasm to offer a genuine cultural experience to the large captive audience of Arctic cruise visitors who stop in there. This kind of cultural tourism is discussed in chapter 2.

My next port-of-call was Whitehorse, in the Yukon, and here I owe a big debt of gratitude to Dave Neufeld, of Parks Canada. Dave came to give a talk at the Pitt Rivers just before I left, and if he had not, I would have missed a great piece of this research, for I had not intended to visit the Yukon until that time. His inspiring talk, entitled "Our Land is Our History Book," was about the Athapaskan peoples who live there, and when I decided to follow up his suggestion to include it in my itinerary, he also introduced me to several of his good contacts among them. Details of the trip we made up to Dawson City can be found in chapter 2, but it would be no exaggeration to say that his local knowledge and his willingness to share it, transformed my visit completely. I would also like to thank Carla, the proprietor of the B&B that Dave booked me into in Whitehorse, who was not only a wonderful hostess, but took me (along with her visiting aunt) up to the Tlingit Cultural Centre in Teslin and introduced me to local architect Gunter Glaeser. Diane Strand, heritage resources officer of the Champagne and Aishihik First Nation, kindly made time to see me at short notice, and we meet her again in chapter 6. At the Tr'ondëk Hwëch'in Cultural Centre in Dawson City, Glenda Bolt, Georgette McLeod, and Freda Roberts were all very generous with their time, despite being in the middle of organizing a huge celebration, and I thank them for that. Their help is evident in several chapters of this book.

After the Yukon, I flew back to Vancouver, where I took a few days off with my son, before heading over to Vancouver Island, and from there down to Washington State. We drove up to the north to visit the U'Mista Cultural Centre that is discussed in several chapters, and I would like to thank Andrea Sanborn for giving me time, both there, and later at a meeting of the FNCCEC where she took the trouble to read and comment on some of the anthropological writings about the place that she had not formerly seen. We did a real flying visit to the Burke Museum at the University of Washington in Seattle, where George McDonald was kind enough to take me to lunch, and to tell me about his considerable involvement with several of the museums that we discuss in the next chapter. I would also like to throw out a thank you to a man named Bruce working in the history section of Blackwells in Oxford who sent me to the Makah Cultural Centre that is the scene of an important point made in chapter 6.

Other visits I made during my time in Canada included a short stay in Montreal, where I thank Margaret and Richard Lock for their very pleasant and congenial hospitality, as well as a fund of local knowledge. Here I visited the Avataq Cultural Institute, which is described in chapter 6, and I thank Sylvie Coté Chew and Taqraliq Partridge for their time and abundant information. I also crossed the bridge to the Mohawk community of Kahnawake, which will be mentioned in several chapters, and I would like to thank Kanatakta, Andrew DeLisle, Melvin Tekahonwén:sere Diabo, Jamie-Lee (or Kanonwiioustha), and Kara Dawne Zeme for sharing their time and knowledge. I also had a pleasant lunch with Toby Morantz and George Wenzel, who were full of good ideas and local knowledge about both Montreal and the Arctic.

I actually set off for the new territory of Nunavut with only a couple of brief introductions from Nelson Graburn, who had worked there many years before, but nevertheless generously shared the names of his contacts with me. Some replied to my e-mails of inquiry, some didn't, so I was particularly grateful to those who were willing to spend time with me. My first acknowledgment must actually be to a person whose only obligation was that I had picked his B&B out of the Nunavut Tourism Guide, however, for Terry Forth, who runs "the Beaches," was a mine of helpful local information. He met me and deposited me at the airport for each of my flights in and out of Iqaluit, which were several and included a period of uncertainty when the whole of southern Ontario was blacked out during a power cut. He gave me an initial general tour of Iqaluit, with specific details about places of particular interest to me, he provided a daily weather forecast, both there, in Ontario, and back home in the United Kingdom, and he helped me to find and contact several people who proved very helpful to my research. I could not have chosen better accommodation. Also in Iqaluit, Pauline Scott of Parks Canada invited me to a delicious dinner and gave me helpful advice, Jim Tegler and Jamal Shirley of the Nunavut Research Institute generously shared information, and Jimmy Ekho, at the Nunatta Sunakkaangit Museum, was a fount of local knowledge. Details of the visit can be found in chapter 6.

In Kimmirut, I had an abundance of attention, for I was met at the airport by both Kyra Fisher, economic development officer in the local government, introduced to me by Nelson, and by Suzie, daughter of the home stay family I had booked, who was also employed in the Tourist Office. Both Kyra and "my family" were wonderfully hospitable, and Kyra furnished me with a list of further names to follow up, as well as a windproof coat to supplement my inadequate clothing! In Pangnirtung, I had no prior contacts to look up, but Pudloo Kilabuk, who ran the B&B I had booked, treated me like a family guest and provided me with two nourishing meals a day as well as the expected breakfast.

On the drive "out West" mentioned earlier, many people were helpful, and I thank particularly Emma Hanson, curator of the Plains Indian Museum at the Buffalo Bill Historical Centre, for responding without prior warning to a request to interview her quite late in the day, to Gerry (Gerald) Conaty, senior ethnologist at Glenbow Museum in Calgary, and to Katherine Pettipas, Manitoba Museum of Man and Nature, Winnipeg, who gave us an advance tour of the new gallery that would open only the following day. I would also like to thank Christine and David McCoy for a fun evening in Calgary, and encouragement to head out into an early September snowfall the following morning!

In May 2004, when this book was already partially written, I set off to take advantage of the remaining portion of my Leverhulme Study Abroad grant to pick up some last vital pieces of information. For this trip I had only a month away from my teaching, but I managed to visit several places that have added greatly to the richness of my materials. First, I went to Hokkaido to see what had become of the "Ainu village" I had now chosen to feature in the Prologue of my book. Nomoto Masahiro (whom we meet in the Prologue) helped out again, for he sent me the name of Hirasawa Ryūji, a dancer and performer who invited me to his house late after a long day's work, so that he and his wife could chat about contemporary Ainu life there. His invaluable contribution to this study is outlined in the Epilogue. I have actually visited Ainu country twice during this research period, and I must also thank Jane Wilkinson of the Royal Scottish Museum for sharing her contacts with me, and for adding her own comments to my work as it proceeds. On the first of these visits, which is the one referred to in the second part of the Prologue to this book, it was a chance absence of one of Jane's friends that put Nomoto Masahiro in the role of looking after me at Shiraoi, and he reminded me that he had been one of the dancers who came to Oxford. He not only gave me a warm welcome to the culture center where he works, but also introduced me to Yoneda Yoshihara, head of the new museum at Nibutani, and sent further information for chapter 7.

My next port-of-call on my last trip was southern Australia, where I visited the Tandanya Institute in Adelaide and then went on to see Bunjilaka, the Aboriginal section of the Melbourne Museum, and the National Museum in Canberra. I would like to thank Howard and Frances Morphy for advice about where I could gather useful information in a very short time and introductions to several helpful people. In Melbourne, a friend from an earlier visit, Wendy Smith, offered me accommodation, helped me to get treatment for an acute back problem that flared up while I was there, and gathered some materials about a new practice in Melbourne of marking Aboriginal places of importance. She also introduced me to Mark Dugay-Grist of Aboriginal Affairs, Victoria, who had been involved in the creation of Bunjilaka, and at the museum, Koori roving curator Lorraine Coutts gave me lots of helpful information about the community consultation process. In Canberra, Kathryn Wells and Sallie Anderson of the Aboriginal and Torres Strait Islander Services of the Australian government were kind enough to spend a long lunch time talking about the Aboriginal art centers that we discuss in chapter 5, and they sent me a very helpful selection of publications.

After the Aotearoa (or New Zealand) part of that trip, I traveled on, via Samoa, to Vancouver again, as mentioned above, and on this second occasion, I was made unusually welcome at the Storyeum attraction, described in chapter 2, where everyone was remarkably cool and cheerful among the last minute preparations for opening the following week. As well as Kyla Leslie and Roberta Voyer, whose jobs probably entailed looking after the press and other interested visitors, president and CEO Danny Guillaume, marketing manager Graeme Drew, show manager Pat Taylor and Dennis Thomas, one of the actors playing Takaya, all made time to see me and chat about the project. Best of all, however, they organized for me to meet the creator of the Aboriginal part of the show, Leonard George (figure 2.1), whom we meet again in chapter 2. I was glad to be able to nip through again shortly before going to press and see the show.

On the way home from this last part of the trip I made a quick, whistle-stop visit back to the Six Nations Reserve, where I was lucky enough that the trip coincided with the opening of the First Nations Art exhibition at the Woodland Cultural Centre. It was great to be able to see again some of the people who had been so helpful the previous year, and Tom Hill introduced me to their guest for the occasion, who was Rick West, director of the new National Museum of the American Indian that we visit in chapters 1 and 7. It was good to catch up with Phyllis and Keith and her large family, and I took the opportunity to stay at the Bears Inn, a local hostelry with Iroquoian themes that had looked so intriguing when I was lodging nearby. A nice visit, except that I was so relaxed that I didn't leave enough time to get to Toronto airport and so missed my morning flight back to the United Kingdom!

Last, but by no means least, I would like to thank a few of the many other people in places here and there who were willing to listen to me turning over ideas for this project, and who contributed their own encouragement and suggestions. Among them were Laura Inoue, in Japan and in the United Kingdom, Tim Ingold, David Anderson, and Allice Legat at the University of Aberdeen, Ian Martin of York University, Ontario, my students Phil Sawkins and Katsunobu Shimizu, who called on me in the summer when I was writing, and by letter and e-mail, Beatrice Medicine, professor of anthropology and head of the Native Centre at the University of Calgary, and Nancy Fuller at the Smithsonian Institution. Several people read parts of the manuscript as it unfolded, and for this and their kind comments, I would especially like to thank Mary Louise Bracho, Ericka Chemko, my mother Beatrice Hendry, Simeon Jones, Keith Lickers, Rob Pope, Judy Skelton, and Felicity Wood. My sons, James and William Kay, have also been wonderfully supportive throughout this project, and I thank them too for their insightful questions and comments, and for continuing to take an interest in the work I am doing.

References and Further Readings

Bedard, Joanna, 1992, "Foreward," in Deborah Doxtator (ed.), 1988, *Fluffs and Feathers: An Exhibit on the Symbols of Indianness; A Resource Guide*, Brantford, Ontario: Woodland Cultural Centre.

Bocock, Robert, 1992, "The Cultural Formations of Modern Society," in Stuart Hall and Bram Gieben (eds.), *The Formations of Modernity*, Cambridge: Polity Press, pp. 229–274.

Dore, Ronald, 1973, *British Factory-Japanese Factory: The Origins of National Diversity in Industrial Relations*, Berkeley and Los Angeles: University of California Press.

Doxtator, Deborah, 1988, "The Home of Indian Culture and Other Stories in the Museum," *Muse*, VI(3): 26–28.

Hendry, Joy, 2000, *The Orient Strikes Back*, Oxford: Berg.

Hill, Richard W., 2000, "The Museum Indian: Still Frozen in Time and Mind," *Museum News*, 79(3): 40–44.

Hill, Tom V., 1992, "Preface" in Deborah Doxtator (ed.), 1988, *Fluffs and Feathers: An Exhibit on the Symbols of Indianness; A Resource Guide*, Brantford, Ontario: Woodland Cultural Centre.

Matsunaga, Louella, 2004, "The Branding of Space," in H. Nakamaki (ed.), *A Comparison of Management Culture in Japan and the UK: Focusing on Religion and Museum*, Osaka: National Museum of Ethnology.

Phillips, Ruth, 1990, "The Public Relations Wrap: What We Can Learn from The Spirit Sings," *Inuit Art Quarterly* (Spring): 13–21.

Sahlins, Marshall, 1999, "Two or Three Things that I Know about Culture," *Journal of the Royal Anthropological Institute* (N.S.), 5: 399–421.

Smith, Linda Tuhiwai, 1999, *Decolonizing Methodologies: Research and Indigenous Peoples*, New York: Zed Books Ltd.

Street, Brian, 1992, "British Popular Anthropology: Exhibiting and Photographing the Other," in Elizabeth Edwards (ed.), *Anthropology and Photography, 1860–1920*, New Haven, Connecticut and London: Yale University Press.

Chapter 1

Museums are Transformed

> If we pay more attention to objects than to humanity, we'll conserve nothing.
> Don't touch, I am very monumental.
>
> George Abungu, Arusha, Keynote Speech

Introduction

The words quoted above were spoken by George Abungu, then Director General of the National Museums of Kenya, as part of a keynote speech on Changing Audiences of Museums in Africa, delivered at a conference held in Tanzania, in April 2002. The gathering brought together scholars from around the world, with a good number of Africans who had done research among their own peoples. The program had been carefully designed to distribute the roles—paper-giving, commentating, and chairing—between 'insiders', or people Native to Africa, and 'outsiders', non-African scholars who had worked there or elsewhere. The content and quality of the papers was uneven, but the discussions were exciting, and during the comments on the speech of Dr. Abungu, who had been describing the way his own museum in Nairobi was opening up to local people, a member of the audience became quite upset. He was African, though not from Kenya, and he was vehement about how much he hated museums: "when I see a drum on a wall, I want to tear it down and *bang* it," he cried, loudly. Dr. Abungu was patient with him, and tried again to explain some of the ways in which he and other museum directors were working to make their museums relevant to their local African public, but his critic was not to be silenced, and he grew increasingly irate. It fell to me, as chair, to find a solution, and as it was the last paper of the day, and late enough to close the proceedings, I chose an easy option and proposed that we continue the debate over supper.

The audience was visibly relieved, and we all moved off, but the exchange illustrated a great tension that has been festering away for some years now between people who work in museums and those who feel that the objects they have on display are somehow grossly misplaced. In practice, many changes have been made, and Indigenous people, such as Dr. Abungu himself, have become involved in the design and display of artifacts to which they have a direct cultural allegiance. Antagonism toward museums has clearly not been completely assuaged, however. This chapter first considers some of the reasons why this change was required, and then it describes some of the trends for change that have been taking place. It also examines the extent to which Indigenous people have become involved in museum work, and presents a few more examples of the kinds of feelings expressed by the angry commentator described above. It will close by presenting some solutions that have been devised to heal the chasm that has for some time now been widening between people who love the objects they collect and show, and those who describe the whole enterprise with words ranging from disrespect to outright theft.

Museum Displays About People—What Do We Learn?

George Abungu's speech actually presented many of the reasons why museums like his own—the National Museums of Kenya—needed to change. Kenya was a British colony, and the museum had been built in the way described in the introduction of this book, as a monument to the British Empire. The contents were the works of the white settlers, he explained, sometimes the products of their hobbies as collectors of natural history, and they were not meant at all for the benefit of black Africans. Indeed, to most Africans, the museum still exuded the idea expressed in his quotation, "don't touch, I am very monumental." Now that Kenya is an independent African country, if still a member of the Commonwealth, the national museum must adapt to serve the public that supports it, he explained. It needs to seek a new audience by changing its visions and missions, by empowering the local community to make it a place of heritage and memories, and by representing the identities of the speakers of the 42 language groups that live in Nairobi, and of the new independent nation.

The grounds of the Nairobi buildings of the National Museums of Kenya occupy an unusually uncluttered position in the busy, bustling city, atop a hill named after the museum itself, its sturdy stone buildings sprawling through attractive wooded grounds. The entrance to the main hall is an imposing architectural creation, lined by three pairs of elephant tusks, and dioramas of Kenya's big native animals greet the visitor as they make their way into the grand hall. A huge stone staircase leads to an elevated gallery, where a series of 17 large well-stocked glass cases display objects pertaining to the lives of the ethnic peoples of Kenya. A collection of watercolor paintings by the naturalist Joy Adamson, which hang on the walls, is designed to show "how traditional costumes and ornaments were worn and depict how many of the artifacts on display were actually used" (http://www.museums.or.ke/gethno.html). The portraits were commissioned by the Government of Kenya "to record the rapidly disappearing traditional cultures," and the images "stand as a substantial historical record of the dress and ornamentation of over forty ethnic groups" (ibid.).

This image is a familiar one, and it will be recognizable to at least the more mature museum visitors in many parts of the world that were settled by European explorers. The colonial museum was a flagship of the British outpost, with monumental buildings, typically set in an elevated park, imposing steps at the entrance, and large spacious halls inside. It would boast fine depictions of local natural history, including species of animals and the ethnic groups of Native peoples, all neatly classified according to 'scientific' findings made possible by the arrival of this 'benevolent' imperial power (cf. Ames 1986: 4). The added advantage in the case of Kenya of a resident foreign naturalist who was also a skilful artist further adorns the display, and to this day her collection of watercolors is even featured on the museum's website. The fact that a disgruntled African employee murdered her is naturally not mentioned.

Other European countries engaged in similar practices, and the capital cities of former colonies around the world have a national museum of this sort filled with their own contemporary displays of nationalism. Indeed, many other cities followed the example and have big, imposing museums, sometimes representing a state or a province as well as the municipality. During this research project I found excellent examples of the genre in Albany (New York), Auckland, Dar-es-Salaam, Honolulu, Jakarta, Kuala Lumpur, Melbourne, Mexico City, Ottawa, Rotorua, Seattle, Suva, Toronto, and Victoria (British Columbia), among other places, and the last two provincial Canadian museums also retain their 'royal' appellation, as well as their regal style. Readers will no doubt have their own favorites, and another prime example is of course Washington, DC, where the line-up of splendid buildings, which now come under the auspices of the Smithsonian Institution, must outrank all other attempts to impress the museum visitor.

Back in the home countries of Europe, even more impressive buildings were constructed to house collections of similar objects, brought back by intrepid travelers, and therefore at the same time to recount the history of the colonial exploits of the nation where they are found. A feature of such museums that always struck me as frustrating was the way displays would faithfully record the name of the collector and the date and place of collection, but sometimes fail entirely to give any information about the person or people who had made the object. This of course reflects the history and nature of the institution, for typically the grand museums were built upon the private collections of people who were, or thereby became, members of the elite of their countries. In the early days of this kind of exploration the objects were gathered as 'curiosities' or 'wonders', and it was only later that they were subjected to the more rigorous so-called scientific classification procedures. Even then, museums could do little about the ignorance of the collector, and this problem even arises in museums that call themselves 'ethnographic' (cf. Ames 1986: 28). From the point of view of Indigenous people who may well now travel to Europe to see the creations of their ancestors, this must seem at the very least to be a very disrespectful way of putting their objects on display. No wonder I felt embarrassed when I found myself showing the Ainu dancers the collection at the Pitt Rivers Museum in Oxford.

Further reasons for my discomfort were made clear during the talk of the young woman named Nokomis Paiz that I described in the acknowledgments. The Pitt Rivers is a museum that is clearly old and somewhat dilapidated, but nevertheless it retains a certain charm for most of those local people who know it, from novelists, through 'friends', to anthropologists. It is a veritable 'museum of a museum'. Yet Nokomis had been made physically sick by what she found there. This young student had come to Oxford from an Ojibwe reservation at Red Lake in the north of Minnesota, and she was first of all disgusted by the human remains. There is a set of shrunken heads, for example, that never fails to elicit a shudder from visitors, but to store any kind of human relics in such a place, rather than to give them a proper burial, seems shocking to me too since I heard Nokomis speak. She was also stunned to find objects that she classified as sacred in full view of the passing public. Nokomis was aware, however, that if ethnographic collections such as these had not been made, there would be little record now of the past of her people, since it was their custom to let old things return to the earth. She was torn, then, and she expressed herself so clearly and movingly that few in the audience could have been left untouched.

There are many Indigenous ideas about museums, and we examine some of them shortly, but Nokomis had the ability to make members of this Western audience put themselves in the shoes of a person whose culture is being portrayed behind the museum glass, and it was not a happy feeling. For one thing, the descriptions being in the past tense, as discussed in the introduction, give the impression that the people no longer exist, rather than just presenting the past of a people who lives on. Then the siting of Indigenous 'Native' people alongside archaeological specimens, or the stuffed animals of the natural history section, suggests a connection that would probably be intolerable to a post-Darwinian European. Indeed, the National Museum of Ethnology in Japan, which displays chairs, bar stools, and needlework as examples of European culture, disturbed me at first, although as there is a Japanese section as well, I became more relaxed. In the array of museums in Washington, DC, however, the Museum of American History is still totally separate from the beautiful new National Museum of the American Indian (which is discussed in chapter 7), though, as we shall see, First Peoples in Canada have specifically asked that this kind of distinction be rectified.

The Changing Face of Museums

Museums have begun to change in the last decade or two of the twentieth century in sometimes quite subtle, but nevertheless very important ways. During my period of research in Canada and the United States in 2003, for example, I noticed several recurring features even in the museums I only went around as a visitor. First, it had become clear that curators must at least consult the local Native peoples whose objects they have on show, and it is now commonplace for the names of an advisory board including such people to be posted somewhere among them. Another common feature is that part of the display will be devoted to objects illustrating the continuity of the people being featured, perhaps by using examples of contemporary art, such as paintings or sculpture. Museums also very often make efforts to add the real voices of contemporary people in one way or another, perhaps by using quotations in the labels, by offering recordings through the medium of a telephone or a portable 'story stick', or by screening films of them. In some cases, there are even Native people on site.

In Pierre, the capital of South Dakota and the heart of Sioux country, for example, the first section of the state museum is called *Oyate Tawicoh'an*, translated as 'the ways of the people', and it presents a historical depiction of the life of the Sioux. It features audio clips, also translated into English, of Lakota, Dakota, and Nakota languages, and a list of Native-sounding names as advisors and consultants for the display. The Journey Museum in Rapid City, on the edge of the Black Hills, recommends viewing a 14-minute film about the continuing sacred nature of the hills to the Lakota people (as well as Custer's conflicting claim), and features a *tipi* into which is projected a picture of a Lakota woman whose voice can be heard reminiscing about how the life of women used to be. The Akta Lakota Museum in Chamberlain, South Dakota, whose name is said to mean "honor the people," has four clear sections, typifying the way periods are represented elsewhere, namely (1) *Precontact Life* (2) *Contact, Trading and Wars* (3) *The Reservation Era*, and (4) *Renewal and Growth*. They all seem to be presented pretty much from a Lakota point of view—a noticeable change, according to my companion, Mary, who had visited several times before. A Lakota man at the entrance desk on the day we went around came over to chat with us, but apparently the museum curator is not Native.

At the refurbished Plains Indian Museum in the huge Buffalo Bill Historical Center in Cody, Wyoming, on the other hand, the curator, Emma Hanson, is not only a trained museum professional, but she is also Pawnee. She took time during my visit to explain that the designs for the new galleries had been very much Native directed. An advisory board of ten people representing the various Plains groups worked with only half the number of non-Natives—who might nevertheless be good at fundraising—to decide on display and contents that would effectively tell their stories. They had drawn up a mission statement that included the words, "the past is best used as it relates to the present and the future," and indeed, each of the four themed sections has an exhibit called *Contemporary Voices* alongside depictions of life as it was in the past. The exhibition actually starts by presenting pictures of six contemporary individuals from the various tribes represented, each successful in a field recognizable to the regular visitor, such as law, art, and architecture, but all set against a huge familiar image of mounted and feathered Plains Indians chasing buffalo. This sets the tone for some quite splendid displays inside, but then this is the museum where descendants of Buffalo Bill himself used apparently to put in the odd appearance!

The Museum of the Rockies, in Bozeman, Montana, entitles its whole exhibit about local Native communities *Enduring Peoples*, and an introductory notice board explains that the use of sweat lodges and pipe ceremonies continues to 'meet central cultural needs' while VCRs, pickup trucks, and satellite dishes are also 'everyday matters'. Each room includes a *TODAY* section as well as historical material, and another notice explains that all the objects on display have been treated respectfully, and have been properly 'smudged' and blessed. Unlike some others, which now avoid the subject, this museum does not shy away from illustrating ceremonial and spirituality 'because it is part of contemporary Indian life'. Indeed, the exhibit emphasizes the revival in Native religious practices, including some, such as the seeking of dreams and visions, which were formerly outlawed by the U.S. government. There is also a notice here asking visitors to bring in objects and information they may like to share for future programs that will focus on individual tribes, and topics deemed important by those people.

A U.S. museum that would be offering something far short of the story of the site if it did not mention spiritual matters is that found at the Pipestone National Park. This is a piece of land that has for long been held sacred by Native peoples as the place where the red stone is found that is carved into ceremonial pipes. The U.S. government has appropriated the land, but it is reserved for Native quarrying, though for some reason using only traditional methods. The museum is very old-fashioned, and showed an explanatory slide-show that was somewhat patronizing, though the chief interpreter was said to be Native, and inside three Native people were to be found working with the stone on the day we visited. They were all quite willing to talk, and one of them—Travis—was quite chatty. He had laid out some postcards of his ancestors, who were wearing beautiful Sioux headdresses, and he spoke of the stories he had learned from them. He also had some interesting ideas about religion, which we recount in chapter 8. All three had examples of their carvings on display.

An interesting smaller museum that makes a feature of providing the 'voices of the people', complete with names and occupations, can be found at Chief Plenty Coups State Park, former home of a man described as the 'last traditional chief of the Crow tribe', near Billings, Montana. The exclusively Crow voices are recorded in devices known as 'story sticks' which may be carried around to accompany and direct a tour of the grounds and buildings, and they explain various aspects of Crow culture and customs, as well as recounting stories, for example about how they came to be living in that part of the country. There is also a traditionally constructed sweat lodge, of the type that Chief Plenty Coups used to use, and a sacred spring where he would bathe. This water source is clearly still revered by local people for the bushes around it are hung with ribbons and other small offerings. Six Crow people apparently work here, but the manager and the owner are not Native.

Over the international borderline in Canada, though some First Nations straddle that line, there are parallel changes to be found. Gerry Conaty, the curator of the newest gallery at the Glenbow Museum in Calgary, has so impressed the Native people with whom he works that they have made him an honorary chief. At the entrance to the gallery, a notice not only announces the 'full collaboration' of the people whose objects are displayed, but also immediately gives the groups they come from their own proper names (Kainai, Siksika, Amsskaapipikani, and Apatohsipikani), though the overall confederacy is still described as 'Blackfoot' (confusingly in the United States called 'Blackfeet'). Representatives of the groups were consulted so extensively about the content, design, and display of the gallery that the relationship is rather described as a 'real partnership'. The exhibits are informative, innovative, and so exciting that the cries of delighted children echo around the area. As language was one of the features the Blackfoot thought important to include, many words can be picked up from the bilingual displays, a series of telephone receivers offer examples of speech with English translations, and one of a series of gallery notes, or take-away flyers, is devoted to language. The museum looks after but does not display some of the medicine bundles and other sacred objects still used in ceremonies, and Gerry is invited to attend the events when they are used, though he himself is not Native.

The Royal Saskatchewan Museum in Regina manages to convey some very powerful messages in its First Nations gallery, including words of wisdom from elders of three different First Nations, and conversational voices issuing from characters displayed in their dioramas whose stories change with time. A notice at the entry proclaims its role of 'paying tribute to Saskatchewan's Aboriginal peoples, *past and present*, whose cultures have *remained vital and dynamic* over centuries of environmental and social change'. The display succeeds in giving a feel for the vast areas of land occupied by First Peoples in this province, for their respect for the land, and for the relative unimportance of humans in the greater scheme of things. Both Cree and Saulteau speakers remind visitors that 'if you took human beings away from the earth, the earth would still live. That is how unimportant we are.' Other moral principles are explained to be encoded in the poles of the traditional *tipis*, values undoubtedly familiar to visitors from any cultural background. Another interesting exhibit tries to summarize the different views of the Crown and the Indians at the time of the signing of treaties.

The Manitoba Museum in Winnipeg, the capital of the next huge province, and with a relatively large urban population of First Nations and Métis, had just opened the new Parklands/Mixed Woods Gallery as we went through. The curator Katherine Pettipas explained that the content had been developed in consultation with several community members. The museum had prepared a small traveling exhibit that circulated throughout the region for feedback, and working with community researchers, they had conducted over 100 interviews to gather information regarding the development of themes and content. Part of the result is a new exhibit on the theme of breaking down the walls of the museum where notices are posted about newsworthy issues. This section is to accommodate temporary ongoing community-generated exhibits that explore themes relevant to them, and the space is also used for public programs, such as storytelling and other types of workshops. On the first day the room was open to the public, I watched a man call his mother on a mobile phone to tell her about an article he had found about his uncles on display. Here too a couple of television screens offer a choice of Aboriginal people telling their (oral) histories, available in Ojibwe and Dakota languages as well as English.

The Museum of Anthropology at the University of British Columbia in Vancouver—on 'traditional' Musqueam territory, as they also concede—has pioneered several forms of creation, display, and storage of their First Peoples' collections. As long ago as the 1950s, they had members of North West Coast peoples come to the site to restore, to copy, and then to carve new poles and houses (Hawthorn 1993), they reserve a place in the museum to display an in-house artist, and they offer almost open access to the vast majority of collections that would in most museums be hidden away in a basement or distant location. There is also a new plan to build accommodation for First Nations research with, and propitiation of, objects in the collection that are important to them, and which it is proposed to classify according to the relevant Native preference. The museum does also display the remains of huge poles 'collected' from villages abandoned after the spread of small pox and other diseases in the area, but willingness to show objects created specifically for the site, as well as the people doing the work, marks a break with usual Western practice (though common in Japan). The presence of an artist carving in front of museum visitors was also a break with tradition, though not unknown in several other Asian countries (see, e.g., Greenough 1995). A North West Coast artist also has a place at the Burke Museum in Seattle.

A particularly interesting item when I visited the Vancouver Museum in 2003 was a boat filled with memorabilia of Maggie Pointe, a Musqueam woman who had recently passed away. The items had been put together for a memorial ceremony, organized by her brother and sister, Shane Pointe and Gina Grant. After it was over, custom deemed that they could be burnt, or given away, and Shane and Gina decided to give them to the museum. The display is a public way of remembering her, and of reminding visitors to the museum that her people are still there. This item was later picked out by Georgette McLeod, a museum specialist from the Tr'ondëk Hwëch'in First People, as a good example of a display that reflects Native ideas, in this case those of Coastal peoples. The Museum of Anthropology also has an exhibit about the way they have helped to revive weaving skills with the Musqueam people, among other things that form part of their strong Native educational program. Finally, although the usual free guides in this museum are not members of the First Nations, the bookings coordinator did manage to find me a Xai:sla student, Frances ("Fran") Bolton, who gave me an excellent and most informative tour. This facility is also sometimes offered to parties of children who visit.

There are many other examples of efforts to recount the views and play the voices of contemporary people in Canadian museums with displays about First Peoples. One that sends a powerful message to children, apparently, is a display of masks at the Campbell River Museum on Vancouver Island. Here the visitor enters a darkened room, designed to give the impression of being under water, and a voice speaking first Kwak'wala, and then English, tells a Kwakwaka'wakw story that involves each of the masks lighting up as they feature in it. A more serious, but equally powerful display, this time for adults, is to be found in the Royal British Columbia Museum, in Victoria, where the story is told of how and why the Canadian government banned and later reinstated the custom of potlatch practiced by the Kwakwaka'wakw, among others. Two collections of masks worn by dancers at potlatch gatherings, confiscated by the government during the period of prohibition, have now been returned to the families of the original owners in Alert Bay and Cape Mudge. The U'Mista Cultural Centre, which houses the masks in Alert Bay, is discussed in more detail later.

Brand new museums are also springing up in cities around the world, so the institution itself is clearly not yet extinct. Indeed some interestingly innovative ideas are being tried out, especially in countries with significant Indigenous populations. The Canadian Museum of Civilisations, in Ottawa, for example, devoted its Great Hall to a display of houses of the West Coast First Nations, and the ceiling is shaped to represent an enormous canoe, its oars forming upright posts that are apparently a sign of peace. The messages of the First Nations Hall there are also loud and clear: 'we are still here, we continue to contribute, we have an ancient and ongoing relationship with the land, and we are diverse'. The Te Papa Museum in Wellington, national museum of New Zealand, not only has a Maori name, but uses a lot of Maori language in the displays and on its website. Indeed, the Maori half of this "bicultural" museum is so impressive and sophisticated compared with the bright, cheerful, but slightly tacky side dedicated to the "passport holders" that many *pakeha*, or non-Maori New Zealanders, have apparently complained that they, the settlers, have been given short shrift (Goldsmith 2003).

At the new Melbourne Museum, there is a striking, specially designed building for the Aboriginal section, inspired by the way that huge sheets of bark were used for shelter in that region (guidebook). Its name—Bunjilaka—means "place (*aka*) of the Creator (*Bunjil*)" in the Woiwurrung local language, and the guidebook includes a message from the Wurundjeri people on whose traditional lands it stands. Among the displays, a reproduction of the well-known anthropologist, Baldwyn Spencer, has been enclosed in a glass case (see figure 1.1) and elsewhere he is depicted in an imaginary filmed dialogue with one of his chief informants, Irrapmwe, whose knowledge and authority were rarely properly acknowledged. Regular tours are offered, with Aboriginal guides who present their bittersweet view of this new venture to allow them a voice, and explain interesting information like the seven seasons Australia had before the Europeans came and imposed their system of only four. The new National Museum of Australia could also boast much Aboriginal input when I visited, though it seems that its Aboriginal director, Dawn Casey, did not have her first three-year contract renewed, so it is unclear how much of it will stay.

Museums Made by Indigenous People

Another movement important to recount is one involving the initiation of museum building by Indigenous people themselves. The museums described above are still largely directed and curated by

Figure 1.1 A model of Baldwyn Spencer, early anthropologist who headed the first museum in Melbourne, is displayed along with some of the objects he collected, and a goanna he named, in Bunjilaka, the Aboriginal section of the new Melbourne Museum (Photograph by John Broomfield, reproduced courtesy of Museum Victoria).

non-Native people, as we have seen, and despite their efforts to add in the voices of the people whose objects they collect, they still often exemplify Western methods of display. In the U.S. case, too, there is almost invariably a list of the names of the rich, usually non-Native people who have endowed the displays, which preserves the element of patronage. Indigenous museums, on the other hand, are quite various, sometimes following these older methods, sometimes reflecting a range of diversity in ideas about the preservation and conservation of material culture and its funding. This section describes some of the differences in the way they are put together, as well as seeking reasons why other museums may have changed little, despite their Native genesis.

The Woodland Cultural Centre provides an excellent example of Indigenous elements in design that were developed over 30 years ago, but are now found in new forms of museum display elsewhere. The people who look after the museum are trained in, and maintain "good museum practice," director Tom Hill explained, but some of their emphases are different. The first is that the museum is "people-oriented," encouraging children to come through, even to handle some of the objects, and it also provides a venue for live events. Second, the priority of the museum is to the communities it represents. It offers a secure place of keeping for objects that people would like to deposit there, and it is a resource for learning about their own culture. For example, children can hear the rationale for where they sit and how they are expected to behave in the ceremonial Longhouses, and they can try their hands at making objects out of the natural materials used by their ancestors. These elements reflect the ideas of George Abungu, discussed above, about opening the museum up to the community it serves, but there is a further crucial difference in the museum at the Woodland Cultural Centre that can be noticed at the very entrance to the displays.

The whole layout of the museum is designed to tell a story, and it offers the visitor the experience of traveling through time, as they follow the trail. 'Your Journey Starts Here' is the notice that guides people into the first display, and they are invited, while observing the materials, to imagine life among people who had yet to be contacted by Europeans. A diorama full of interest opens the exhibit, and there is an intriguing arrangement using perspective that creates the atmosphere of a precontact home. The arrival of the first French missionary in the area is depicted in a stunning painting, created for the museum by the Native artist Bill Powless who still helps to create temporary exhibits in the center. I found myself spending quite some time in front of this painting, trying to imagine the thoughts of the friendly, curious, but slightly nervous people waiting to greet the first foreign visitor.

A display of trade materials follow, and the story goes on to recount how these First Peoples accommodated and adapted to the new arrivals, sealing an agreement peacefully to respect each other's ways in a (displayed) two-row wampum belt (see figure 1.2). There is an explanation, through material evidence, of their preexisting political system, and a reconstruction, with maps and diagrams, of how the local community came to be formed in the area. Different types of documentary evidence display how the Canadian government has tried to reconstitute the lives of these people, and there is even a section that presents stereotypical representations of the 'Indians', as they were for long seen by outsiders. The story continues through to the present day, with another powerful exhibit about the crucial contribution of the Mohawk people to the construction of contemporary high-rise cities (see figure 1.3), and the visitor is turned out into the latest temporary exhibit.

MUSEUMS ARE TRANSFORMED 41

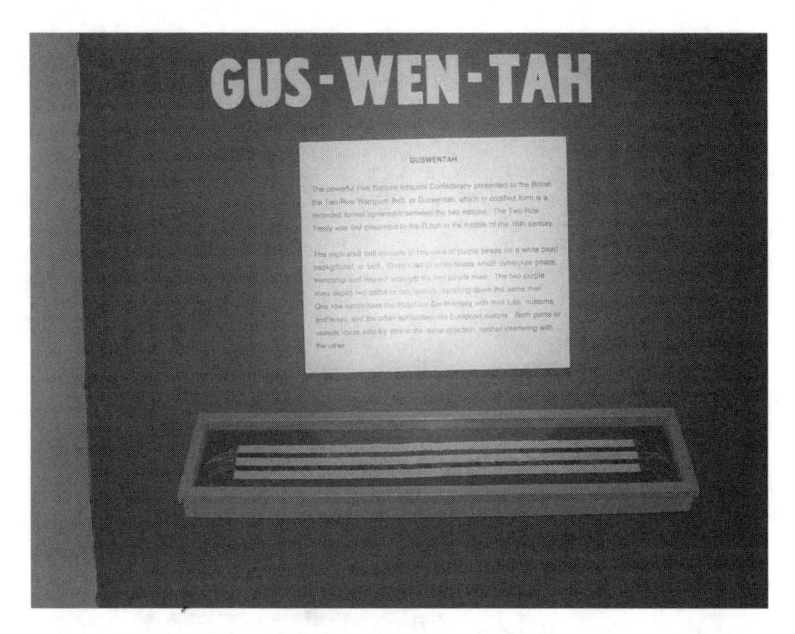

Figure 1.2 A depiction of the *Gus-wen-tah*, or two-row wampum belt, in the Woodland Cultural Centre (Courtesy of the Woodland Cultural Centre).

These temporary displays also often illustrate the principle of creating a story line to contextualize the objects around a particular theme. For example, during my stay, Keith Jamieson put on an exhibition of photographs of the Haudenosaunee people, unusually taken by a non-Native, and he spent a long time seeking to understand and present the motivations of the photographer alongside his work. Previously, Keith had designed a display of objects originally collected by a nineteenth-century Mohawk man, Dr. Oronhyatekha, who, as Peter Martin, was also qualified by American standards of the time. Most unusually, he had become accepted in both worlds, he spent a term in Oxford, and was apparently at ease in the court of Queen Victoria. Keith designed the display to illustrate not only the story of this man's life and times, but also to demonstrate his crucial role as a cultural broker.

Another temporary exhibit, which displayed old and new examples of beautiful Iroquoian beadwork, presented the materials in the context of an incredibly powerful message that could be a blueprint for world peace. This is the Great Law, passed down amongst the Iroquois (Haudenosaunee) people as the rationale for their alliance of first five, and then six nations, brought to them by an ancestor they

Figure 1.3 This display at the Woodland Cultural Centre portrays the dangerous role of the Iroquoian ironworkers, in demand to this day to build the skyscrapers that characterize many North American cities (Courtesy of the Woodland Cultural Centre).

call The Peacemaker who, in turn, is recorded as having been sent by the Creator. The message is said to extend to 'all nations on earth', and 'to shed the light of understanding upon the minds of all people'. The contemporary work on display was made through the collaboration of 'people of all ages from a wide variety of ethnic and national identities', it is explained, and these apparently included altogether 'over 500 people of at least 25 countries'. This cooperative venture used techniques and designs passed down through generations of Iroquois people, along with their philosophy. A rich collection of examples were displayed, along with photographs of the way the work is done, how it is worn, and how it was sold to Victorian visitors to Niagara Falls.

Another important aspect of the displays put together by Indigenous people, again illustrated in the Woodland Cultural Centre, is the respect accorded to objects regarded as sacred, or in some other way inappropriate to have on show in public. Thus the actual *Gus-wen-tah*, or two-row wampum belt, which played an important role in the history of the Haudenosaunee people, is stored safely elsewhere, and the agreement it codified is illustrated by the use of a similar, but specially made artifact. For these people, such a device does not detract from the value of the object; on the contrary, it ensures that the real, historical record is maintained in the hands of those who have inherited the right to guard it. Indeed, since this material object is also a mnemonic to assist in the passing on of oral history, for centuries an efficient record-keeping device alternative to the written word, it could be said to be too valuable to put on display.

It was mentioned in the previous section that objects relating to the spiritual are sometimes displayed, and sometimes not, and it is of course a crucial part of self-representation, that people can make these decisions for themselves. For the Kwakwaka'wakw people, of the northwest coast of Canada, the masks dancers wear at potlatch ceremonies are regarded as sacred, almost living artifacts, and they must be given special care. This does not preclude their display in public, however, and, as already mentioned, special museums were built to house them in two locations on the coast of Vancouver Island. In the Great Hall of the Canadian Museum of Civilisations, in Ottawa, some of these masks have been set out behind a specially commissioned dance screen, an arrangement devised through cooperation between the (non-Native) curator, Andrea la Foret, and a representative of the Kwakwaka'wakw people, Gloria Cranmer-Webster.

In the Dr. Oronhyatekha exhibition, which was also a joint venture with Trudy Nicks at the Royal Ontario Museum, Keith Jamieson added a display that might now be described as 'interactive', where visitors could write about what their relatives were doing at times depicted in the exhibition. The information the Six Nations people provided eventually contributed to the sum of knowledge being collected by the Woodland Culture Centre, and this activity played an important role that has not until recently been part of the remit of a Western-style museum. It is comparable, however, to the innovations described above for the Bozeman Museum, where visitors were asked to bring in objects and information they may like to share for future programs. It is also something along the lines of the exhibit on the theme of 'Breaking down the walls of the museum' that had been instituted in the new gallery of the Manitoba Museum of Man and Nature.

This idea of 'opening up the museum' to the local community is reminiscent of the words of George Abungu cited above, that a museum needs to empower local people to make it a place of heritage and memories. He noted that black leaders have been busy with basics like water and roads, but now have new visions and new missions, and museums can move from being houses of wonder to being places of shared experiences. They can provide a platform for dialogue, be a place where people can express difference peacefully (especially in war-torn areas like contemporary Africa), and—as we have seen elsewhere—they can bring knowledge of the past to educate for future social interaction. Abungu even had a scheme to bring children off the streets into the museum compound to do artwork for the tourists.

The national museum of Tanzania in Dar-es-Salaam has instituted a scheme to offer different tribal people who live in the country the opportunity to present their culture through an Ethnic Days Programme. These take place three or four times a year at an open-air site known as the Village Museum, where groups of people come and build an example of their housing, prepare food, demonstrate their dances, and introduce visitors to their games and other pastimes. The houses remain as exhibits, and some of them display characteristic objects inside, as well as explanations about the forms of life they support. Some of these days have been filmed, available for purchase on video, and some are also documented in museum books. The program is gradually growing, according to Dr. Kayombo, who explained it to me on my visit, and people are now clamoring to take part at a rate greater than they can accommodate.

But How Much of this is Self-Representation?

These situations appear to empower local people, but we must be cautious before we describe such schemes as 'self-representation' because the tribal people in this case are again being 'consulted' and 'invited' rather than initiating their own forms of display. Indeed, in

Tanzania, the Ethnic Days are put together under the advice of ethnographers, most probably African ethnographers, but the overall events are controlled by the museum. The museum too may be largely in the hands of Africans, but these may or may not be members of the ethnic groups being 'empowered', and museum employees are still very often trained in the methods created and approved of by Western museologists.

A similar situation may be observed in Mexico, where many 'community museums' (or *museos communitarios*), have been constructed. These are officially owned by the local people, who are much involved in their design and construction, but they are also somewhat controversial as they are influenced by the *Instituto Nacional de Antropologia e Historia* (National Institute of Anthropology and History or INAH), which offers support and scholars to oversee the projects. I was taken to visit such a museum in a Zapotec village in Oaxaca State, and the local people in charge of it were clearly very proud of what they had created. The president of the museum committee told me that they had wanted to stop archaeological remains and other treasures found locally from being taken away to distant museums, so they decided to open their own. They had thus approached the INAH for help. The collection and design of the displays had been a collective effort on the part of the inhabitants of the community, but advice had been received from the INAH representative, Teresa Morales. The result is a nice enough museum telling the history of the local people and illustrating their activities and their festivals, but the form of display is fairly similar to that of the National Museum of Anthropology in Mexico City, partly because they were given some furniture from there.

My guide for the day was the same Teresa Morales, who has also published several articles on the community museums that she and her husband, Cuauhtémoc Camarena Ocampo, have helped local people to create. She emphasized that the input of the local people is always their guiding force, and the different museums reflect the differing ideas of the people they represent. One of their articles includes a quite lengthy appendix quoting the words of several of the Indigenous people who have become involved, and their ideas certainly resonate with those of Indigenous people I met in other parts of the world. For example, Jacinto Simón Leocadio, of the council of the communal lands of a town in the Mixtec Highlands of Oaxaca, describes the community museum they have built as "a cornerstone around which we are going to try and build another future for ourselves" (Morales, T. and Camarena C. 1999: 89). Of Shan-Dany, the

Zapotec museum I visited, an ex-president of the committee, Victor Garcia Garcia, had described it as an "a heritage of our own," "an example for our children" (Morales, T. & Camarena C. 1997: 25). Another local venture in the same community—a *Casa de la Cultura*, or a 'house of culture'—is discussed in chapter 3.

This situation in Mexico is not dissimilar to that described elsewhere as the ecomuseum project. An informative article by Nancy Fuller (1992) presents in this context her experience working for the Smithsonian Institution with the Ak-chin Indian Community of Arizona. The mission of the Smithsonian was to 'share its resources and to be a catalyst for stimulating original thinking and innovative practices in the museum profession' (ibid. 363), so it certainly leaves open the possibility of harnessing Indigenous ideas. The project was to *help* Native communities to build or upgrade their own museums, but Fuller emphasizes the extent to which power and control is transferred to the community. This is of course the broader idea underlying the concept of an ecomuseum, which Fuller describes as 'both a framework for examining the nature and structure of cultural institutions and a process for democratizing them' (ibid. 328). Developed in France in the late 1960s, it sought to open up the concept of a museum to involve the whole life of a community and its people in the depiction of their own heritage, an idea that was ratified by the International Council of Museums in 1974 (ibid. 329). The Mexican project started at around the same time, and 'people's palaces' (a name used in Glasgow) have appeared in many localities around the world in its wake.

In both Native cases, the aim of identifying and fuelling Indigenous pride would seem to be met, although the stimulus for building a museum still comes from outside, and the 'education' offered is probably largely 'Western'. This is perhaps inevitable if the model of cultural display is in fact a 'museum', and it applies even more strongly if Native people are given as a condition of repatriating their own objects that they build such a place. The U'Mista Cultural Centre already mentioned above is an example of this, and in Alert Bay, as in Cape Mudge, buildings were necessarily constructed to conform to the requirements of 'proper' museum conservation techniques. The masks are displayed in a way that differs completely from the enclosed glass-case style, however, and it is explained in a video shown at the center that they had spent long enough 'locked away'. They are thus arranged in a big open hall, which forms the inside of a building modeled on a former Chief's Big House, and visitors may examine them closely from a variety of angles. They are also taken out for use at appropriate times. Here the required 'museum' has become a 'box of treasures' for local people.

Other Native museums are built with the intention of retelling a story that they perceive as having been distorted, and the choice of display style is made deliberately to attract members of the wider public. An excellent example is the Museum of Wounded Knee, which has been placed close to the hotels and other facilities in Wall, South Dakota, a popular watering place (literally, as the Wall Drug Store offers free iced water) for visitors to the nearby Badlands. This museum, an attractive building put in place by the Chamber of Commerce of the nearby Pine Ridge Indian Reservation, offers a good selection of Native artifacts, but also tells the painful story of the massacre of Wounded Knee using the first-hand accounts of French, Lakota, and U.S. commentators. It places the tragic event in the context of local history, with several powerful exhibits, such as a television that scrolls through the dates and places of broken treaties, and a map of the United States that shows, over the period from 1492 to the present, how Native land has been diminished. When we visited, a young Lakota Sioux student on a summer job was looking after the museum, and his response to my question as we entered, 'does this museum present the Native point of view?' was telling: 'no', he said, 'this is the history'.

Members of the Allegany Seneca Reservation in Salamanca, New York, use a museum they have built in a parallel way. Located in the vicinity of some popular local gaming halls and visited by many members of the non-Native community in the area, this Seneca National Museum again has an attractive decorated exterior. Much of it depicts the life and history of the Seneca people who lived in Upper New York State before European settlement, and it also offers a variety of contemporary Seneca art, crafts, and music for sale. An important part of the display also tells the story of the building of a local dam, which flooded a vast area of the Seneca land, and although people were rehoused, they are clearly not as happy with the new location as they had been with the one that is now lost to them. The display also suggests that the dam was unnecessary for its alleged purpose. Some other museums located in the grounds and buildings of Native-run casinos are discussed in the next chapter.

What do Indigenous People Think of Museums Anyway?

Despite all the changes described above, there are still many Indigenous people who have little time for museums. They too have picked up the association between museums and cultures long gone, and they prefer to keep their memories in different kinds of places. In the village of Teslin, for example, a place in the Yukon territory with a population of between 400 and 500, the Tlingit people—who represent some 70 percent of that figure—have built a new Heritage Centre despite the fact that there is already a museum there depicting their past. A notice in the new building explains that the people are in a period of cultural rejuvenation, trying to adjust to a combination of traditional and contemporary lifestyles, and the center helps them better to understand the past, appreciate the present, and plan for "our" future. It does have displays of masks and other objects, and a shop for tourists, but it also serves as a meeting place for elders, a site for dance performances, and a place to practice blanket-making and other arts and crafts. Out at the front, a row of brightly colored poles stand for the five clans of the people, and although I visited only a few years after they were constructed, the Tlingit woman at the reception said that they were almost ready for a new coat of paint.

An influence for this center was apparently a well-known older site of Native heritage on the Skeena River in the interior of British Columbia at the 'Ksan Historic Indian Village, near Hazelton. This 'Village' comprises a house presenting the precontact past of the Gitksan people, another showing how it changed after the arrival of the Europeans, a training center for young carvers, a Today House of the Arts offering Gitksan goods for sale, and an exhibition center. The whole represents the expansion of a much smaller collection that dates back to 1960. It is reported that when Alfred Douse, one of the Gitksan people most involved at the time, was asked to think of a name for it, he replied as follows "It shall not be called a museum, for we are not a dead people; let it be called the Skeena Treasure House" (Simpson 2001: 153). A similar point was made by Freda Roberts, the coordinator of the Dänojà Zho Cultural Centre in Dawson City that is discussed in more detail in later chapters: "This is not a museum," she said, "our culture is living and we want to mark that."

In the South Pacific, too, this point was made quite forcibly by Emmanuel Kasarhérou, cultural director of the Jean-Marie Tjibaou Cultural Centre in Nouméa, New Caledonia. He said that he wanted the contemporary artists who display work there to benefit from both their Kanak past and the European influence brought to this French colony. "The Pacific people need to be proud of what they are doing now and not worried that they are not like their grandfathers were."

In Port Vila, Vanuatu, there is a small 'national museum', but its director Ralph Regenvanu explained that it is largely for tourists and to bring in a bit of an income. The wider activities of cultural display found in Port Vila are discussed in the next two chapters, and that of the Jean-Marie Tjibaou Cultural Centre in chapter 5. According to Lissant Bolton, Melanesians find it hard to see the point of decontextualizing objects by placing them in a gallery, and they are more concerned to conserve the space and place where they have meaning (Bolton 1997).

I was told several times in North America that objects that people regard as alive would die if they were locked up, especially in glass cases. According to Gerry Conaty at the Glenbow Museum, even the Blackfoot peoples who were involved in putting together the new gallery described it as a Death Lodge, a place for keeping things that are no longer used. Some of their compatriots that I met elsewhere even disapproved of the whole venture. When a traveling version of the exhibition was brought to Manchester in England, some of those involved came to the Pitt Rivers to speak about the experience. Frank Weasel Head, a founder of the Mookaakin Cultural and Heritage Foundation to promote and preserve the culture and language of the Blood/Kainai people, said that he felt uncomfortable looking at the objects in the Pitt Rivers Museum. Instead, he spoke enthusiastically about the joy of repatriating sacred objects to the tribe. Once returned, they can be cared for, and used for education and appropriate ceremonial by those who are qualified to be their "keepers," who will also then pass them on for future use.

In the light of such views, I wondered why these people agreed to get involved with a museum at all, and their answers were very revealing. First of all, an exhibit in a museum is a good way to tell a story, and they wanted to make sure that theirs was told properly, and in their own words. At the Pitt Rivers talk, both the non-Native curator Beth Carter and Frank Weasel Head spoke positively about the long and intensive collaboration that had taken place in order to build trust, and then to design and build the display. Many of the items had been made specially to help visitors understand, or they were on loan, which meant that they still belonged to a recognized keeper and were being kept alive in that way. The exhibit is not simply a display of old artifacts, and Andy Black Water, who was in charge of language interpretation in building the displays, explained that these should properly be recycled by being returned as offerings to Mother Earth. Andy's voice is one of those that may be heard in the Glenbow Museum in Calgary offering visitors just this kind of information. He also reiterated what Gerry Conaty had told me, namely that the offerings that used to be made are now often stolen, so to deposit them in a museum is safer.

A similar point was made by Linda Pelly-Landrie, head of the Saskatchewan Indian Cultural Centre in Saskatoon, who said that their arts and crafts and medicine bundles were being used by every other organization but themselves. "I think it is time that we showcased our own culture," she said, though they prefer to call the place where they will do that a "Keeping House" rather than a museum. There were several attractive displays in the cultural center when I visited and they are planning eventually to have four galleries open to the public to represent the eight language groups they cover, and much of the content will be contemporary works of art and craft. An archive gallery, which will house sacred objects for ceremonies, will have access only to the elders.

This is of course another important issue for First Nations, and negative attitudes to the display of sacred objects range from displeasure to outrage. In the Museum of Man and Nature in Winnipeg, alongside the new gallery described above, there is an older section where an exhibit entitled Seeking Harmony with the Pipe suggests a situation quite opposite to that implied in the title. It marks out a huge transparent box containing nothing but a notice that reads as follows: "Due to the sacred nature of the pipes in this exhibit and in consultation with Elders from Manitoba and Saskatchewan, the museum has removed them from public display." The older sections of this museum actually still make much use of the past tense in the displays of First Nations' materials, and some of the notices juxtapose 'Reality' with 'Myth' in a way that does not immediately express respect for the First Nations' stories that are contrasted with 'science'. In later chapters of this book we look at activities of First Nations people in Saskatchewan, Winnipeg and elsewhere that offer alternatives to museum displays such as these.

Repatriation, NAGPRA, and the Canadian Task Force

I have left until the end of this chapter one of the most powerful reasons why Indigenous people dislike museums, although it was raised earlier, and that is because they often house the human remains that were collected by biological anthropologists and other 'scientists' for their research. This is one of the reasons why anthropologists are none too popular either, for these so-called 'research materials' are in fact the remains of someone's grandparents, or more distant ancestors. According to the beliefs of many such peoples, these ancestors cannot rest in peace until their remains are given a proper burial, or another kind of ceremony of transfer to the afterlife, and there has been a strong movement around the world for people to reclaim these lost ancestors.

In the United States a federal law was passed in the 1990s called the Native American Graves Protection and Repatriation Act (NAGPRA), and museums are now obliged to declare to all the people concerned what their collections comprise. The sanction for failing to make this declaration is the loss of federal funding, and most of the big museums have also entered into a process of returning many of the human remains in their care. Other countries have reacted in different ways, and some are still agonizing about what to do with the demands they receive regularly from Indigenous people to return the human remains that they believe could be important for research. Some, like the British Museum, even fear that opening the floodgates will deprive them of a large part of their collections, for the repatriation process not only applies to ancestral remains, but also to any number of other objects that people claim were stolen or obtained in an unacceptable manner. In Japan, the National Museum of Ethnology, a relatively new museum, has largely avoided this problem by commissioning new or simply copied items for the display and explanation of other cultures.

The issue is a large one, and it has been discussed in detail in many publications. I will close here simply by recounting the reasonably positive story of the Canadian response to a bitter dispute that arose when the Glenbow Museum in Calgary began to prepare an exhibition for the Winter Olympics in 1988. The plan was to offer a showcase to the visiting world of the beautiful early artistic achievements of the Native people who had been living in the surrounding parts of Canada at the time of first contact. A team was appointed, visits were made to museums all over the world to identify, and then request loans of their most stunning material for the occasion, a title was chosen, and, as discussed in the introduction to this book, a logo was designed. Unfortunately, however, there was very little consultation of the First Nations people whose ancestors' creations were to form the display.

One local group—the Cree of Lubicon Lake in Northern Alberta— were particularly annoyed to discover that the exhibition had received funding from an oil company with whom they were already in dispute over the exploration of a piece of land they had regularly used for hunting. Their chief started a protest. He rallied the support of other First Peoples, the Canadian Assembly of First Nations, and Native people and Indigenous groups in the United States and elsewhere.

Letters were sent out to the same museums that had been approached by the Glenbow seeking a boycott of the exhibition, and a few—in Sweden and Holland—agreed to their very reasonably phrased request. Most did not, however, and the controversial exhibition that went ahead, under the title *The Spirit Sings: Artistic Traditions of Canada's First Peoples* was object of much further protest and a great deal of academic discussion. Eventually, when the exhibition moved to Ottawa later in the year, a symposium was organized at the invitation of the Assembly of First Nations by themselves and the host to the display, the Canadian Museum of Civilisations, to thrash out the issues.

The agreed outcome of the symposium was the establishment of a national Task Force to discuss and devise strategies about the relationship between cultural institutions and First Peoples in Canada. Jointly organized by the Assembly of First Nations and the Canadian Museums Association, the Task Force was made up of 25 individuals from Aboriginal and museum communities across Canada, who met with others in their own localities, and then together, to define and discuss the issues. The main ones identified were: increased involvement of Aboriginal peoples in the interpretation of their culture and history, improved access for Aboriginal peoples to museum collections and research, and the repatriation of artifacts and human remains. A report published after deliberations of two years laid out the details of the agreements in a tone of great mutual respect. It emphasized, in contrast with the solution devised in the United States, 'that partnerships should be guided by moral, ethical and professional principles and not limited to areas of rights and interests specified by law' (Task Force Report: 4).

Some of the recommendations—like needing access to greater funding for displays and for training—have probably not yet met the aspirations of the members, but as we have seen above, there does seem to have been a genuine move toward fulfilling many of the others. The Task Force sought to stress "the role of First Peoples in Canadian history," which should replace "stereotyped exhibitions that depict First Peoples as dying, primitive and inferior," and an Appendix at the end of the Report lists several existing partnerships that they hope are working toward such an aim. Certainly, I was lucky enough to witness ongoing good relations between the leaders of the Task Force, Tom Hill, the museum director of the Woodland Cultural Centre, and Trudy Nicks, of the Royal Ontario Museum.

For First Peoples, museums may now be seen as places to tell their stories, a much better situation than when their stories, along with their objects, were entirely appropriated by others. In the new cultural centers they have created themselves, museum-type displays still sometimes form part of the project, if often with different names, but they have many other aspects, and these will form the subject matter of much of the rest of this book. Chapter 3 gives an overview, and introduces the reader to some of the types of cultural display put together entirely by Indigenous people. Other chapters focus on other parts of their work. In the meantime, museums have opted to add the history of this process to their displays. As described above, the potlatch items that were confiscated have been replaced at the Royal BC Museum in Victoria by an account of the banning and reinstatement of potlatch, and both this museum and the Burke Museum at the University of Washington in Seattle, now have exhibits about the repatriation issue. We return to look at the role of museums in cultural exchange in chapter 7.

References and Further Readings

Abrams, George H.J., 1994, "The Case for Wampum: Repatriation from the Museum of the American Indian to the Six Nations Confederacy, Brantford, Ontario, Canada," in Flora E.S. Kaplan (ed.), *Museums and the Making of "Ourselves": The Role of Objects in National Identity*, London and New York: Leicester University Press.
Ames, Michael, 1986, *Museums, the Public and Anthropology*, New Delhi: University of British Columbia Press, Vancouver, and Concept Publishing.
——, 1992, *Cannibal Tours and Glass Boxes*, Vancouver: University of British Columbia Press.
Bolton, L., 1997, "A Place Containing Many Places: Museums and the Use of Objects to Represent Place in Melanesia," *The Australian Journal of Anthropology*, 8(1): 18–34.
——, 1999, "Radio and the Redefinition of *Kastom* in Vanuatu," *The Contemporary Pacific*, 11(2): 335–360.
Brown, Alison, 2001, "Artefacts as 'Alliances': First Nations' Perspectives on Collectors and Collecting," *Journal of Museum Ethnography*, 13: 79–89.
Conaty, G., 2003, "Glenbow's Blackfoot Gallery: Working Towards Co-Existence," in L. Peers and A. Brown (eds.), *Museums and Source Communities: A Routledge Reader*, London: Routledge.
Coombes, Annie, 1994, *Reinventing Africa: Museums, Material Culture and Popular Imagination in late Victorian and Edwardian England*, New Haven: Yale University Press.
Doxtator, Deborah, 1985, "The Idea of the Indian and the Development of Iroquoian Museums," *Museum Quarterly* (Summer): 20–26.
——, 1988, "The Home of Indian Culture and Other Stories in the Museum," *Muse*, VI(3): 26–28.

Eoe, S., 1990, "The Role of Museums in the Pacific: Change or Die," *Museum*, XLII(1): 29–30.

Fforde, Cressida, Jane Hubert, and Paul Turnbull, 2001, *The Dead and Their Possessions: Repatriation in Principle, Policy and Practice*, London and New York: Routledge.

Fienup-Riordan, Ann 1998, "Yup'ik elders in Museums: Fieldwork Turned on Its Head," *Arctic Anthropology*, 35(2): 49–58.

Fuller, Nancy J., 1992, "The Museum as a Vehicle for Community Empowerment: The Ak-Chin Indian Community Ecomuseum Project," in Ivan Karp, Christine Mullen Kreamer, and Steven D. Lavine (eds.), Ch.12.

Goldsmith, Michael, 2003, " 'Our Place' in New Zealand Culture: How the Museum of New Zealand Constructs Biculturalism," *Ethnologies Comparées* (Printemps) 6 <http://alor.univ-montp3.fr/cerce/revue.htm>.

Greenough, Paul, 1995, "Nation, Economy, and Tradition Displayed: The Indian Crafts Museum, New Delhi," in Carol A. Breckenridge (ed.), *Consuming Modernity: Public Culture in a South Asian World*, Minneapolis: University of Minnesota Press.

Hakiwai, A., 1990, "Once Again the Light of Day? Museums and Maori Culture in New Zealand," *Museum*, XLII(1): 35–38.

Hawthorn, Audrey, 1993, *A Labour of Love: The Making of the Museum of Anthropology, UBC, The First Three Decades 1947–1976*, Museum Note 33, Vancouver: University of British Columbia Museum of Anthropology.

Kaplan, Flora S. (ed.), 1994, *Museums, and the Making of "Ourselves": The Role of Objects in National Identity*, London and New York: Leicester University Press.

Karp, Ivan, Christine Mullen Kreamer, and Steven D. Lavine, 1992, *Museums and Communities: The Politics of Public Culture*, Washington and London: Smithsonian Institution Press.

Leggett, Jane, 1999, *Restitution and Repatriation: Guidelines for Good Practice*, London: Museums and Galleries Commission.

Mihesuah, Devon A. (ed.), 2000, *Repatriation Reader: Who Owns American Indian Remains?* Lincoln, Nebraska: University of Nebraska Press.

Morales, T. and C. Camarena, 1987, "La experiencia de constitución del Museo Shan-Dany, de Santa Ana del Valle, Tlacolula, Oaxaca," *Antropologia* (May–June).

——, 1997, "Los museos comunitarios y la conservación del patrimonio cultural," paper presented at the Conference "Bilateral Protection of Cultural Heritage along the Borderlands," National Park Service, San Antonio, October 23–25.

——, 1999, "Oaxaca's Community Museums: A Door to the Future," *Voices of Mexico*, 49 (October–December).

Pannell, Sandra, 1994, "Mabo and Museums: The Indigenous (re)Appropriation of Indigenous Things," *Oceania*, 65: 18–39.

Pearce, Susan (ed.), 1994, *Museums and the Appropriation of Culture*, London: Athlone Press.

Peers, L. and A. Brown (eds.), 2003, *Museums and Source Communities: A Routledge Reader*, London and New York: Routledge.

Phillips, Ruth and Christopher B. Steiner, 1999, *Unpacking Culture: Art and Commodity in Colonial and Postcolonial Worlds*, London and Berkeley: University of California Press.

Simpson, Moira G., 2001, *Making Representations: Museums in the Post-Colonial Era* (revised edition), London and New York: Routledge.

Task Force Report on Museums and First Peoples, 1992, A Report jointly sponsored by the Assembly of First Nations and the Canadian Museums Association, Ottawa.

Chapter 2

Aboriginal Tourism and that Elusive Authenticity

> On more than one occasion visitors have arrived at our reception desk and have refused to go into the exhibition halls because we did not "look Indian."
>
> Tom Hill, Seneca, *Fluffs and Feathers*

Introduction

While writing this book, and after spending the best part of a year in Canada, I met a woman who was about to head off from Scotland for a five-week holiday, largely organized by her husband, which would take her up the northwest coast of America from Vancouver to Alaska, and then back across the Rockies to Calgary. When I told her about my interest in that part of the world, she took up an invitation I threw out casually to come round for a cup of tea and hear about some of the First Nations culture centers she might be able to persuade her husband to include in the trip. I spent an hour or so describing various possibilities, and showing her the photographs I had taken, and she went off cheerfully exuding some of the same kind of enthusiasm I had clearly expressed in my suggestions.

About a week later, on the eve of her departure, I rang to wish her a good time, and inquired whether her husband had agreed to incorporate any of my suggestions into their itinerary. She explained politely that they would need to see how things went, but she recorded that her husband had already included a site of Native tourism into their tour. It was one that I had not thought to mention because it is located 100 miles or so south of Calgary, but I had visited the place with my novelist friend, Mary, who at the time had proclaimed that if all Indigenous culture centers could capture the appeal of this one, they would be awash with visitors. The place in question is called Head-Smashed-In Buffalo Jump, clearly a name to conjure with, and it can boast several attractive features.

Head-Smashed-In is the site of steep natural cliffs, a sudden drop of 10 to 18 meters in the otherwise flat countryside that characterizes the plains and prairies that used to teem with the large herds of bison (or buffalo) that formed the mainstay of the Native economy. Cunning techniques were used to lure and trammel large herds of the beasts into stampeding over this cliff, where they would plunge to a rapid death below, and lie ready to be transformed into tools, shelter, and food for many months to come. Archaeological evidence gathered in the area has demonstrated the use of this and other similar cliffs for some 10,000 years for this purpose, until the bison herds were destroyed by white settlers in the nineteenth century, and Head-Smashed-In is such a clear and well-preserved site that in 1981 it was chosen by UNESCO as a site of World Heritage.

Since 1987, there has been a very impressive interpretive center there, and the publicity put out about it is also extremely striking. The website, for example, has rows of bison running across the screen, and colorful illustrated leaflets are available in several languages. There is a comprehensive educational program for schools and other large parties, and the individual tours, offered on arrival, are well organized and informative. Visitors are encouraged to take an elevator up to the top of the building first, and to walk the 200 meters over to the precipice of the "jump," where various features of the site are pointed out. Then they come back and gradually make their way down through five levels of displays about the life and ways of the people who lived here, the skilful methods they used to channel the buffalo over the cliff, and the uses to which all the parts of the animals were put. There is a dramatic film that recreates the careful preparations, shows how men disguised themselves as wolves to discourage the bison from straying off the path, and illustrates the tremendous force and excitement of the stampede. The film ends with a gunshot and the next display documents the outcome of the arrival of the Europeans, whose sport hunting, among other things, put an end to the long-standing practice.

Another feature of the site, which was important for this study, is the fact that most of those working in the interpretive center looked as though they were Native people, and I felt that this was even clearer evidence than the notices in museums that the people had not died out along with their traditional economy. I arranged an interview with Lorraine Goodstriker, who was the supervisor of on-site interpretation, and she explained that although the whole area, including surrounding trails, is operated by the government of Alberta, the majority of people working there are Peigan (or Blood, a branch of those still more widely known as Blackfoot or Blackfeet). They do the guiding and explanations, and they look after the *tipis*, both those on display, and others that can be rented out to visitors like hotel rooms. They also take on seasonal workers and summer students and provide them with training courses.

This last aspect of the site is clearly not the one that attracts visitors from as far as Scotland, because it is not information available in the publicity, and other places I had suggested to my acquaintance had even more Native involvement. So what was it about this place that had it firmly on her husband's agenda before they had even left home? There is a good story about the name, for a youth apparently scrambled down behind the cliff to watch the buffalo fall, but then had his head smashed in by the sheer weight of animals that came over it. This may have been a factor, but I suspect that there were several others, probably included in my description above. However, I propose to defer judgment about this until a bit later in the book. We will return to Head-Smashed-In.

Clearly, then, museums are not the only place where we can learn about different peoples of the world. Indeed, there has been an enormous increase in the possibilities for Indigenous cultural display during the 30-odd years of the focus of this study. These have grown alongside the burgeoning popularity in travel and tourism, and brochures regularly draw on the most colorful depictions of people who happen to live in the areas they advertise. Shows of performing arts are offered as special outings, some are even brought inside the expensive hotels, a range of local 'arts and crafts' are readily available for purchase, and in many locations, 'villages' or more elaborate reconstructions of local life are offered. It has become part of the visit to almost any country to 'take in' some of the cultural variety that lingers on in a world that many people feel is getting more and more homogenized.

In fact, as I have already asserted in the introduction to this book, cultural variety is refusing to being extinguished, and in this chapter I hope to illustrate some more of the visible ways in which the rekindling process is catching rather well. Tourists and other travelers are often wary of what they are presented, however. They are not sure whether they are seeing 'real people' playing 'authentic' roles for them, or whether the shows have somehow been created to please them. They worry also that the wares on sale are not 'real products' of the people, but inferior goods made especially for tourists. Some of the museum-buffs who prefer the kinds of places we discussed in the last chapter avoid altogether the recreated 'village', even though it is called an 'open-air museum'. Somehow it is not 'the real thing' that they have been educated to expect a museum to offer, though as we saw, the practices of museums often leave a lot to be desired.

These reservations may again be based on that same erroneous assumption that the 'real' people whose lives and works they seek are in the process of dying out, or being assimilated into the wider society. Or, to put it more precisely, the assumption is that the *culture* of the people concerned is dying out, as if culture were something fixed and unchanging until the invention and dissemination around the world of Coca-Cola and other Western commodities. What some 'purist' travelers are perhaps seeking, then, are remnants of an imagined past when the cultural features were 'pristine' and as yet unaffected by the invasion of almost every corner of the earth by Western goods (and sports). In fact, change is an integral part of every culture, and visitors who worry about this kind of 'authenticity' would again seem to be trying to freeze living people at a time in their ancestral past. Worse, they are doing that freezing at a time decided by them, the visitors, as 'pristine', simply because it was prior to contact with the societies from which they, the visitors, came.

Fortunately for the tourist industries in general, and Indigenous people involved in presenting their cultural jewels to the wider world in particular, the purists I have just described are not the only travelers. There are many who are happy to enjoy a good show, wander fascinated through a recreated village, and choose to take home a few unusual souvenirs, whether they worry about authenticity or not. The possibilities for examining cultural difference may be the highlight of a trip, or indeed, the very reason for selecting a destination in the first place. Less fortunately for some of the people who become objects of their interest, there are other kinds of 'purists' who want to go beyond the sites of display and find the 'real people' living their 'real lives'. And some of these visitors give little thought as to how their explorations might impact on the lives of the people they seek, or indeed, how they themselves might appear to the local people whose lives they invade. A conference was held in Indonesia in 1996 precisely to address this problem of world tourism (Nuryanti 1997), and some Indigenous people have found a solution that is also a response to this wish, as we see later.

This chapter examines the variety of cultural tourism on offer. It describes examples of the kinds of display that tourists and other travelers pay to enjoy. The focus is largely on the producers of the displays, rather than the tourists themselves, but we later address again the question of whether good-intentioned people are still seeking to imprison others at a point in their past, and thereby influence detrimentally the displays they see. We also look a little at the thorny question of 'authenticity', to see how such a thing might be judged, and whether one group of people is again trying to impose their assumptions on others. We examine how much of the profits from tourism reaches the people 'on show', and by presenting the views of some of the people putting on the displays, I hope the chapter offers the reader some new, better-informed ways of evaluating cultural experiences they may choose to visit.

A Potted History and the Formation of Stereotypes

Some of the wariness of the contemporary traveler can be traced to ideas they hold before arriving in a place about how the Native people they will find there should be. The quotation at the start of this chapter refers to the disappointment expressed over the years by some visitors to the Woodland Cultural Centre because those who greeted them, although bona fide members of the Haudenosaunee and Ojibwe Woodland Peoples, did not fit their expectations. At one point, whenced the possibility of attracting large numbers of the tourists could be seen as a substantial source of income to support the center, those involved even discussed responding to the expectations of the visitors by wearing the feathered headdresses they sought (Hill 1992:6). Some Indigenous peoples elsewhere have taken such an approach, as we see later, and they may satisfy some of their visitors, but the Woodland Cultural Centre decided to take a different tack. They chose instead to think about the sources of the stereotypical ideas held about them, to make an exhibition around them, and to demonstrate their erroneous origins. The result was entitled *Fluffs and Feathers*, and I will try to summarize the story, as published in the *Resource Guide*.

These stereotypes were born in a period that is now noted for its malignment of the 'other peoples' who were colonized and systematically 'put down' as part of the justification of this colonization. As we discussed in the introduction, the material culture of First Peoples who had been dominated was carried to and displayed at the well attended World Fairs and Exhibitions, sometimes with a group of the people themselves arranged alongside. At the turn of the twentieth century, there were traveling shows as well, and the one put together by Bill Cody, or Buffalo Bill, was probably one of the best known and most influential in several countries of Europe as well as North America. As the author of the *Resource Guide* explains, the presentations always depicted Indians as wild and bloodthirsty, threatening and dangerous, but ultimately to be defeated by a swashbuckling epitome of American manhood, such as Buffalo Bill (Doxtator 1992: 16–18). Worse, the shows were often presented as 'educational' and 'authentic' representations of pioneering history (ibid. 19).

The stereotypes were perpetuated in an abundance of cheap paperbacks, known in the United States as 'dime novels', as well as in more highbrow literature and poetry, epitomized perhaps by Longfellow's Hiawatha. In Canada and Europe, the 'Indians' were often presented more sympathetically, but always poignantly, as losing their culture and bemoaning their past (ibid. 29–30). Later, the 'movie industry' for years drew mercilessly on the themes of Cowboys and Indians to present thrilling, romantic depictions of their various encounters to an apparently insatiable enraptured public. The traveling shows had at least offered employment to 'real Indians', who could depict themselves, even if in stereotypical activities, but film directors as often chose non-Indians to play their parts. Indeed, in the 1950s and 1960s, it almost became a vital step in an actor's burgeoning career to play such a role, depicted by 'big names' such as Elvis Presley, Tony Curtis, and Rock Hudson, as well as Audrey Hepburn, Anne Bancroft, and Mary Pickford (ibid. 38).

Fluffs and Feathers was a brave exhibition that presented to tourists and local people alike images that may well have already been firmly fixed in their minds, but it invited them to question them. For the Native people, it was a way of making fun of the romantic images of the Eurocentric view, for the non-Native visitors, it was a salutary lesson in how misplaced their images were. The permanent exhibition that continues in the Woodland Cultural Centre Museum intends to do the same, although discrete observations I made of passing visitors did not convince me that they always understood that intent. It's a complicated issue, and will take time to resolve, but examining the presentations of First Peoples of material culture that they regard as stereotypes of themselves must certainly be an authenticity of the best kind.

Meanwhile, it was still possible for Native people to make a living by responding to the expectations of the wider public, and it is important to remember that these same people were perfectly capable of making business decisions about what would bring in the greatest income. Shops and stalls set up in locations visited by travelers were selling genuine "Indian art," in that the art was made by "real" Indians, but the kinds of objects they made were designed precisely to appeal to the visitors. Frank Ettawageshik, who inherited such a shop in the north of Michigan from his father, has argued that it was precisely by responding to change in this way that his people resisted the attempts of the American government to assimilate them into the wider society. To suggest that the objects are not "authentic" is to suggest that the people are not "authentic," he argues, while his family has been in this area since the early 1700s. As Trudy Nicks has pointed out, this kind of "creative accommodation" is a two-way process that dates back to the earliest Indian-European encounters (1999: 302), and I would add, to all intercultural encounters.

Nicks describes the successful traveling shows of the Mohawk Indians of Kahnawake, a village not far from Montreal, who consciously adopted the more elaborately feathered headdresses of the Plains Indians, or in their own words the "Sioux look," to appeal to their European and white American audiences (ibid. 305). These same people had previously appeared in Europe in their own Iroquois attire, but the legacy of Buffalo Bill was a strong one. In Kahnawake, too, an early example of a tourist "village" was created, and its creator also chose to include West Coast totem poles to attract his customers (ibid. 306). The village was a good outlet for the beadwork featured in the Woodland Cultural Centre exhibition described in the previous chapter, beadwork that was also carried to resorts such as Niagara Falls, and sold quite widely in Toronto and Ottawa. Indeed, the ability of these people to adapt to the taste of their customers undoubtedly contributed to the preservation and elaboration of the art. This is an early example of what has now come to be called Pan-Indianism, a conscious cooperation among First Peoples, which has also probably contributed in no small way to their survival and revival across the land of America.

An early illustration of this cooperation was the display in the *Indians of Canada* Pavilion at the EXPO in Montreal in 1967. Keith Lickers, my host at the Six Nations, described it as a turning point marking the Canadian government's move from a policy of integration to one of cultural education. I was lucky enough also to meet Andrew de Lisle, the Mohawk Chef de Mission for that project, and long-time chief of the community of Kahnawake. He described in some detail the process by which they, the "Indian" people themselves, managed to put together for the first time a depiction of their own history. This meant resisting the ideas from the Canadian government that they should display only "cultural things" such as dancing, crafts and customs, and instead they portrayed their own systems of government and how it had been eroded over time by the Indian Act and the imposition of Canadian laws. The pavilion contained stunning photographs of the land as it was before contact and the story was told in the compelling way that characterizes the work of people who have for long privileged oral traditions. It was also staffed by hostesses from Indian communities of all the regions of Canada. It told a heart-rending story, but the pavilion offered an example of the tremendous power of good tourism.

The (Economic) Value of Cultural Display—Who Benefits?

The stories of Indigenous people, past or present, can clearly provide a wealth of wonderful material for the traveling public to enjoy, and that experience can be beneficial for "hosts and guests" alike, as anthropologists of tourism have for some time pointed out (Smith 1977/1978 was seminal). For a price, the visitors can become temporary "guests" in the homes and lives of any number of local peoples around the world, learn of their activities, watch and even participate in their celebrations, and buy or bargain for examples of their goods. With a modicum of luck and good practice, the visitors will travel home with a positive view of the experience. The "hosts," on the other hand, not only have a chance to show off their skills and treasures to the visitors, but many of them can also make a living by doing it. One question to ask, however, is how far the total tourist income is actually distributed among the people whose culture forms the focus of their interest, and whether this issue is the one most important to them anyway?

This is a thorny issue again, for many of the most popular shows of Indigenous people in the world were not put together by the people themselves, though they do provide work and a way of life for them. Would we want to take away that work because outsiders had the enterprise and international knowledge to put together something that would succeed? Cultural shows may not only be sources of quite big money in themselves, the visitors they bring can also help to revitalize and replenish the broader economies of large swathes of the countries concerned. The shows can also offer further education to the Indigenous participants, as we see later. Even when cultural displays are established and run by Indigenous people, they may benefit only a few individuals, if they succeed, and others still participate as employees, who may anyway influence the visitors more than their bosses. Let us turn over these ideas by examining some examples, this time during a whistle-stop tour of some islands in the Pacific Ocean.

A famous and very successful case of cultural tourism is to be found on the west coast of the main Hawaiian Island of Oahu—at the Polynesian Cultural Center (PCC). Opened in 1963, and built around a lake that runs the length of the 42-acre site, this park was an early example of the reconstruction of 'traditional' villages now found in many tourist destinations. There are collections of houses from Samoa, Tonga, Tahiti, and Fiji, as well as Aotearoa Maori (New Zealand), Hawaii, and the Marquesas, built with materials brought from those islands, and each with 'cultural presentations' to visit. These include storytelling, demonstrations of Indigenous technology, dancing, singing, and illustrations of games characteristic of the particular peoples. There is also a 'canoe pageant', that presents 'ancient legends' of Polynesia, with reenactments by characters in period costume, and an IMAX reproduction of the Polynesian sea odysseys. Thus, for the tourist, a fascinating day may be spent learning of islands scattered through such a huge area of the Pacific Ocean that would practically take weeks properly to visit them, and to gain this amount of cultural knowledge about. On a full-price ticket, with a cost well in excess of US$100, the visitor may also partake in a splendid supper buffet, and enjoy a highly professional and spectacular evening entertainment. There is also a big shopping plaza, so this one center offers all the excitement of Polynesian cultural diversity in a single daylong visit. Over a million visitors a year take up this offer, and the place has become a prototype for many others (Stanley 1998: 39).

So, what of the performers and other participants who present the cultural display at this popular tourist venue? When I visited the PCC, Mele Ongoongotau, who is a senior member of the staff there, undertook to take me around, answer my questions, and introduce me to many of her colleagues. She herself was from Tonga, and she worked full-time at quilting and other activities of a recreated nineteenth-century mission house, where visitors learn about the Polynesian branch of the Church of Jesus Christ of Latter Day Saints, whose members, in fact, designed the park. Most of the performers are students of various subjects at the neighboring Brigham Young University, and taking part in these shows helps them pay for their education. Parishioners of their local Mormon churches, they have traveled from the islands that are represented here, and although some say that they had to learn their traditional dances and culture when they arrived, they certainly seem to enjoy sharing the PCC's mission of "preserving the cultural heritage of Polynesia." There is some changing of roles, so that 3 of the 16 people I saw performing in the Maori house were not Maori, and Mele's husband, also a full-time member of the team, is a Tongan who plays the part of a Fijian drummer. Nevertheless, each "village" has a "chief" from the island concerned, and the Polynesian Studies department of the university is said to pay great attention to the authenticity of the displays.

To travel to the actual islands of Polynesia does not necessarily bring displays that are more beneficial to the people represented, or that are put together by local people, although there is usually similar contact with Indigenous guides and performers. In Fiji, for example, I visited three cultural centers that display precontact Fijian culture for tourists and they were all staffed by Fijian Native people, who act as guides, and who perform dances and other entertainment. Two of these parks are ultimately owned by white settlers, who made the investment to build the parks and reconstruct and maintain houses that are no longer lived in, and they clearly pick up any profit that is to be made. However, work is provided for local people, and for some (black) American visitors who were touring the first center with me, being able to ask questions of a Native guide was enough for them to deem it "authentic." Our guide was certainly willing to express his views on any number of subjects ranging from the colonial history of his country and the legacy of the British, to the (controversial) contemporary political situation. I left Fiji three days before the coup that hit the international news in 2000.

The largest and most flamboyant Fiji Cultural Centre at Pacific Harbour also had a Fijian manager, a Mr. Yaragumudu when I was there, who called the place a "living museum." He was also positive about the active role he had been able to play in determining its content. Here visitors are greeted by serenading Fijian guides, who lead them, all the time singing, to the auditorium of an open-air theater, where stories, dances, and festivals are introduced across a shimmering lake. The ensuing path leads through reconstructed houses, where Native people demonstrate some of the same skills that were shown in Hawaii, and a boat ride enhances the atmosphere of being in a real village. There is a museum within the center, an interesting display of Fijian native herbs and their healing properties, a restaurant, and some shops. Mr. Yaragumudu explained to me that an income for the park derives from international visitors, of course, but they also want to respect local culture, and preserve their traditions for the younger generation. They thus invite local schoolchildren to visit, and they encourage the employees to interact with visitors, and explain, or even teach, their Indigenous skills.

In Vanuatu, another set of islands in the Pacific, which were not represented at the PCC, there is a somewhat different attitude to tourists and the sharing of cultural knowledge. The 'national museum' and its activities are discussed in the next chapter, in which the focus is on Indigenous ideas behind cultural display, but an interesting version of the tourist village is worth discussing here. This attraction is billed as one of the 'Adventures in Paradise' offered to visitors, and it comprises a complete out-of-town tour. Although only a short drive from Port Vila, Ekasup Cultural Village is approached by leaving the bus and setting off down a narrow path into the relative darkness of the tropical forest. This environment sets the scene for what is described in advance as a traditional welcome ceremony, but it starts abruptly with an alarming sudden appearance of fierce-looking men in near-naked Native attire. This apparently constitutes an inspection by the chief, who needs to check all visitors before they are allowed to enter. Needless to embellish, we were all approved and then welcomed!

Once inside, the village becomes a friendly place, with women and small children engaged in the activities which are explained to have been perfected by their ancestors for life in the forest. These included the collection of water, the preparation and preservation of food, details of baby care, and an interesting system of forecasting the weather. The presenter was charming and amusing, relating each technique to their equivalent in city life, and pointing out that with this basic knowledge one can survive in the forest, whereas in the city one needs money for even this basic purpose. He also explained hunting techniques, arts such as weaving, and the use of medicinal herbs for healing, but he points out that knowledge like the last is sacred, and not therefore available to everyone. This idea is an important element of customary life in the islands of Vanuatu, and we see in the next chapter that it underpins the way that the 'museum' is run.

In the meantime, basic information about life in the forest is not only explained to tourists, but Ekasup Village has also been set up as a venue for elders of the nearby communities to pass on the same knowledge to their own children and youngsters. Some of the people, who are in the forest to welcome the tourists, were there for this educational purpose, then, and Ralph Regenvanu, the head of the museum, described the whole venture to me as a "two-way process," which also offers local people contact with members of the outside world. This combination of local education and tourism appears again in many of the culture centers we visit later in the book. In the meantime, there is an interesting spin on the concept of value here, for Vanuatu is an independent country that has discriminated quite carefully about the introduction of Western knowledge and technology, just as they have tried to discriminate about who is entitled to hold their own. This local, and sometimes exclusive, value attached to cultural knowledge is another important subject that recurs in later chapters of this book.

Some Examples of the Transfer of Control

In the last chapter we talked of the way that museums are involving the producers of their collections in their activities, and how some Indigenous people are setting up their own museums. Likewise, with tourism, there are examples of both sites set up by non-Native people being shared with or handed over to those who provide the attraction, and of Indigenous people setting up their own shows. In this section, we examine some examples of ways in which the sharing process is taking place and whether they constitute a genuine transfer of control. In the next, we turn to programs initiated by Aboriginal people themselves. In both cases, it is also interesting to consider the costs and benefits to ordinary members of the communities that become involved.

The first situation is exemplary, and takes us back to Africa, where a solution has been found both for visitors who spurn recreated villages and want to witness the life of a real working community and for the villagers who receive their visits themselves. This is a system of "cultural tourism" that I explored in the Arusha region of Tanzania. It was initiated in 1997 by the Netherlands Development Organisation (SNV), but by the time of my visit in 2002, the project manager was a Maasai man called Tom Ole-Sikar, and he was about to hand over the project directly to the villagers. He explained that the Dutch assisted local people to initiate the project in two important ways. The first was a form of liaison, where they would identify a village with plenty to offer tourists, and then train a senior member of the community to coordinate the program and a person who could speak English to work as a guide. The second form of assistance was the marketing of the program, and they funded the production of brochures, newsletters, a website, a travel guide, and even a promotional video. They advised about the price that they thought tourists would pay and the local community proposed development projects that the income would support. Ultimately local culture is to be preserved rather than changed by the international visitors whose interest has fostered a renewed sense of pride in it.

One village I visited was Ng'iresi, a community of Waarusha people who are said to be related to the Maasai, but they are settled and grow crops, as well as keeping cattle. A party of six, we were picked up from our accommodation and driven to the home of the village coordinator, Papa Loti, who greeted us with soft drinks, and introduced us to his family. We chatted for a while, learning how the interest of tourists had enabled the village to build two new classrooms for their school, and supply desks and chairs for the teachers and pupils. All the children could now count on seven years of education, although still in classes as large as 85, and only the best 5 percent would proceed to secondary school. Papa Loti had previously worked with tourists in a Serengeti game park, so he had been ready and willing to use that experience for the benefit of his home community.

We then set out, on foot, with our English-speaking guide, Emmanuel. We learned of the local natural resources, their beauty, and how they are used. We heard of the history of the area, and we were introduced to people at various kinds of work. We were shown inside a couple of "traditional houses," where the way of life was explained. We also saw the school, now out, for we were followed and regaled by a gaggle of excited small children. Two of them, who introduced themselves as Nelson and Stanley, cleverly saw the visit as an opportunity to practice their English, and they charmed us all with their experimental phrases. Other villagers called across the wide valley to Emmanuel, and the clearly witty exchanges that ensued suggested a fun form of long-distance communication that long predates the Internet! We felt privileged to share it, and even tried one or two such greetings of our own. Our fascinating walk lasted for nearly three hours, probably a snip for local people used to the terrain, but for us it was quite exhausting. Exhausting, but a brilliant introduction to the lives of 'real people'.

Up in the northwest of Canada, a different kind of transfer is taking place. This is an illustration of the recently designed policy of the Department of Canadian Heritage to incorporate the views and the history of the First Peoples of their country into their overall programs of protection and commemoration. At first I felt uncomfortable about this association. If First Peoples are being protected and commemorated by "Canadian Heritage" doesn't that relegate them to the past? A visit to the Yukon for the midsummer celebration of National Aboriginal Day convinced me otherwise. As my guide, David Neufeld of Parks Canada, has pointed out (Neufeld 2002), for many years the sites and events that were chosen for such attention were all about "discovery" and the adventures of "pioneers" in the area. Now, at last, the *idea* of Canadian heritage [purposely lower case] also acknowledges the history of the First Peoples who lived in this area, made famous by the Klondike Gold Rush, and still drawing tourists because of this association. Parks Canada works in partnership with several of these First Peoples, and David was kind enough to introduce me to some of them.

We spent June 20 and 21 in Dawson City, a strange town that was built to support the gold seekers, made particularly famous by the poetry of Robert Service. To maintain its economic base, it preserves and displays the architecture and atmosphere of the time to amuse and educate the many visitors who travel through, along the Alaska Highway. Thus, most of the streets remain unpaved, the buildings are reminiscent of a theme park, and some of the residents are to be seen in period costume. In stunning contrast, a new construction on the bank of the Yukon River called the Dänojà Zho Cultural Centre (see figure 5.2) invites those same travelers to witness the ongoing cultural activities of the Tr'ondëk Hwëch'in people. The lives of these original local residents were shattered by the arrival of the gold seekers, but fortunately their leader of the time, Chief Isaac, was a wise man with considerable foresight. He moved the community to a new settlement a few kilometers down river, and, as he feared much of their culture would be displaced, he even made arrangements for songs, dances, and stories to be carried further down river to relatives who lived in Alaska.

The culture center displays tell this tale, as well as recounting the everyday lives of the people then and now, and on June 21, National Aboriginal Day, we and other passing visitors were privileged to join the Tr'ondëk Hwëch'in people on a very cheerful occasion. Part of the reason for this was the music played throughout the afternoon by a visitor from Alaska, Trimble Gilbert, accompanied by local musicians, and there was a parade and plenty of dancing. However, the people of the Dänojà Zho Cultural Centre were also celebrating a land claim agreement that had been initiated over 30 years before, when they and other Yukon First Nations had presented the former prime minister Pierre Trudeau with a document entitled, *Together Today for Our Children Tomorrow: A Statement of Grievances and an Approach to Settlement by the Yukon Indian People*. The occasion was also marked by the publication of their history by Helene Dobrowolsky (2003). We discuss the reclamation of land in the Yukon in chapter 6, but this day at this superb culture center was a veritable expression of the ongoing lives of these people and their children. Two young graduates, Leon and Lynette, stood up to thank their community for the help they had received, and the previous day I had been shown round Dänojà Zho by Patricia Lindgren, a great grand-daughter of the wise Chief Isaac, a fact of which she was justifiably proud.

There are 14 First Nations in the Yukon, and they have formed a Tourism Association to promote and market a variety of ventures in different parts of the territory. Their mission is to maintain the cultural integrity of each First Nation, however, and they are active in lobbying all levels of government to pursue that aim (YFNTA brochure and www.yfnta.org). Business membership is graded according to the level of self-government by Aboriginal people, and voting rights are limited to those that are majority owned (ibid.). Aboriginal tourism in the area includes river trips to fish and learn of Aboriginal life, "wilderness" camps to experience the way "Native culture, cuisine and activities blend perfectly with the natural environment" (ibid.), museums, culture centers, and outfitters for travel in the region.

The distinctions put in place by this organization express the desire of Indigenous people to run their own shows, at the same time as recognizing the reality of steps that need to be taken to achieve this goal, and the value of cooperation with wider tourist ventures. In some big preexisting tourist attractions, the control of an individual Aboriginal component may have been handed over recently just as museum curators have started consulting First Nations people. One example I witnessed was to be found at the American theme park, Knotts Berry Farm, located in Anaheim California, where there are two Native dance shows, and a reconstructed Haida house to visit. In each case, the show was preceded by an explanation about the particular First People by a member of the group involved, and at the Haida house, the audience was asked to observe certain protocols of respect. In Hawaii, at the Bernice P. Bishop Museum, there is a demonstration and class about how to make the ubiquitous *lei* used there. The Hawaiian instructor, described as Aunty Mary Lou, explained that the role gave her the opportunity to revive activities that might otherwise have been lost because early missionaries had told them not to make the feather capes worn by traditional aristocratic Hawaiians.

In Vancouver, there are several tourist sites that have offered concessions of one sort or another to First Nations people. There are Haida carvers, who are willing to chat and explain their situation, and also dance, at the site of the suspension bridge in Capilano Park, and reconstructions of several important totem poles along with a Visitor Centre in Stanley Park. Perhaps the most spectacular is the evening entertainment offered at the Hiwus Feast House way up above the top of the cable car lift on Grouse Mountain. Visitors book for this dinner-show in advance, and are met at the terminus by a Coast Salish hostess who leads them up through the trees to a red pine, decorated "longhouse." Once inside, we sat either side of a central fireplace and were regaled with a number of humorous stories, a variety of dances, and a feast brought out to us on a series of small plates. We were introduced to considerable explanation about Salish culture and several words of the Salish language, and we were all also allocated one of the Salish clans, and taught to take part in the dancing according to that allegiance. The show was fun, and interesting, and even the children present seemed to get quite involved. The Squamish branch of the Coast Salish people claim this land as their own, so it was a good opportunity for the presenter to describe their Aboriginal allegiances, although apparently the Grouse Mountain Corporation had at first issued a general invitation to local First Nations people to present a show at this site, and it was only after a few years that the appropriate people came to run it (Scarangella 2004).

A new venture that opened in Vancouver in the late spring of 2004 also offered a space to local First Nations people, and they seemed to have been well consulted. This is an indoor entertainment feature entitled Storyeum, a series of nine enacted stories about the history of British Columbia, located in the heart of the tourist-area known as Gastown. The first story is about the environment, and the salmon that run through it, but the second and third are entirely about activities of the Coast Salish people before the arrival of new settlers from the outside world. One of these presents a young boy named Takaya, in the forest seeking to carry out a ritual associated with achieving adulthood, and the other, set inside a Wolf clan longhouse, shows a granddaughter being prepared by her grandmother for a naming ceremony that passes on much important cultural information.

I happened to be in Vancouver the week before Storyeum opened, and I was lucky enough to meet Leonard George (figure 2.1), the local Tsleilwaututh First Nation chief who had worked with the president, Danny Guillaume, as part of the team that designed and built the attraction about the First Nations part of it. He had come up with the ideas for the Coast Salish stories, and written the scripts for the actors. He was showing his family around the installations on the day that I met him and they were clearly all impressed with what he had produced. They regarded this as a great opportunity to make the visiting world aware of their history, and of their continuing presence, made clear in the conclusion to the show. Further tourist facilities are being set up by members of his community, and these are to be advertised in the lobby, so although Storyeum is not entirely under their control, they have certainly had a productive input into its creation.

I also met one of the actors who would play the part of Takaya, the boy seeking to become an adult, and he had traveled back to

Figure 2.1 Leonard George in the offices of Historical Xperiences, creators of Storyeum, in Vancouver, British Columbia. The panel behind him is the work of Leonard Scow (Courtesy LG).

Vancouver after completing a prestigious acting course at the Lee Strasbourg Theater Institute in New York to portray this period in the history of his people. Also a member of the Tsleilwaututh First Nation and son of one of Leonard's cousins, Dennis Thomas explained how delighted he was to be able to portray "our real story." "It shows how much we appreciate our land, our Earth," he went on, recounting how Takaya needs to fast for four days and nights and to smudge himself with cedar smoke while trying to find the perfect tree to cut down to build a canoe for his family, at the same time praying to the Creator and to the ancestors so that through that cedar tree he can connect with the spirit world. Dennis also talked to me of his personal spiritual journey as a young Tsleilwaututh man in the contemporary world, so I was particularly pleased when I managed later in 2004 to pass through Vancouver and see the Storyeum show for myself that Dennis was playing the part of Takaya. The show lived up to all expectations, and presented very positively the role of the First Nations of British Columbia in dealing with the abrupt arrival of the Europeans and their industrial developments, though the behavior of the latter was truthfully presented as more mixed.

Aboriginal Initiatives

There are many kinds of self-initiated Aboriginal tourism in different parts of the world, some more successful than others, and wider local organizations promote them with varying degrees of support. In New Zealand, I discovered a number of Maori shows, presented in different locations, which I had not seen advertised in New Zealand tourist brochures. Clearly Maori initiated, some were quite zealous in insisting that visitors engage in ritual greetings before they could be admitted to the *marae*, or ceremonial meeting space. On one occasion this entailed our tourist group choosing a representative man who engaged on our behalf in a series of shouts and threatening face-makings with a much more threatening Maori man who came out to greet us (see figure 2.2). As at Ekasup Village, once we had gone through this routine, there was friendly exchange, and the show began. Apparently tourists enjoy this kind of audience interaction, and I heard that a couple of Maori brothers had returned from a life in Sydney, Australia, to set up overnight tourist accommodation that features Maori food and further examples of ritual interaction (*Tamaki Tours brochure*).

Some visitor centers in North America offer overnight stays in *tipis*, along with Native food, but the only one I experienced was

Figure 2.2 Greeting for visitors at the Maori Arts and Crafts Institute in Thermal Valley, Rotorua, New Zealand (Courtesy NZ Maori Arts and Crafts Institute).

disappointing. The *tipi* was made of canvas, rather than the original buffalo skin, not in itself too much of a problem as Native Americans also adopted canvas when they were introduced to it. However, the inside of the tent contained nothing but a place in the middle for a fire and a pile of sleeping bags. No beautiful buffalo hide rug on the ground, no inner tent to divert the smoke out at the apex of the tent, in fact not one of the many resourceful features that were explained in the museum display at the very same location. Wanuskewin, near Saskatoon, is made much of in the tourist literature, but it is not owned or managed by the several First Nations people whose culture it represents, though there is a Board of Elders apparently, and there are several Native employees. Our host for the *tipi* experience was not Native, though he did explain that the usual Cree guide was off that evening, and at our request, we met him in the morning.

In Southern Ontario, there seems to be considerable cooperation between ATASO (the Aboriginal Tourism Association of Southern Ontario) and the broader Southern Ontario Tourism Association, and the two even share a building in Brantford, where the Woodland Cultural Centre is located. This is a reasonable state of affairs to expect, because the very town and its surrounding Brant County are named after Joseph Brant, who led his Mohawk people and other members of the Six Nations there in support of the British during the American War of Independence. Their story is part of the Woodland Cultural Centre's display, and the picturesque qualities of the Grand River where they were granted "six miles on either side, from source to mouth" to settle, is a prominent feature of the local presentation for tourists. Actually, much of that land was taken away again by the wider settling community, but the Reserve of the Six Nations, where I stayed, and the adjoining New Credit home of the Algonquian Mississauga people seem now to be included proudly in the overall tourism literature. Leaflets are offered at all the sites of interest, so that visitors to one place, not necessarily associated with First Nations, are made aware of the possibilities for visiting First Nations sites as well.

Attractions in the area include the homestead of Alexander Graham Bell, the Scottish immigrant attributed with inventing the telephone, Chiefswood House, birthplace and childhood home of the half-English-half Mohawk poetess and author, E. Pauline Johnson, and Her Majesty's Chapel of the Mohawks, originally dedicated for the Native settlers in 1788. There is also a reconstructed seventeenth-century Iroquoian enclosure, named Kanata Village, its promotion material explains, after the Mohawk word for "community," also adapted slightly to be the nation as Canada, and used by several other Aboriginal enterprises. Many such enterprises in this area choose intriguing names such as the Stone 'n Bone Galleries (offering the work of local carvers), SpiritWare (with original designs in leather and suede), and Iroqrafts, which boasts a large number of books and handmade gifts. It is also possible, with a little luck that they be available, to see local sculptors at work, and consult an expert in native flora at the Sweetgrass Garden Centre. On the main road that skirts the Reserve, there is a building marked Six Nations Tourism that can offer guided tours through the attractions, and, when open, offers information and souvenirs for sale.

This area is also the home of a large community of people, however, and although they offer a variety of enticements to passing visitors to drop by, there is no guarantee that any of the offerings are more 'authentic' than any other. That First Nations people initiated them is a good point in their favor, and visitors can usually be assured of this aspect of their quality. However, among themselves, people may disagree about their relative value, just as people in any community will. The Kanata Village, for example, that reconstructed seventeenth-century complex "complete with longhouse and palisade" (tourism literature), must have upset someone, for in the year I was there the longhouse burned down, an event attributed to arson. This is clearly a fun place to visit, with storytelling, dancing, and Native food, popular with local schoolchildren, for whom a sojourn involving an overnight stay can be arranged. However, it has some critics. Although apparently initiated by the White Pine Native Centre, an Aboriginal Friendship Society in Brantford City, it was run by a non-Native man, and it employed dancers and storytellers who, though members of other First Nations, were not of Iroquois descent. The popularity of the place was possibly disconcerting then to people who thought it presented false ideas.

Probably a good bet for a visitor to this or any other Indigenous area is to visit a place, or attend an event, put together largely by and for Indigenous people themselves. The Woodland Cultural Centre is one of these, and so is Dänojà Zho Cultural Centre in Dawson City. In the next chapter, we consider these and more, though from the point of view of their prioritized activities, which are usually not tourism. However, First Nations people also enjoy visiting and traveling, and events that they organize for this purpose have become increasingly popular in recent years. A big occasion that I attended in the Sky Dome in Toronto was the annual Canadian Aboriginal Festival, complete with Aboriginal Music Awards, but smaller versions of the same kind of activities are held throughout the area at the annual round of powwows. These are quite spectacular dance competitions, with competitors attired in the full ceremonial regalia appropriate to the class of dance they are entering, accompanied by groups of musicians who sing as they beat the exciting rhythm of dance time around a communal drum. Between competition events, visitors may also join the dancing, and many happily shuffle their way around the large arena.

These gatherings also usually draw a plethora of stalls, offering all manner of goods for sale, cheek by jowl with representatives of local Indigenous organizations such as the Six Nations Writers, the Good Minds.com book service, and the Jake Thomas Learning Centre in the case of the Six Nations events. For those who want them, tourists or otherwise, objects and information are thus available from First Nations people, about First Nations people, and put together by First Nations people. The powwow scene (see figure 2.3) may not fit the stereotypical image a non-Native visitor might have acquired through reading, films, and even museums, but these events represent the contemporary activities of genuine Native people, who travel from different First Nations, and Tribes in the United States to celebrate their cultural heritage together.

Figure 2.3 Men's Fancy dance at the Grand River Powwow, Ohsweken, Ontario.

Two other interesting sites of Aboriginal tourism that I visited during my stay in Canada are apparently operated out of the same Curve Lake First Nation, located in the central Ontario Kawartha (Shining Waters) lakelands. The first, the Whetung Ojibwa Centre, situated on site at Curve Lake, comprises a gallery of work created by Native artists from all over Canada and the United States, a huge gift shop packed with these and other interesting Native products, a small museum, and a Tea Room, where Native foods can be sampled. The now quite large enterprise started out as a family business, run by Eleanor Whetung from her living room, where she made crafts and ran a gift shop. In the early 1960s, when unemployment was high, she encouraged her children and other members of the band to make goods for her to sell, and in 1966, with the help of a loan, she built her first craft shop (http://www.whetung.com/history.html). Shortly afterwards, Michael, her son, opened the Tea Shop, and the business, which now attracts customers from all over the world, took off from there (ibid.).

The second site that seems to have a head office at Curve Lake, in the Turtle Island Tourism Company, is actually situated on a prime piece of land in the heart of Ottawa. Entitled Aboriginal Experiences, this is another example of a reconstructed village where parties of tourists may watch "a vibrant and exciting program of First Nations dancing," try the "high-quality Aboriginal cuisine," and engage in interactive "hands-on" workshops. An evening visit offers all this set against "sunset on the shores of the Ottawa River" (promotional brochure). I actually encountered this site, by chance, as I was walking past its location on Victoria Island on my way back to Ottawa from a visit to Heritage Canada in Gatineau, Quebec. It was too early in the season for any of the events, but I did meet a member of the team who gave me all the information and explained the satisfaction of the First Nations people running the show that they had regained control of this piece of land, literally in the heart of Canada's capital city.

The Natives Strike Back: Casinos and Cultural Display

Probably the single most successful type of Indigenous tourism, if it can be called such, would have to be attributed to the casinos that have appeared in North America in the last few years. In the United States, these establishments take advantage of differential legal arrangements for gambling on Native reservations, and large numbers of non-Native people travel to these sites to push their pennies into the vast banks of slot machines. So successful have they been in some areas that beautiful new schools, tribal government offices, and health centers attest to the renewed fortunes of the local Native communities. Funds are not always distributed so fairly, and there have been internal disputes about the use of this new wealth, but one positive outcome relevant to this study has been the construction of cultural centers to record local history, and revive traditional activities.

The Seneca National Museum described in the last chapter stands beside a local gambling hall in Salamanca, New York, and another splendid culture center I found in upper New York State marks the presence of a successful Oneida Casino. Shako:wi tells the story of the Oneida people who remained faithful to the new American state when Joseph Brant traveled north with the British and other members of the Six Nations. Housed in an impressive new pinewood building, the center offers free entry and information about the Oneida nation, as well as several interesting displays, a gift shop, and an educational program. Ideologically inseparable from this establishment, though some distance away, is the large casino, hotel, and restaurant complex that has brought fortune to the Oneida people through one of their number who gained a business degree from Harvard and came back to put his learning into practice. The building is enormous, and the car park so big that a bus service runs around to pick up visitors and take them to the attractions. As is apparently typical, there is a good deal in all-you-can-eat dining, which serves as a friendly draw to the place that then offers rows and rows of clanking, twinkling slot machines to draw in the visitors' cash.

Probably the most famous and fabulous of these casinos is Foxwoods, another great complex of indulgence and entertainment in Southeastern Connecticut that was put together by people who call themselves the Mashantucket Pequot. A smallish group of around 350, though now with hotly contested entry requirements, they have become so well off that the state-of-the-art museum and research center they have constructed is claimed by their brochure to be "America's largest tribal museum ever" (brochure). It does take a whole day to see it properly, and much effort has been spent in offering all kinds of impressive display techniques, as well as frequent reference to archaeological and oral evidence for the history asserted. The presentation starts with the illustrated story of the recent reclaiming and equipping of tribal lands that the rest of the museum describes historically, and archaeologically. Even in the casino complex, itself, there is a taster display, with directions to the culture center, and a huge spectacular statue of a single Indian that lights up every hour on the hour to shoot laser beams from his bow and arrow into the sky. There are some skeptical voices about the 'authenticity' of this and other tribal peoples who have done so well in the U.S. context, with all its melting pot ideology (see, e.g., Clifford 1988: 277–346), but their success may have sparked some jealousies. Like others, these are people who are supposed to have died out, and some of their descendants don't look much like their supposed Native ancestors. Some look very white, and in other cases their skin color rather resembles that of the slaves imported to North America by the English invaders, who incidentally get a real rough press in the museum. One or two First Nations people I spoke to in Canada felt that the Mashantucket Pequot phenomenon is a case of non-Natives surfing on a tide of Native revival. They may be right, or they may not. Either way, the success of Native casinos in North America has brought wealth and other benefits associated with cultural pride to many groups of people who were formerly sorely disadvantaged, and that can't be bad.

The Mashantucket Pequot people's choice and emphasis in their displays also possibly contains a clue to the reason why Head-Smashed-In is such a draw, but we return to this in chapter 6. In chapter 7, we consider again the issue of personal identity as a member of a group of First Peoples.

References and Further Readings

Clifford, James, 1988, *The Predicament of Culture: Twentieth-Century Ethnography, Literature and Art*, Cambridge, Massachusetts and London: Harvard University Press.

Cruickshank, J., 1999, "Negotiating With Narrative: Establishing Cultural Identity at the Yukon International Storytelling Festival," *American Anthropologist*, 99: 56–69.

Dobrowolsky, Helene, 2003, *Hammerstones: A History of the Tr'ondëk Hwëch'in*, Dawson City, Yukon: Tr'ondëk Hwëch'in Publication.

Doxtator, Deborah, 1992, *Fluffs and Feathers: An Exhibit on the Symbols of Indianness: A Resource Guide*, Brantford, Ontario: Woodland Cultural Centre.

Ettawageshik, Frank, 1999, "My Father's Business," in R.B. Phillips and C.B. Steiner (eds.), 1999, *Unpacking Culture: Art and Commodity in Colonial and Post-Colonial Worlds*, Berkeley: University of California Press.

Hill, Tom V., 1992, "Preface," in Deborah Doxtator (ed.).

Hitchcock, Michael, 1999, "Tourism and Ethnicity: Situational Perspectives," *International Journal of Tourism Research*, 1: 17–32.

Kirshenblatt-Gimblett, Barbara, 1998, *Destination Culture: Tourism, Museums, and Heritage*, Berkeley: University of California Press.

Neufeld, David, 2002, "The Commemoration of Northern Aboriginal Peoples by the Canadian Government," *The George Wright Forum*, 19(3): 22–33.

Nicks, Trudy, 1999, "Indian Villages and Entertainments: Setting the Stage for Tourist Souvenir Sales," in R.B. Phillips and C.B. Steiner (eds.) pp. 301–315.

Nuryanti, Wiendu (ed.), 1997, *Tourism and Heritage Management*, Yogyakarta: Gadjah Mada University Press.

Phillips, R.B. and C.B. Steiner (eds.), 1999, *Unpacking Culture: Art and Commodity in Colonial and Post-Colonial Worlds*, Berkeley: University of California Press.

Richard, Butler and Thomas Hinch, 1996, *Tourism and Indigenous Peoples*, London: International Thomson Business Press.

Scarangella, L., 2004, "Narratives and Counter-Narratives of 'Nativeness' in Tourism: Reclaiming Place at Hiwus Feasthouse," *Anthropology in Action*, 11(2/3): 9–21.

Smith, Valene L. (ed.), 1978, *Hosts and Guests: The Anthropology of Tourism*, Oxford: Basil Blackwell, 1977; Philadelphia: University of Pennsylvania Press.

Stanley, Nick, 1998, *Being Ourselves for You*, London: Middlesex University Press.

Stanton, Max E., 1978, "The Polynesian Cultural Centre: A Multi-Ethnic Model of Seven Pacific Cultures," in V.L. Smith (ed.), *Hosts and Guests: The Anthropology of Tourism*, Oxford: Basil Blackwell.

Webb, T.D., 1994, "Highly Structured Tourist Art Form: Form and Meaning of the Polynesian Cultural Center," *The Contemporary Pacific*, 6: 59–85.

Yamashita, Shinji, 2003, *Bali and Beyond: Explorations in the Anthropology of Tourism* (translated by J.S. Eades), New York and Oxford: Berghahn Books.

Chapter 3

Indigenous or Alter-Native Forms of Cultural Display

> Culture is the basis for an identity, without it one is lost.
> Mary Jamieson, Mohawk, "For Us to Decide"

Introduction: Some Truly Indigenous Examples of Cultural Display

In this chapter we turn away from the point of view of tourists and museum visitors to look at some examples of what Indigenous people, given a free reign, choose to do themselves in representing and displaying their culture. In the last chapter, we saw some cases of self-representation, but these were linked to raising funds through tourism and entertainment. If the resources were otherwise available, would people really care about putting their culture on display to outsiders? Indeed, would they want to be on display at all? In the first chapter, we saw some of the political associations of cultural display, often demeaning to the people whose objects were on show, representing their past, and until recently ignoring their continuing existence. To invite members of the cultures represented to advise on these displays was a step in the direction of recognizing them and we also introduced one or two examples of museums founded and run by Indigenous people themselves. In this chapter we turn to examine in more detail some of the things that happen when Indigenous people reclaim control.

In fact there is considerable variety in the response, and we look at several cases to see how different peoples define culture, how they choose to preserve it and to foster it, and whether or not they decide to display it. The coverage includes places called culture centers, heritage sites, and a museum, though this one could just as well be called a film collection. We also look at a Tribal Information Center, and an example that translates as a House of the People. In this chapter, we are concerned with the reasons people give for what they do and why they want to do it in the first place, and after a few shorter examples, there is a longish section examining one case in some detail. We also take a look at some plans for future constructions. In each case, we examine the forms of rationale that different people give for setting up their *own* culture centers, the purposes they serve, and *why* they are thought to be needed. When we come to compare these explanations across the world, despite the variety in form that we observe, we find that they are remarkably similar.

Some World Variety

For my first piece of research on this project, I set out to find as many *different* centers of cultural display as I could, always with the proviso that people should be doing their own representations. I was particularly looking for arrangements that had been set up to replace the old connotations of museum display, and a part of the rationale that informed my choice of locations was that these be perceived to be *alternatives* to museums. The play on the word, written "alter-Native," in the title of this chapter has been borrowed from Keith Jamieson, who helped me so much at the Woodland Cultural Centre [which we visit shortly], because it nicely expresses the Indigenous aspect I was also seeking. The process of this exploration is described in the acknowledgments and methodology section of chapter 1. In this one I aim to present a few of the places I visited as far as possible in terms that the people I met there expressed to me. I am presenting the first examples in the order in which I discovered them, for that way I can also share my learning experience.

Red Lake Nation: A Tribal Information Center

The first example is located at Red Lake Nation, North Minnesota, in the home community of Nokomis Paiz, the young Ojibwe woman whose visit to Oxford I described in chapter 1, as well as the acknowledgments. The full name of this particular center is Tribal Information Center, Archives and Library, and it houses a collection of books, papers, photographs, and objects, which document the history and traditions of the local Ojibwe (or Chippewa) people, along with general information about American Indians. It was my first encounter with a proper Native alternative to the displays I had seen before in museums, and I was impressed. It is located within the Tribal Offices, and is clearly primarily for the people whose resource it has become, although they also made available to me—a foreign researcher—an abundance of literature relating to themselves and their current activities.

Nokomis's mother, Jody Beaulieu, is responsible for the center, and she took on the task of explaining its rationale and present purpose. The center is first of all concerned with collecting and conserving reports, records, and information for passing on to the next generation. "We are the ancestors of those who are yet unborn" is the theme of the project, and the establishment of a proper archive of material for their use is a primary purpose. There is a political element to this, of course, and such information provides evidence and support for negotiations with the state and federal authorities, as we see in greater detail in chapter 6. Thus the archive also included a set of U.S. laws regarding Native issues, and records of past treaties. Red Lake residents are proud of the sovereign status they claim to retain for the reservation because their ancestors refused to participate in a local arrangement called the Dawes Allotment Act of 1887.

There is also a strong sense of taking responsibility for their own records, and this was clearly expressed in the way Jody bemoaned the fact that too many books had been written about them in the past by outsiders. The library holds all these books, but another part of the project is to collect oral history from the elders of the community to add primary material to this resource. This included cultural knowledge, for example, about methods of healing that had been handed down, and their relevance to contemporary diseases, some of which had been induced by contact with outsiders. The library also holds a collection of fiction about Native Americans, particularly by Native authors such as Tony Hillerman, although he is Navajo rather than Ojibwe.

There is also a collection of photographs, and some of these have been returned to the community from places like the Minnesota Historical Society, where they had been stored for many years. The task of identifying and properly naming the people depicted had been a satisfying part of the process, for many of the pictures, though beautifully produced, had simply referred to those portrayed as "an Ojibwe man," or a more demeaning title such as "Wild Rose" for a young woman. Elders had been called in to try and identify all those pictured, and several were now displayed with their names returned to them.

Some objects had also been returned from the Historical Society, but Jody noted that they did not want to make this place another museum, and the Historical Society has much better facilities to store the older things. They had brought some representative items, however, because many local people did not have a chance to get down to the Twin Cities. These include a beautiful beaded waistcoat, and some handwritten missionary descriptions of Red Lake at the time of first contact. Jody and her colleagues maintain good relations with the museum there however, and play an advisory role about the use of their things.

Santa Ana del Valle, Oaxaca, Mexico: *Casa de la Cultura,* or House of Culture

The second example I visited was in Mexico, where there are many national programs to allow (advise and control) Indigenous people to do their own cultural displays. My research therefore proceeded through several government offices, where I was shown beautiful maps peppered with tiny colored markers, illustrating how many villages had built their own museums and "houses of the people." In chapter 1, the Zapotec community museum in Santa Ana del Valle was described, and I explained that my visit had been made possible through the kindness of Teresa Morales, from the National Institute of Anthropology and History, who had been advisor in the construction. While I was there, some members of the local government came out to find me, however. They had heard of my arrival through a communication from one of the government offices I had visited, and they were very keen to show me their *Casa de la Cultura*, formerly the *Casa del Pueblo* (house of the people).

This was quite a different venture from the museum, for various reasons. It was also part of a government plan to encourage continuity of cultural variety, and support was provided, here as elsewhere, for people to practice traditional arts on a regular basis. This village boasts a particular form of dancing that is valued widely as an unusual form in Mexico, and the headdresses for this art are stored in a room in the house. Moreover, they had developed a successful children's band aged 8–14 years, *La Banda Infantil Amanecer*, which traveled regularly to other cities of the country to perform. The achievement of which the local people were most proud, however, was the acquisition of a *fonoteca*—a collection of CDs from around the world that allowed them to listen to a whole variety of other music. This they had received as a donation from a local man named Francisco Toledo, who has made a name for himself as an artist, and who was keen to put some of his newfound wealth back into the community.

This was a situation somewhat different to that found in Red Lake, then, for although the Mexican government was busy putting resources into the preservation of cultural difference, through the museum and the encouragement of traditional practice, what local people themselves wanted to do was to place their own rather well-known music in a global context. The extra resources they received from Francisco Toledo had allowed them to develop this desire. Actually, this community has many international links, for several members of the population hold down jobs in California, which provide another source of outside income. A device of the local council to bring some of this U.S. wealth into the municipality is to make it compulsory for every adult householder to do service in the community, so this brings them back on a regular basis if they want to keep their Zapotec home.

One of the men showing me around traveled to the United States to work when he was not doing this "service," and he explained a dilemma he had been experiencing about rearing his children. On the one hand, he wanted them to keep up their Zapotec language, and all the cultural strength they had living here, and on the other, he wanted them to have facility with English, a language that he thought would be of more use in the world at large. So he was considering taking them with him the next time he left for California. Almost the opposite of Red Lake, then, for Native Americans who happen to live in the United States are lucky if they still have a language to keep, though they know English as well as anyone. The important factor, of course, is that this man had a choice and the community at large had benefited from their own source of nongovernmental income.

Port Vila, Vanuatu: The Film Collection of
'Museum blong Vanuatu'

The next example of cultural self-representation that I visited had a major advantage over the first two in that it is located in a country now independent of the colonial powers that occupied it. The collection of islands in the South Pacific, where we visited Ekasup Village in the last chapter, Vanuatu is also relatively isolated from its neighbors. It has of course received much influence from the outside, the lingua franca is a Creole, and as part of the world of nations, it has constructed recognizable institutions that include a 'museum'. I had heard before I arrived, however, that foreign anthropologists, including those who helped to establish it, had been expelled for a period after independence, and it was running according to local ideas. The director, Ralph Regenvanu, a local man, though trained in Australia, was keen to point out that "everything here belongs to the people." Although various objects were out on show, he explained that this was the least active part of the museum, and the displays, which have labels in English and French, are maintained largely for tourists, and the associated income.

Much more active is the film and sound unit, for people all over the scattered islands of this nation want to record and conserve much more than a few objects that have anyway been removed from their meaningful context (Bolton 1997). Local fieldworkers have thus been trained to use the equipment, and they record ceremonies and other practices as examples of their ways of life. As many people still cannot read, they are also better able to enjoy the films made, Regenvanu explained, and these offer more interesting television for them than the Australian programs they can now receive. The arrival of cameras may also encourage workshops of cultural revival, and people who get involved become aware of the value of their long-standing, but threatened *kastom*. Derived from English (custom), this word subsumes all manner of ideas and activities, including a system of law that is often still preferred by people to that administered by the European-style courts.

The collected films are housed in a place at the museum called the *Tabu Room*. This is to recognize that knowledge in a local view is not simply available to all those who might seek it. Certain types of knowledge must be earned, and access to it granted after local versions of training, at a grade-taking ceremony. Rights to view films and other materials are, therefore, given only to those who can demonstrate that they have achieved the appropriate status, and the means to gain the status are at the same time being carefully recorded. This practice makes clear various issues about the value of esoteric tribal knowledge that is not available to all insiders, let alone outsiders, and in Vanuatu care is being taken to exercise controls over those who would export natural products for healing and other practices. These ideas are not restricted to the people of Vanuatu, and the management of this film collection illustrates an important issue of concern to people in many parts of the world about the way their local knowledge is appropriated by outsiders who fail properly to respect their ways of life.

I visited several more places on that first trip, and some of them are mentioned in later chapters so I refrain from making the list too long at this stage. My next port-of-call was Nouméa in New Caledonia, to the Jean-Marie Tjibaou Cultural Centre, which was mentioned briefly in chapter 1. We discuss this wonderful place in more detail in chapter 5. I also visited several interesting cultural centers in Aotearoa (Maori New Zealand), and one of these is featured in chapter 4. I traveled back via Malaysia on that first trip, where I found an abundance of what could be described as cultural display, set up by different groups of people, but as I explained in the acknowledgments, none of them really fitted the remit for this book.

The Case of Canada

After my first initial explorations into the world of Indigenous Forms of self-representation, I decided that it was time to investigate one case in more detail. My research suggested that Canada had not only been in the game for a reasonably long time, and that there was an abundance of examples within Canada itself, but that there had also been some relatively supportive government policies there. In this broad section, I describe, first, the place where I spent the longest time investigating the rationale for and the activities of such a cultural center. Then I look a little at a confederacy of such centers through describing the events of an annual meeting I attended, interspersed with visits to three further centers. Last, I describe some places that are still at the design stage to see how far they have been able to build on the experience of their forebears.

The Woodland Cultural Centre

The Woodland Cultural Centre (see figure 3.1), on Six Nations land in Brantford, Ontario, is one of the oldest and largest cultural centers created by Native people themselves, and it has in the library excellent records of its establishment, and of all the history that lay behind it. Indeed, the library is itself part of that history, and on a good day, Keith Jamieson (see figure 3.2), the man in charge of the resources when I was visiting, would point out blemishes in the wall and would speculate about their origins. These are not gunshot holes, however, not even the results of severe storm damage. The marks in question are the rebellious embellishments of small children, strictly contained sons and daughters of Woodland Indians who were pupils of the Mohawk Institute, an Anglican residential school known locally as "the Mush Hole." That name derives from a persistent quality that the food was said to have, but it expresses a negative attitude that goes much deeper, a subject that is discussed in more detail in the next chapter.

Figure 3.1 The Woodland Cultural Centre in Brantford, Ontario, converted in 1972 from the original building of the Mohawk Institute (Courtesy of the Woodland Cultural Centre).

Figure 3.2 Keith Jamieson in the Library at the Woodland Cultural Centre, Brantford, Ontario (Courtesy of the Woodland Cultural Centre and KJ).

For now let us record that no visitor to the Woodland Cultural Centre goes away without being made aware of the origin of the buildings, and most quickly learn that it was burnt down twice—by pupils—since its first construction in 1830, and before it was closed as a school in 1969. Annually, there is a reunion of the "survivors" of that educational institution, though there are said to be a few former pupils who so hated it that they will not even enter the new positive place it has become. Almost everyone there knows someone who went to the school, and they all have their stories, some good but many bad. A rounded study, full of quotations and personal stories, is to be found in the library (Graham 1997), as is the Anglican report that recommended the closure of all such residential schools and that the federal government should start listening to the Indians themselves about their needs for education (Hendry, C. 1998). In 1969, the buildings became the property of the Six Nations, and a discussion began about how to use them.

Documentation of the outcome of these deliberations can be found in the 1972 report of a feasibility study, which was carried out to assess the idea of converting the buildings into an "Indian Culture Centre." In 1971, the federal government instituted a Cultural and Education Centres Program to fund proposals from Native political organizations to revive the language and culture that had been threatened almost to extinction by the residential school system. Tom Hill was working for the Indian Affairs department at the time, and he and Keith Lickers, who was a local schoolteacher, were both involved in the feasibility study, supported locally by the Association of Iroquois and Allied Indians. This organization comprised some 20,000 people from bands in eight communities in the southern part of the province of Ontario, and the introduction to the document points out that the location was thus centrally located both to Native people of Southern Ontario and to several universities. Near the banks of the Grand River, Brantford is a site of significant historical and cultural meaning, and supports a strong Indian identity. Culture is a product of all elements that give people a sense of identity, the report continues, and language is the medium of culture.

Further compelling reasons for the overall proposal are immediately laid out. The Indians were the first demographic group in Canada, their knowledge of roots and herbs cured European travelers of their scurvy, and their staple foods of corn, squash, and potatoes sustained the life of the early settlers. Their gifts of snowshoes and birch bark canoes enabled travel and exploration, and even in war, the Indian art of camouflage was soon widely adopted. "These are only a few of the

Indians' contributions to the life and culture of Canada. Where is this acknowledged in Canadian history?"

> It is not sufficient to depict the Indian's achievements in museums, as though he was already a relic of the past.

Thus it was argued that a culture center would offer the means not only to display these achievements, but also to preserve the heritage of the Indian people and to keep alive their languages, rituals, costumes, and dances to pass on to the next generations. Steps must be taken now to maintain and enhance this cultural identity, the paper argues, suggesting again that the storehouse of information they would create would also be easily accessible to researchers at universities. "Here the true history of the Indian's contribution to Ontario and Canada could be written."

The report goes on to lay out in considerable detail the precise objectives of such a center, the personnel, facilities, and furniture that would be needed to achieve them, and the roles and responsibilities envisaged for employees and the overall administrators. A board of governors would include representation from each of the participating bands, as well as from local universities and the Royal Ontario Museum. Within the center, there would be a library, with personnel to establish and build up a collection of relevant materials and to coordinate research; there would be a museum and gallery to store and display artifacts, some of which would need to be returned from existing non-Native establishments; and there would be a communications director to set up links, do public relations, and organize recordings and videotapes of language and cultural events. The cost of staffing and equipment is calculated, suggestions are made about financing, and it is noted that a training program will be required so that Native personnel can eventually replace any non-Native experts that need to be employed in the first instance.

The report is extremely impressive, not only in terms of its comprehensive coverage of the needs, and its vision for their fulfillment, but also in the sense of excitement it conveys for such a project to be realized. It stints on nothing and the range of equipment it lays out as required sounds like a dream for any organization to acquire. I found myself wondering how much of the proposal was funded, and when I came home that evening and posed the question to Keith, he surprised me by confirming that everything had been agreed. It was a good time for the development of culture centers, and this one benefited from visionary people to put it together.

Joan Greenbird, an Anishnaabe from Walpole Island, was the longest serving member of the Woodland Cultural Centre when I was doing my research in 2003, and she described the "round-the-clock" activities of setting it up. There were field researchers from each of the support bands, collecting artifacts and all their background history, and a mobile unit was set up, with library, small museum, and audio-visual facilities to share the resources with people who lived too far away to visit. Members of all the bands were asked to collect materials, and a newspaper clipping file was established to record mention of Indian issues from all over Canada. Students on summer employment helped to catalogue these, although over the years it became expensive to keep up the subscriptions, so they cut down the coverage to Woodland issues. Joan, herself, took on the task of putting all the Six Nations material on microfilm. She has since carried out several other jobs that made use of technological aids as they became available, and she is now in charge of desktop publishing. Although Walpole Island has now set up its own heritage center, Joan remains in Brantford, where she designs and produces the newsletter (*Wadrihwa*), language publications, forms, reports, and brochures, and many of the exhibition posters and tickets.

Another long-standing member of the team is Judy Harris, from Six Nations, who manages the museum collections, recording and cataloguing the objects as they arrive, and maintaining and regularly checking the atmospheric conditions. She also described the excitement of the initial acquisition activities when funding allowed travel to seek important artifacts and the purchase of a collection that would enable them to tell their own story and to present information from their own perspective. In 1975, they had the idea of hosting their own art show, she went on, which at first was mainly "Indian art," but now includes "everything, all kinds of art" [though usually by First Nations people]. Over the years they have built up "quite a reputation," and they are approached by museums and galleries around the world for loans, recent ones being from Frankfurt, New York, Banff, and Montreal. These days funding is tighter, however, and acquisitions tend to be from donations, rather than purchases, though an attempt is made to buy some of the best of the art produced for the now annual exhibitions.

Other achievements of the Woodland Cultural Centre over the years have been many, and some of these are discussed in later chapters of this book, as is a bold new plan for the future. There is a broad range of activities for children and other visitors, organized by Tara Fromen, the education officer, as well as an educational outreach program, which sends a speaker—usually Bernadette Wabi—out to schools and other venues. These and the unparalleled program of language revival will form part of the subject matter of the next chapter. Further aspects of the arts program, including exhibitions, shows, cooperative ventures and performance plans for the future, that of the following one. Some of the important international links of the center will be discussed in chapter 7. One recommendation of the initial feasibility study that was not implemented, however, was the representation on the board of local universities, and this may have impacted on a withdrawal of activities that was announced in the spring of 2004 (*Wadrihwa* 18,4, p. 7).

This was the closure, except by special permission, of the Library and Resource Centre that had been such a strong foundation at the beginning, but that had been somewhat sidelined by the time I was working there. Keith (Jamieson), whose 2003 forward plan to the board was not supported, though he was receiving around 120 inquiries a month from around the world, had left when I visited in 2004. In fact I had already approached some of the board members about this and other issues, and they had expressed varied views, depending partly on the political situation in their own communities, since each of them contributes to the funding. One complained that 90 percent of those inquiries are from outsiders so why should they support that? However according to vice chairman, Philip Franks, who supported the bid, there are three main roles of the center: first, to preserve heritage and culture, second, to educate members of the participating bands, and third, to share with mainstream society. Thus, responding to inquiries is an integral part of the remit. Philip's suggestion was that some rethinking was required, not about the goals, but about how to achieve them in the current environment. Taking advantage of technology, as it becomes available, might enable them to work out a new way to do their own education, for example.

In late 2003, Janis Monture was appointed as the new executive director of the Woodland Cultural Centre, and she came with a fund of ambitions and ideas, which included an increase in IT provision. Top of the list of the priorities she outlined in an interview she gave me before I left was the crucial issue of funding. She wanted to move away from being so grant dependent, she explained, and was thinking about contracting out the role of fund-raising to a professional, preferably someone of First Nations ancestry. She was also keen to raise the profile of the center in mainstream national and provincial organizations such as the Canadian Museums Association and the Ontario Arts Council. She planned to consult members of the four remaining supporting communities, and find out what they wanted for the center. Another aim was to build partnerships with some of the thriving Aboriginal businesses—some of these within their communities—and that way they could perhaps gain corporate sponsorship.

Janis had some other, more specific ideas for the Woodland Cultural Centre, and it will be interesting to watch her progress as she seeks to put them into action. She suggested that something new is needed to recapture its vitality. In a way, this long-term stalwart center had fallen victim to its own success by the time I visited, for it had reclaimed the cultural heritage of its people so well that most of the threats that fed the initial enthusiasm for its establishment had been banished. It had addressed all the issues raised in my first variety of world examples and more by the time I arrived, and it was a great place for me to examine the problems and procedures that had laid the foundations of their achievements. The Woodland Culture Centre may well retain its leading role in the world of self-representing Indigenous people, but the most explicit plans to date are those of the previous director, Amos Key, who resigned his job to put them into place. We return to these in chapter 5.

The First Nations Confederacy of Cultural Education Centres

The Cultural and Education Centres Program initiated in 1971 by the federal government of Canada has continued in one way or another since that time. By 1978, 51 centers had been set up in different parts of Canada, and an independent evaluation of the work of their program (Evalucan 1978) recommended that it should be given even higher priority and increased resources. The report maintained that the Indian (and Inuit) people had clearly demonstrated that they were able and willing to carry out appropriate programs, the centers were efficiently and effectively organized, and they were having the expected positive effect on the people and their communities. The program should continue, for the Indian and Inuit people saw the Cultural Education Centres as "the main vehicle or opportunity for the preservation of their cultural tradition or heritage." "It is our opinion that the Programme must give higher priority to the Indian/Inuit people's input to the direction it should go" the evaluators commented. Moreover, the financing should be guaranteed for periods of three to five years, they advised, for the quarterly situation they were observing was not conducive to forward planning.

Governments change, however, and that first federal munificence didn't actually last very long. Over the years, funding for Cultural Educational Centres in Canada has continued, but in variable sums decided by the government, and with variable lengths of guarantee. Soon after the Cultural and Education Centres Program went into action, the directors of the larger centers formed a national committee to address these and other concerns. Over the years, the growing committee has changed its name a couple of times, but in 1993, when it took on the present one, it became the First Nations Confederacy of Cultural Educational Centres (FNCCEC). At its annual conference held in 2003 in Mi'kmac territory, at Kjipuktuk (The Great Harbour), otherwise known as Halifax, Nova Scotia, which I was permitted to attend as an observer, the continuing lack of secure funding was a recurrent theme.

Another one, which was still simmering away in the questions and comments raised in response to an apparently munificent speech by a (non-Native) representative of Canadian Heritage, had been the main topic of a report commissioned by the organization back in 1982. The title puts it in a nutshell: "For Us to Decide, Our Culture, Our Survival, Our Future." This document (from which the quotation at the start of this chapter is taken) examined the importance of Indian control of Indian Cultural Centres (as they were called at the time). It related the paucity of appropriately designed education, and a sense of identity undermined by the regular Canadian school system that Indian children must attend, to their higher than average figures for dropouts, delinquency, suicide, petty crime, and drug and alcohol abuse. "Culture is the very spirit of the Indian people and cannot be ignored as the central focus for all Indian development programs" (ibid. p. 18). In the next chapter we see some of the outcomes of schools that have become independent, but in 2003, representatives of the culture centers still felt that decisions were being made about their funding needs without due consultation.

Despite these major drawbacks, the organization holding its annual assembly did by this time represent the interests of 87 centers scattered throughout Canada. It serves as a national organization and coordinating body for these centers, and its mandate is to advocate for the recovery, maintenance, and strengthening of First Nations culture on behalf of its membership (www.fnccec.com). One of its main roles is to promote and assist First Nations' cultural identities by serving as a funding agency for participating centers (ibid.), thus the issue of the diminishing government resources that it distributes is a theme continually emphasized as hampering its other roles. These include assisting in the development of new centers, and of training programs and the provision of technical assistance to existing ones, as well as the provision of publicity about them to the government and other public bodies (ibid.).

We have already encountered some of these member centers in earlier chapters, and others appear in later ones, but it will give a flavor of the composition of this big national body if I describe a small selection here. Between them they represent a great range of styles, reflecting the diversity of the First Peoples who live in Canada, and they engage in a multitude of different activities. I had visited a number of these places, and so at the conference I recognized delegates who had previously granted me interviews.

From furthest afield was Andrea Sanborn who had traveled from the U'Mista Cultural Centre, which, as described in chapter 1, was constructed for the express purpose of bringing home ceremonial dancing masks confiscated during the Canadian government's ban on potlatch activities. U'Mista, in the Kwak'wala language, holds the meaning of something precious returned, and the large decorated Chief's Big House that holds them now occupies a dominant position on the seafront at Alert Bay, where the 'Na̱mgis First Nation lives in northern Vancouver Island. The center also offers displays about its own history, and encourages the viewing of a video in which Gloria Cranmer Webster explains it, noting that this "Box of Treasures" is not a memorial to a dead past, but a symbol of the survival of her people. The center also houses a gallery of Kwakwa̱ka̱'wakw art available along with local crafts and other goods for purchase, and it runs a busy program of educational and other cultural activities. The language classes boast pupils from the ages of 3 to 93, Andrea had explained when I visited, and on that same day I watched a boat of ceremonially attired people leave from the shore to help celebrate the opening of a new Big House on a nearby island.

Also present at the conference was Lawrence Ambers, band manager of the 'Na̱mgis First Nation, who was representing the local school, for the educational activities of the U'Mista Centre had outgrown their facilities, and both school and a newly constructed recreational center had now become venues for many of them. Some of these are discussed in the next chapter. Andrea also talked, when I was there, of a tourism project that had been proposed, for it seems that visitors to the island are generally attracted by the First Nations, and they are not far from a high end resort named Nimmo Bay. A cooperative venture involving a four-day package of Aboriginal tourism could perhaps provide a lucrative source of nongovernmental support for the cultural and educational activities. Actually, the U'Mista Cultural Centre has been the focus of several visits from other anthropologists over the years, and the fascination of the consumers of their books (e.g., Clifford 1991, Lévi-Strauss 1988, Stanley 1998) and classes may be another draw to this charming spot.

Linda Pelly-Landrie, a former national coordinator of the FNCCEC, was also an active participant at the conference. She was at that time president of the Saskatchewan Indian Cultural Centre, which was the first provincial center, and is still one of the largest, with a mandate to the chiefs of the 74 bands in the huge province of Saskatchewan. Its biggest role is to provide educational support for the languages and other cultural skills of the eight First Nations—Woodland Cree, Swampy Cree, Plains Cree, Dene, Saulteaux, Dakota, Nakota, and Lakota—and to promote awareness about them in Canadian society. They have a good collection of books, prints, maps, and audio and videotapes in and about the various languages, and they are also able to provide computer software for language lessons and for the fonts required for the transcription of each language. Beautiful calendars are also produced for each of the peoples and some are available in English as well as the original languages.

This Saskatchewan Indian Cultural Centre is located in quite a different situation to the U'Mista, in the heart of the city of Saskatoon, and it is geared almost entirely toward supporting members of the local First Nations rather than attracting visitors. However, once visitors find themselves inside the rather unremarkable building, there is a large, open gallery space with stunningly attractive objects and artwork on display. Some of these are the products of a successful program of training First Nations art teachers, but another project of the center is to open a First Nations Keeping House to safeguard and protect all manner of cultural treasures including songs, stories, and sacred bundles as well as artifacts. There is also an active program for elders of the community. The center is planning a storefront to showcase their products, they have a good library, and they published a book about all the culture centers of Canada for the FNCCEC.

Another familiar face for me at the meeting was Kanatakta, who had been executive director of a culture center I had visited in Kahnawake, Mohawk home of the traveling show and the "Indian village," described in chapter 2. Here, the situation was different again, for there is only one Aboriginal language in this community, and for most people it is their second language if they know it at all. Indeed, for some learners it may be their third language because this federal Mohawk territory is surrounded by the province of Quebec so French is an important part of school life. Revival activities are robust, then, almost fierce, and the name of the center makes no concessions. It is Kanien'kehaka Onkwawén:na Raotitiohkwa, which Kanatakta (whose name is also in the vernacular) explained to me in some detail, as it contains concepts at the heart of Mohawk thought. Putting it briefly, and undoubtedly incompletely, it denotes a place of language and thought for all Mohawk people, so pretty much a culture center, but firmly in the Mohawk tongue. Kanatakta emphasized that the center is very much geared toward the community and its needs, and the building also houses a local radio station.

Kanien'kehaka Onkwawén:na Raotitiohkwa is not large, but it has an art gallery and a permanent museum presenting the history and political system of the Kanien'kehaka (Mohawks or, literally, "keepers of the Eastern door"). It opens with a painting of the Tree of Great Peace, which originally symbolized the League of Five Nations, formed at the instigation of a Huron man named Tekanawí:ta (Peacemaker) who thereby brought peace and a system remarkably like democracy several centuries before the arrival of Europeans in the area. These peoples, later to incorporate one more and become Six Nations, were named by the French as the Iroquois. They lived in a large area now straddling the United States–Canada border, and the longhouses they inhabited were described by Jacques Cartier when he first sailed up the St. Lawrence to the island that later became part of Montreal. Documentation and further detail about their story is to be found in a library/resource center similar to that of the Woodland Cultural Centre, except that this one had two young people taking care of it when I was there, and visitors could come in and be helped. One of these, Jamie-Lee (or Kanonwiioustha), was a fluent speaker of her native language, having attended an immersion school throughout her childhood, and we will return to her case in chapter 4, where we also visit the Kahnawake Language Centre.

To return to the meetings of the FNCCEC, there were plenary gatherings, with speeches, and sessions for representatives of the centers to discuss local issues in smaller regional groupings. On the last morning, each of these local groups brought resolutions to the full gathering again, and they were formalized for further action. The meetings had been opened and closed with ceremonies led by the Mi'kmac people, hosts for this event in Halifax, which is part of their traditional lands. An important part of the first day had been addresses by Giles Rochon, head of INAC (Indian and Northern Affairs Canada), and Norman Williams from Canadian Heritage. Both spoke much about funding for language revival and fielded questions and comments about the lack of consultation and continuing patronizing attitudes, among other things. There was also a formal dinner, after which a moving speech by a Mi'kmac teacher who had worked locally to have the Mi'kmac language replace the requirement to learn French was followed by presentations to people who had made a significant contribution to the continuity of their languages. Then we were entertained by a great and happy show of Mi'kmac dancing and stories.

During dinner, a tree just visible outside the window began demonstrating dramatically the arrival of Hurricane Juan, predicted to hit The Great Harbour at midnight that evening. This turned out to be a devastating natural phenomenon that kept delegates up most of the night, some in nervous huddles, some running in and out excited by the power of the wind, reporting on its latest destruction. In the morning, this charming seaside community looked completely ransacked. Mature trees in the park were uprooted, the shoreline deck was unearthed, bus shelters and car windows were smashed, and at one end of the hotel we were staying in, a façade of bricks lay scattered on the grass. At the opening of the meetings, President Gilbert Whiteduck had put a positive spin on the expected arrival of the hurricane. It will keep everyone at the conference, he pointed out, and perhaps it will bring the "refreshing energy" we need. After only 30 years of rebuilding cultural identities ransacked through up to four centuries of European invasive arrivals, I was impressed by the energy I had already witnessed around the country, but if more is needed, let more roll in.

Projects Preparing for the Future

As witness to the continuing energy among Canada's First Nations, this last section describes some examples of planned projects not yet completed, but gradually making headway toward a start in the next few years. The aims are still clearly recognizable, though again the forms are quite variable, despite contact between their protagonists through Aboriginal associations such as the FNCCEC. One project that I heard about at the meetings, for example, was from one of my tablemates at the opening meetings, who had traveled from Alberta. Morris Running Rabbit, tribal councilor from the Siksika First Nation, near Calgary, told me of their plans to build a new museum and interpretative center to be a showcase of their culture and its achievements. They already have a cultural education center and the group appeared full of life and energy. The men's cowboy hats and boots gave them an appearance of people who could successfully cross local cultural divisions in that "stampede" town, and the center looked set to be an interesting place to visit when it opened in 2005.

The Qay'llnagaay Heritage Centre and the Kluu Laanas Cultural Development Project are plans of quite a different order, for they are both located in the Haida Gwaii, islands some distance off the extreme west coast of Canada named by settlers as the Queen Charlotte Islands. Thriving Haida communities with beautiful wooden houses and striking totem poles were decimated by the arrival of Europeans and their diseases only a couple of centuries ago, but the Haida people still form a sizeable part of the population of the Haida Gwaii. They are in the process of claiming back their lands, an issue we discuss in chapter 6. In the meantime, Haida material culture is on display in many parts of the world and rarely fails to impress. One of the West Coast houses that form such an important display in the Canadian Museum of Civilisations is Haida, and in chapter 2, we heard about another one that has been reconstructed at Knott's Berry Farm, in Anaheim, California. In that chapter, too, we met some Haida carvers at Capilano Park in Vancouver, who work in a Haida constructed building, and present a dance show at advertised points during the day.

My own first introduction to this distinctive material culture had been in the Pitt Rivers Museum in Oxford where a huge Haida pole stands in the center at the back of the hall, stretching from the ground through the height of all three floors. There are various carvings on the pole, and a neat Haida watchman at the top proudly surveys the entire cramped collection of objects beneath him, brought, like he was, from distant parts of the world. On the second floor is an old postcard that illustrates the original location of this pole, at Old Massett in the Queen Charlotte Islands, and I had memorized its provenance. I thus made arrangements to drive to this community when I was visiting Haida Gwaii, quite a distance from the hotels and other facilities, but interesting as the place where many Haida settled after they were forced to leave older communities depleted by disease. The settlement does not look particularly welcoming to an outside visitor yet, and there is a tumbledown building marked MUSEUM, that is clearly defunct. There is a well-stocked gift shop, however, and there I asked whether there were any plans to rebuild the sorry building.

It was late in the day, and I was extremely fortunate that Vince Collison, the cultural development coordinator agreed to come back to his office and talk to me about the Kluu Laanas Project. This is to be a "living museum," he explained immediately, with artists' workshops and a community feast house. It is still at the planning stages, though they had raised the funds for a feasibility study, and he showed me the materials that had been drawn up already. These listed "functions, programs and services" it is proposed that the cultural center will offer, which include just about everything we have touched on already, and more. Among them are documentation of the Haida lineages of the past, present, and future, teaching centers for language and living Haida culture, carving and artisans' space, meeting places for Haida and other First Nations, and dedicated space for potlatch feasts and other ceremonies. It is planned to erect a totem pole in front of each building. The name, *kluu laanas*, is Haida too, meaning "canoe village" to mark the canoe as an integral part of Haida culture that also represents the independence of the Haida and their source of power in war, food gathering, trading, and exploring.

The project also includes a tourism center, with a presentation of Haida culture and history, and an "Old Massett Heritage Trail Interpretation Centre." This last will allow visitors to share the "immaculate milieu of rainforests and sandy and rocky beaches," but also "control and increase respect for the sensitive and pristine environment" of this part of the northwest coast. Vince explained that doubts have been expressed about the tourism, because people are afraid of "selling out," of losing a focus on themselves by catering to the visitors. He emphasized, however, that local people need to find a way to make a living and a lifestyle, and this source of income and employment, if managed properly, could be the answer. It would also enable Haida people to manage their own resources, and present themselves as living people, rather than the long-gone creators of museum specimens. A big part of the overall project is to establish good relations with museums around the world, and to bring Haida materials back into their proper context. I asked about the pole at the Pitt Rivers, which Vince had actually visited, but he was noncommittal. First, they would bring home and properly bury the ancestors whose bones have been the focus of Western research, and this is procedure is well underway.

The Qay'llnagaay Heritage Centre is a sister project, considerably further ahead, that represents the Haida people who live in and around Skidegate, in a more central part of the islands. Here five splendid new totem poles have already been raised, with great ritual and celebration, ready to stand at the entrance to the planned buildings, and a carving shed houses the construction of new bentwood boxes to accommodate the ancestral remains as they are returned.

The site for the center is adjacent to the Haida Gwaii Museum, which displays information about the repatriation process, acts as custodian for objects of Haida and Tlingit origin, and displays materials in consultation with "the Hereditary Leaders and Elders of the Haida nation." Working in the museum alongside the director, Nathalie Macfarlane, I met one of the prime movers behind the Qay'llnagaay project, namely Nika Collison, cousin of Vince, and granddaughter of the now rather well-known Haida artist Bill Reid. Nika has already written a fairly extensive report about the planned project, entitled "Communicating Who We Are," which I quote from below, but she was willing to spend time telling me about it in person too, and her excitement and enthusiasm were quite infectious.

According to the report, the Qay'llnagaay Experience is to bring to fruition an idea that has been "a dream of the Skidegate community for over 40 years." It will enable members of the Haida community "to celebrate their living culture" and to share with the world the "relationship with the land and sea that shapes, nourishes and sustains them." The exhibits are planned as "one flowing experience," and they will "strive to awaken all senses: sight, sound, smell, taste, touch, and a heightened awareness of the sixth sense." The outdoor part of the experience—where visitors are "to feel and smell the earth, the sea, the air"—is to be as important as the indoor one, and even the reception desk is to be placed in a welcome atrium "with natural light and wide open space." A "trading house" will provide a gift shop and gallery to promote local artists, and an "eating house" will offer the experience of "traditional Haida cuisine and food preparation," along with cooking classes and a display about sources of food.

Two classrooms are to be constructed for a variety of educational programs still being designed, but one will house an orientation about the conservation agreement between the Haida people and Parks Canada before visitors set out to explore this ancient and unique natural environment (see chapter 6). The other space will be flexible enough to be used for the activities of various partners, which already comprise universities and schools from around British Columbia, including the one specializing in art and design named for local artist, Emily Carr, and the on-site Bill Reid School of Art. At the latter, courses and workshops will be available in skills such as wood, bone, and stone carving, gold and silver smithing, and bentwood box making. For casual visitors, the payment of an entrance fee will grant them admission to several further display areas where they may study for themselves aspects of Haida life and history, observe the marine life, and relax and reflect on the resources that are managed here.

There will also be a Performing House, available for theater, music, and lectures, as well as community ceremonies, food sharing, song, dance, and storytelling. Children are to be welcomed throughout Qay'llnagaay, but there will be an area with activities specifically geared to appeal to them, where they may find discovery boxes, games, and an arts and crafts play space.

The report, from which all these descriptions have been gleaned, has a side column running through it quoting ideas and suggestions from members of the community, with their names, and an Appendix at the end, which lists all the people consulted and their organizations. This is clearly to be a great collaborative venture, and Nika talked me through some of the long, hard process over the years since the land had been allocated for a heritage site "back in the 50s or 60s," to ignite a broad interest, raise the necessary funds, and reach this exciting stage of detailed planning. In fact, it all started sometime before she became involved, but with her training in cultural resource management, and her ability to bring on side a range of influential people, she now occupies a place at the heart of the program. Before the first museum was built, the planning committee, which represented all the communities in the islands, was not majority Haida, but it is now, and the non-Haida people I met are thoroughly on side. Nika has a way of getting on with people, and she and Nathalie, who is actually training her in museum management, seem to speak with a single positive voice.

Many Forms, One Story

We have seen many examples of cultural display in this chapter, many ways of reclaiming control over the presentation and re-presentation of the heritage that people around the world cherish as their own. Sometimes this takes the form of emphasizing material culture, sometimes it seeks to collect and record the continuing use of language and ritual performance, and sometimes the activities are more concerned with revival than conservation. Often an important part of the display is outside, recognizing the harmonious links between a people and their long-standing environmental context. In many cases people are involved in repatriating objects and the bones of their ancestors, collected by outsiders for their own purposes, but there is also a sense of seeking to establish good relations with those whose forebears took so many liberties in the past. Thus museums that cooperate with the descendants of those who provided the prizes of their collections can now count on support in having them properly cared for. In other places, there is encouragement for living artists to produce work that reflects both their ancestral heritage and their contemporary situations and we consider these in some detail in chapter 5.

In all cases, however, people are united in a desire to take responsibility for their own records and, to conserve their shared heritage for the future generations of their own people. They are often willing to share their cultural treasure with outsiders as well, keen to set right historical records that ignored their contributions, but they all emphasize first the need to understand themselves, to value and to retain their own rich sources of identity. If we, as outsiders, at last allow and support the world's Indigenous people as they do this, I feel certain that we too will be surprised and rewarded with the splendid abundance of cultural variety that the world we all live in has conserved for posterity.

References and Further Readings

Bolton, L., 1997, "A Place Containing many Places: Museums and the Use of Objects to Represent Place in Melanesia," *The Australian Journal of Anthropology*, 8(1): 18–34.

——, 1999, "Radio and the Redefinition of *Kastom* in Vanuatu," *The Contemporary Pacific*, 11(2): 335–360.

Clifford, James, 1991, "Four Northwest Coast Museums," in Ivan Karp and Steven D. Lavine (eds.), *Exhibiting Cultures: The Poetics and Politics of Museum Display*, Washington, DC: Smithsonian Institution Press, pp. 212–254.

Collison, Nika, 2002, "Communicating Who We Are: The Qay'llnagaay Heritage Centre Preliminary Content Development Report, Phase 1," Qay'llnagaay Heritage Centre Society.

Eoe, S.M. and P. Swadling (eds.), 1991, *Centres in the Pacific*, Port Moresby: Papua New Guinea National Museum.

Evalucan, 1978, "Evaluation of the Cultural/Educational Centres Programme," Calgary, prepared for the Department of Indian and Inuit Affairs.

"For Us to Decide: Our Culture, Our Survival, Our Future," A Report on the Findings of Consultation on Indian Control of the Cultural Education Centres Program, presented by the National Committee of the Indian Cultural Education Centres, March 1982.

Graham, Elizabeth, 1997, *The Mush Hole: Life at Two Indian Residential Schools*, Waterloo: Heffle Publishing.

Hendry, Charles E., 1998, *Beyond Traplines*, Toronto: The Anglican Book Centre.

Jonaitis, Aldona (ed.), 1991, *Chiefly Feasts: The Enduring Kwakiutl Potlatch*, New York: American Museum of Natural History.

Lévi-Strauss, Claude, 1988, *The Way of the Masks*, Seattle: University of Washington Press.

Stanley, Nick, 1998, *Being Ourselves for You: The Global Display of Cultures*, London: Middlesex University Press.

Vianney, A., 1991. "The Vanuatu Cultural Centre," in S.M. Eoe and P. Swadling (eds.), *Centres in the Pacific*, Port Moresby: Papua New Guinea National Museum.

Chapter 4

Language and Formal Cultural Education

> Culture is the Education for your life.
> — Lesikar Ole Ngila, Maasai
>
> They put you through hell just to save you.
> — Vince Bomberry, Cayuga artist, on Christian residential schools

Introduction: *Raising Our Voices*

In November 2003, the annual conference of the Sweetgrass First Nations Language Council, organized by members of the Woodland Cultural Centre, had outgrown the premises in Brantford, and was transplanted to the roomy facilities of the University of Western Ontario. Plenary sessions took place in a large lecture theater, with raised seating to accommodate an audience of several hundred, and a substantial stage at the front. Again, I had received permission to attend as an observer, and one particular event made a strong impression on me. It involved a group of four young people who had been invited to speak about the experience of learning the original language of the Indigenous group into which they had been born. The languages—Cayuga and Mohawk—are now seriously endangered, and many adults in the communities where the speakers had been raised know little of them. They had tackled a lonely task then, and Lottie Keye, the teacher who presented them, was justifiably proud that they had made good progress. She asked them to speak for just five minutes to say how knowing their language had made them better people and how they would use it in the future.

First, none of the speakers was able to confine their talk to five minutes, and they were all remarkably sanguine about speaking in such a large auditorium. At only high school leaving age, they demonstrated extraordinary confidence, a common theme of their presentations being that they "knew who they were." The first one up, Andrew Thomas, said that a short answer would be that his language had given him an identity, but he went on to describe how positive he felt about taking part in ceremonial activities, and about the responsibilities he felt toward becoming involved. Mike Bomberry also spoke of the importance of ceremony, and how powerful he finds Cayuga words that cannot be translated into English. "My culture is there for me," he said, "and I am there for it." Unlike the first two, who had been sent as children to immersion schools, Wesley Miller was learning his language in adult immersion evening classes, and he encouraged others to follow suit. Kawennahén:te Cook, the only girl, spoke of the "firm base" the Freedom School in Ahkwesáhsne has given her, and she compared the respect they have for their teachers there with the generally "disrespectful and stupid" attitude of kids in the wider community. Each of them confirmed that they would certainly bring up their children to know their own tongue.

A large man in the front row of the audience, whose name—Tom Porter—crops up again in chapter 6, had tears running down his cheeks by the end of the speeches. He jumped to his feet and appealed to the "elders" present to walk down and shake the hands of these children. The atmosphere was thick with emotion as people rose to follow his lead, and when Tom had lined the four speakers up at the front, there was no age bar on the queue that formed to congratulate them. The audience was disappointingly small, but not one member of it remained seated, and there were few dry eyes among them as they filed by. Some of the reasons why four school leavers should provoke such turmoil in the adult audience of the Sweetgrass annual conference, *Raising Our Voices*, becomes clear as this chapter unfolds.

Residential Schools and the Assimilation Policy

The film *Rabbit Proof Fence* has made the world aware of the iniquities of the residential school system imposed upon Indigenous peoples' children by colonial governments. Set in Australia, *Rabbit Proof Fence* tells the story of three small girls who escape from such a school, and who embark upon a horrendous journey back home by following the rabbit-proof fence that runs over the 1,000 odd miles between the school and their village. They are at first chased by a fellow Aborigine who has been employed to bring them back, but they manage to evade his tracking by heading off through water and doubling back. They endure miles and miles of incredible hardship and deprivation, and one of them loses her life altogether, but two of these girls do actually make it back to their home town, where their relatives are overjoyed to see them. Many more children in Canada, Australia, New Zealand, and other colonies were less lucky. Most were forced to live out their formative years almost entirely separated from their families and the cultural background into which they had been born. Some didn't survive at all.

The film *Rabbit Proof Fence* also does a reasonable job of explaining the rationale behind the late-nineteenth-century policy of assimilation that underpinned the school program. In a nutshell, the idea was that taking young children away from their Native parents and bringing them up within the education system developed for white children would assimilate "problem natives" into the wider society within just a couple of generations. Schools that were originally set up by overseas missions to educate local children, often in their own languages, were exhorted to implement this assimilation policy by becoming residential and by using only English. The pupils were sometimes taken by force from their communities, they were rarely, if ever, allowed to return home, and they were forbidden to use their native tongues. Indeed, to make it more difficult for children to escape and to discourage them from using languages other than the dominant English, they were often sent to schools far from their homes, where they were mixed with children from many other linguistic groups. Hence the long journey of the three little girls in *Rabbit Proof Fence*.

Children within these schools who were caught using their own languages were punished, and some of the stories I heard in Canada well illustrate the strength of this prohibition. The first was regularly told to visitors to the Woodland Cultural Centre about the regime that had been meted out to the local people who attended the Mohawk Institute as children. They reported that the punishment for using their own language was to have their mouths stuffed with rags, apparently only marginally less painful than having a needle stuck through your tongue, which was said to have been practiced at other schools. Tom Hill, whose grandmother had been sent to the Mohawk Institute when her own mother passed away at an early age, recounted another fate. She had been beaten for speaking her own language, though she still knew little English, and she was put on a regime of salt and water for two weeks. Fortunately for this particular child, her grandmother heard of her plight and removed her from the school to raise her at her home.

According to the history of the Mohawk Institute, retold in *Wadrihwa* (Froman 2003), the school was sought after by Six Nations parents for their children for quite a long while after it opened in 1828. Associated with the nearby Mohawk Chapel, where the Mohawk language is proudly displayed behind the altar, and windows depict stories of the people, it also provided them with a trade and with some facility for working in the wider society. People also chose to send their children there, for they thought that they would be better looked after than they themselves could manage in the relative poverty that surrounded them at home. Orphaned children were taken in as well. Later, children were sent from different parts of Canada, and, as numbers increased, the regime grew stricter. All the children were expected to work for their living, boys in the fields and girls in the kitchen and laundry, but funds were tight and the fresh food they produced was largely sold to raise the income to pay the staff. The children were apparently often fed porridge three times a day—hence the name Mush Hole—and even the quantities of that were inadequate, so many reported feeling constantly cold and hungry.

They did receive the basics of reading, writing, and arithmetic, and some of the graduates were subsequently employed as teachers, which apparently also saved on costs (ibid.). One such teacher, Susan Hardy, is depicted for her long and patient contribution in one of the stained glass windows of the Mohawk Chapel. She taught and encouraged several generations of young people, and my host, Keith Lickers, told me that his father had benefited from her support. Susan Hardy was instrumental in helping Norman Lickers to continue his education at the University of Western Ontario where he became interested in becoming a lawyer. He pursued his academic study at Osgoode Hall in Toronto and got his call to the Bar in 1936 when he became the first qualified Native lawyer in Canada. An ironic twist was the fact that he became chairman of the board of governors for the Woodland Cultural Education Centre, the transformation of the Mohawk Institute, when it was closed by the Canadian government as an Indian Residential School in 1969.

For most children, however, life was tough in these schools and they learned little more than to be confused by the contradictory cultural messages they received. A series of short personal stories published about a school in Vancouver Island recounts vividly how devastated girls felt when the long beautiful hair they had grown to cherish as a source of pride and self-identity was cruelly lopped off on arrival. Boys who had been diligently learning manly skills of fishing and hunting while their sisters tended crops were thrust out into the fields to labor at "women's work." Tiny children who had known nothing but the comfort of a huddle of brothers and sisters when they fell asleep at night were separated into hard, single beds, with regulation bars at head and foot. If anyone lost control of their bodily functions, they were made to parade around the school with their soiled sheets, to be shamed by the laughter of the other children.

This kind of regime sounds harsh enough now to those of us who were prepared for boarding school in the United Kingdom by parents who shared the values of strict discipline, and to whom we returned in the holidays. For children who were simply lifted out of all prior experience, it is hard to imagine what kind of damage was inflicted upon them. An almost universal consequence was that when they had children of their own, they did not even try to pass on the language that had brought them such suffering, which accounts for the large numbers of people who know little of their native tongue today. A couple of mature Mohawk women I met at the Anglican Church on the Six Nations Reserve reported that their parents spoke the language, but not around their children, as if they were ashamed of using it. The father of one of them had been beaten for using Mohawk at school, with the words, "you don't bring any of that heathen Indian stuff into the Church." Graduates of these schools had also been denied important cultural knowledge about making homes in the traditions of the elders of their own communities. Hence the phrase "lost generation," used about Aboriginal people in different parts of the world who were subjected to this feature of the colonial assimilation programs.

Fortunately for the ultimate survival of languages and cultural knowledge, some people were lucky enough to avoid these schools, and others were rebellious enough to persist in the use of their own languages. Schools around the world continued to be run by churches, which were expected to implement the policies decided by governments that oversaw them. Probably, then, local experience would reflect the personalities of those appointed to run the schools—certainly the history of the Mohawk Institute would suggest the same (ibid.)—and many horrific stories are now emerging about the abuse that some children were subjected to. Vince Bomberry's quip, quoted at the start of this chapter, was made in reference to the involvement of the church with residential schools. Ultimately in the case of Canada, it was also a church report by Charles Hendry—referred to in the last chapter—that was influential in bringing the system to an end, and throughout the 1970s, most of these schools were closed down. In any case, according to Jody Beaulieu, at the Red Lake Tribal Information Centre, an unexpected aspect of the mixed schools in the United States was to unite people from different tribal groups in their resistance to government policies, and many of those who occupied Alcatraz had met in this way.

Some Native schools still exist in the United States, but they have been forced to change their remit considerably, and the Akta Lakota Museum described in chapter 1 is actually part of such a school, which now also publishes language and other Lakota cultural materials. Run by the Roman Catholic Church, St. Joseph's School does present a Christian education, but on the Sunday that we visited the museum there were few children around as they were said to be allowed home on this day. Other museums in the United States and Canada now have displays about the residential school system, relating the poor conditions and the loss of language, as well as the connection with the Christian church. At the U'Mista Cultural Centre, as at the Woodland Cultural Centre (see figure 3.1), the buildings of the old residential school still stand as witness to the system that was imposed, and although they are architecturally not particularly attractive, it has been decided in both cases to preserve them so that it will not be forgotten. Elsewhere old schools have sometimes been converted into community colleges.

Immersion Schools and Adult Language Programs

A vital part of the cultural education programs reported throughout the world, then, is the revival of languages so brutally removed from the tongues of those who would ordinarily pass them on. Different languages have of course been subjected to different degrees of devastation. People in areas remote from the large, important settlements of the colonizing powers have been better able to retain their native tongues, and in Canada, languages like Cree and Inuktitut are less endangered than many others, though still under threat. Indeed, at the meetings of the First Nations Confederation of Cultural Education Centres (FNCCEC), when names were being put forward for awards to those working to retain their languages, the delegate from James Bay reported that so many people know and use Cree there that she had not been able to isolate one single such name. Elsewhere, languages have died out altogether as the older speakers—for whatever reasons—failed to pass them on. In many places, however, even only a few remaining speakers of an Indigenous tongue become highly valued teachers in the present positive climate of language revival.

A program that has been adopted in several different parts of the world builds on the basic ability of small children to absorb the languages they hear around them. In the places I visited in East Africa—Tanzania and Kenya—local people I met could routinely use at least three languages. They were all fluent in the lingua franca Kiswahili, the national tongue in those two countries, they had learned at least one tribal language in their family homes, and those who were available for employment with foreign visitors also had good working English. In these cases, the local languages are not yet threatened, and people learn them in a natural way as they grow up. Based on this principle, then, various peoples around the world have instituted "immersion schools" to give children the opportunity to pick up the languages that their parents were not taught, but which underpin their cultural identity.

In Aotearoa, more widely known as New Zealand, there is an active program of preschool immersion in Maori language, and in a community in Lower Hutt, a short train ride from Wellington, I watched the children of such a group chat as they ate their lunch. Patsy Puketapu, who was showing me around the *marae* where the children meet, explained that this *kohangareo* (literally, language nest) was then (in 2004) in its twenty-first year, so some of its "originals" were now teaching there. Some such groups are home-based, some are school-based, but this had been the first one to be operated from a *marae*, she explained. *Waiwhetu Marae* is a beautiful ceremonial house that her father-in-law had built back in 1960 as a spiritual home for the community, and photographs of the many activities based there, displayed around the large eating area at the back, bear witness to its continuing important role. Lower Hutt's proximity to the seat of government has worked in their favor, it seems, for when a group of elders decided in the 1970s that the state of their language needed attending to, Lower Hutt was funded to pilot the scheme.

In North America, too, I found many examples of immersion schools for preschool level children where native languages are under threat, and at the People's Center, in Pablo, Montana, I met a young Salish woman teacher, who explained that the system had been introduced to allow small children to meet the elders. Aggie was born of a Salish father and non-Native mother, but on the reservation where she grew up, her mother had found it useful to learn Salish as well. Kootenai is another language used in this area, so most local schools offer them both on an elective basis, and the tribal school requires one or the other. In Ohsweken, on the Six Nations Reserve, all the schools offer Mohawk or Cayuga as a second language, but there is full Cayuga immersion through one high school, and 50/50 Mohawk immersion in another one. There is immersion school support for Mohawk language in Kahnawake, as discussed in the last chapter, and the Freedom School in Ahkwesáhsne has been a model for many others.

It should be noted, however, that language immersion schools are not the choice of every parent living in an Indigenous community, and many worry that if they put their children into such a specific educational establishment, they will fail to make good grades in the English part of the curriculum. Some say that the First Nations have already been too far assimilated into the wider society, others simply worry that teachers with native language ability may not be properly qualified in other subjects, and academic standards will fall. Many parents who choose to send their children to an immersion primary school, therefore, move them into the mainstream system for the high school part of their education. On the Six Nations Reserve, numbers drop off dramatically at the high school level, but many children also have to travel off reserve to high school where they complain that they are discriminated against in other ways. The Cayuga and Mohawk classes taught in regular school also present the language in a written form that is unfamiliar and off-putting, according to one mother I spoke to about this. She felt that as these were originally oral tongues they should be taught orally, not through a foreign writing system.

In practice, the results of the children who stick with immersion in their own native languages seem to be good in English classes as well, and all of the speakers we mentioned at the beginning of the chapter confirmed that this was the case for themselves and their classmates. I met one boy on the Six Nations Reserve who had been persuaded by his parents to move to the mainstream system at ninth grade, after attending Cayuga immersion from kindergarten to eighth grade, and he gained an average of 92 percent within one year. Having proved that he could do that well, he convinced his parents to let him move back to the immersion high school on the reserve. He had just graduated when I met him and he was planning to train as an immersion teacher so that he could use his Cayuga and "pay back the teachers who had taught him." Tove Skutnabb-Kangas, a Danish linguist who gave the keynote lecture at the same Sweetgrass Language Council conference addressed by the youthful speakers, confirmed that children who learn their native tongue generally do better across the board, in English as well as other subjects.

Immersion language schools must of course teach subjects other than language, but use of the native tongue offers the opportunity also to pass on an understanding of cultural knowledge. A report about the Kanien'kéha (Mohawk) Program in Ahkwesáhsne makes this point in reference to the strong Haudenosaunee (Iroquois) component in both science and social studies, the former relating the teaching to the local environment, the latter to community values (Cook-Peters 2003: 4). Jamie-Lee, whom we met in the last chapter, reported that in her immersion school in Kahnawake she learned the history of the community and of the Mohawk people in general. She also learned the importance of respect: respect for other people, and for all that they had, so each morning in class, they would give thanks for the world that gave them light and warmth and food.

In the village of Kimmirut, in the new Inuit territory of Nunavut, I watched a group of secondary school children prepare for a summer "science" camp that would combine teaching about plants, animals, rocks, and minerals with the experience their elders can still pass on of living off the land. A highlight of the camp experience is the hunting, killing, and dissecting of a caribou, which offers the children hands-on participation in the activities that were vital to traditional life, as well as introducing the new "scientific" knowledge associated with animal anatomy and biology.

Such a combination of 'new' and 'old' allows children to become familiar with both the curricula of the wider Canadian world to which their province belongs and their own traditional worlds. In Nunavut, the traditional world is not as far removed as that of the Haudenosaunee people, whose lands have been more effectively taken over, and it is possibly more difficult to establish ideas that are shared within the community about how the teaching should be presented. Cathy Jamieson, deputy head of the 50/50 Mohawk immersion school, told me about a new teacher, trained in an Aboriginal education program, who had sat down in a circle with the children in his classroom. His methods had met with opposition from colleagues trained in a more European style of straight rows and quiet kids. In the Ahkwesáhsne report, evidence is presented that some children learn better if they are allowed to be moving, even chewing gum, and observers had already noticed that the Kanien'kéha classes are noisier and busier than the English ones (Cook-Peters 2003: 10). Possibly factors such as these may explain why First Nations children have trouble moving to outside high schools.

Indigenous language programs also include classes and other activities for adults who want to learn the native tongue they were never taught, of course, and culture centers around the world offer support for local language study. Parents whose children acquire fluency form one important group that is motivated to learn, and Jamie-Lee told me that her mother had just completed a Mohawk teaching course, although she is not yet completely fluent. The case of Kahnawake provides a good starting point for this subject, because the community has set the goal of achieving 80 percent bilingualism within 20 years. The head of the Language Centre, Melvin Tekahonwén:sere Diabo, explained that people had been worried about the fate of their tongue since the mid-1970s. They had lost their land and their means of livelihood, so if they lost their language what would be left of their culture? They started in a small way, but it was not enough, and in December 1999, they made a Declaration of Languages, followed by the passing of a law by local counselors. Now organizations within the community give their employees time off to study as well as paying for the classes, and people come every day. The first goal is to have 30 percent fluency among community employees in five years, something of an increase over the present 5 percent.

If this seems an optimistic idea for people whose languages have been so severely curtailed in their use, it might be worth glancing at revival programs that have been going a little longer. In my own lifetime, for example, the Welsh language has undergone a remarkable transformation. In the late 1950s, when I was at school in North Wales, it was spoken largely within communities of people who had grown up together, and most of the people I heard speaking the language were engaged in menial tasks. Now, schools and universities require bilingual stationery and brochures, outsiders who take up all kinds of employment are expected to master the tongue, and roadsigns throughout the principality are in Welsh. Immersion schools turn out children who switch easily between the two and Welsh is heard widely on the streets. There has also been a revival in the use of the Gaelic language, in both Scotland and Ireland, and efforts are being made to bring back the use of Cornish in the extreme southwest of the United Kingdom. In mainland European countries, parallel movements may be observed in various cultural regions, and languages such as Catalán and Basque are vibrant right through to university level and beyond.

At the Sweetgrass conference, Amos Key summarized the history of the struggle to revive First Nations languages in Ontario since 1984, when he had become involved in setting up an immersion program at the Six Nations. He spoke of the support of local chiefs, of the generosity of language speakers who freely gave their time, and of the success of the children who came through this program. The private school board that was set up to administer the Cayuga immersion program has the best retention rate in the province, he announced, and students who enter the high school go right through to grade 12 and into postsecondary courses beyond that. He also spoke of his involvement in founding a radio station on the reserve, and the large collection of CDs and tapes of Longhouse ceremonies that had been gathered. There had been plenty of local critics and detractors, he said, but the graduates who had stood up the day before had done something many adults would find difficult.

The Canadian government had offered varying degrees of support, but often short-term and unreliable, with much evaluative surveying, and when the Sweetgrass Language Council was entrusted with distributing funds for language revival throughout Ontario, this burden of constant auditing added to their struggle. This Aboriginal Language Initiative had been the result of a 1995 Royal Commission on Aboriginal Peoples that recommended that a foundation be created to address the loss of Aboriginal languages and cultures. By the 2003 conference, a Task Force committee was being selected to advise the government on the setting up of a new Aboriginal Languages and Cultures Centre to continue this work *under the stewardship of Aboriginal peoples* (*Canadian Heritage News*, April 2003). This was clearly a response to claims of the sort we touched on in the previous chapter at the meetings of the FNCCEC—that decisions are constantly being made by the government on behalf of First Nations. The outcome of the Task Force remains to be seen, but as Amos Key has been invited to take part, the Sweetgrass First Nations Language Council, through him, will be close to the process.

The mood of the conference was that language teachers in Canada should be remunerated at the same level, whether they teach Cree, Cayuga, or the much favored French. The principle of giving First Nations languages in Canada a status equivalent to that of the official ones of French and English has formed the basis of various proposals put together by the Assembly of First Nations since 1990, and it underpins discussions at provincial level too. At the Sweetgrass conference, the linguist Ian Martin, from Glendon College, York University (Ontario), presented a paper that looked in some detail at the models Canada already has embedded in its legislation, both federally and in the provinces of Quebec, Northwest Territories and the newly created Nunavut. The last case is a good one, for with an 85 percent Inuit population, it has been necessary to make Inuktitut an official language, though the Francophones already have a school for the

50 French-speaking children. Martin also spoke of the importance of initiatives such as the Kahnawake one described above, and encouraged members of First Nations to use the power already invested in their local bands to revive their languages.

Courses Beyond Language

Many more aspects of culture and history are taught at schools around the world as people seek to reclaim and take control of their own heritage. Reviving spoken language is a vital part of the process, but its teaching is anyway supplemented with music, stories, and pictures, that introduce secrets a dying language would otherwise take with it to its grave. The work of Margaret and Teddy Peters, active participants in the Sweetgrass Language Council during my visit, well illustrate the point, and they were demonstrating materials they use at the same conference. Margaret makes books, pictures, and other teaching aids for Mohawk language teaching, and as she grew up in a Mohawk-speaking family, she is well aware of the culturally specific images. These include clan names, ceremonial and ritual recitations, and details of the original calendar used in this part of the world (Peters and Jacobs 2003). Teddy's grandparents reared him in the Mohawk tongue and he teaches by using songs in Mohawk, which he plays over the air on the local radio station. Apparently people also call in to contribute to the program by telling stories (Peters 2003). At the Sweetgrass conference, teachers of other languages such as Ojibwe and Cree shared similar teaching materials for their own tongues.

Dancing is an important part of the curriculum at the T'lisalagi'lakw School in Alert Bay, which was designed with the performance room visible through glass from the main entrance hall. Kwak'wala dance is taught from the Headstart Aboriginal program, which children enter at four years of age, through grades one to seven of primary school, and they also learn to make the regalia that bring it all to life at the Big House feasts. According to their teacher, Alexandra Willie, who called in when I was there, the children have the same level of dancing ability as the adults on these occasions. Prizes are awarded every year to the pupils who achieve most in dancing and singing, and their names are entered on the roll board displayed in the school entrance alongside those who have shone in areas such as citizenship, diligence, and academic work. The dance room itself is organized to indicate the same four cardinal directions as the big house, each associated with a different season, so the children can easily adapt their learning to the public ceremonial functions that are held there. The dance teacher also offers classes to adults if they need them.

In New Zealand, I came across a culture center in Rotorua that offered training in various Maori arts, such as carving and weaving, but only to those who could claim at least one-sixteenth Maori blood. At the Maori Arts and Crafts Institute in the Te Whakarewarewa thermal valley, non-Maori visitors were welcome, for a price, to come in a watch the trainees at work and learn from a guide about the importance of the skills that were being imparted. Carving was a way to tell stories, he explained, when the Maori language had no writing. He also demonstrated how to extract thread from the flax plant for making ropes and fishing nets, and to prepare the materials for weaving baskets and mats. Paying visitors were shown how to make a ceremonial Maori greeting before being admitted to a show at the *marae*, but the more practical skills were reserved, free, for those of genuine Maori background.

In Nibutani, Hokkaido, in the north of Japan, I was introduced to a group of women practicing the appliqué work that characterizes the clothes the Ainu wear for ceremonial occasions, similar to those I had seen in the Ainu village described in the prologue to this book. These skills had been lost to many people, just as their language had, and the local authorities have now organized for those who retain them to teach their neighbors during a month long course at the village hall. They seemed to be a cheerful group, sharing ideas about the wearing of the garments once they would be made. Men present in the same hall were relearning how to carve fine wooden plates, and when I jumped out of my host's car at the station, some 20 minutes drive down the road, I discovered they had followed us to make me a gift of two of their plates and an appliquéd headband!

Back at the Six Nations, at an establishment called the Jake Thomas Learning Centre, founded in 1993 "for the conservation of traditional Iroquoian culture," Native and non-Native people may sign up to participate and learn the skills required to make items such as cow horn rattles, traditional outfits, moccasins, corn husk masks, beadwork, wampum beads, and wampum belt reproductions. Yvonne Thomas, widow of the eponymous Jake, teaches these skills in the context of their meaning to the way of life of the Iroquoian people, and she stocks a selection of audiotapes and videotapes recorded by Jake before he died. This remarkable man, a former museum curator of the Woodland Cultural Centre, could speak all five of the Iroquoian languages, and recite from memory ceremonial knowledge such as that contained in the Great Law, the Code of Handsome Lake, prayers of thanksgiving, and ceremonies for the Longhouse calendar year. Yvonne told me that some people criticize her for making this knowledge too widely available, and for the sale of books and audio/videotapes, nevertheless these tools are a critical component that enables the learner and ensures that the Longhouse ceremonies go on, she explained. Moreover, Jake was concerned to conserve things that could otherwise be lost forever, and since he devoted much of his life to recording for posterity, she feels responsible for making his work available (see, e.g., Thomas and Boyle 1994).

During the summer of 2003, when I was visiting the Six Nations, a conference entitled *Restoring Our Peace* was held in Chiefswood Park, an open meadow at the entrance to the reserve. It was a fine sunny day, so most of those present parked the lawn chairs they had brought in the shade of a large spreading tree. The speakers were under a pergola-style umbrella, their voices relayed clearly across quite a large area that also included a tent where food was being served, and another where massage and *reiki* treatment were being offered. Water was freely available, and the serious presentations were interspersed with a performance of contemporary dance during the lunch break, and an amusing series of skits presented by a youthful drama group. The event was organized by the family assault support service named *Ganohkwásra*, a Cayuga word meaning "Love among Us," and it was funded by the Aboriginal Healing Foundation.

This conference was a follow-up to one held a couple of years before that had addressed issues of Haudenosaunee history and its consequences for the present population. It had been entitled *The Disruption of Our Peace*, and had apparently been a great success (*Ganohkwásra Newsletter* Summer 2002). This one was moving on to the positive process of reclamation, which according to the *COD* definition quoted by Tom Hill, who introduced the Sunday session, means "to win back, away from vice, or savagery," an interesting expression, he noted, since that was precisely the term that had been used by non-Natives about themselves. The concern was to reclaim "our culture, our status, our artifacts, our voice and our lifestyle," he said, and speakers addressed several issues pertinent to this aim.

As much as the content of all the addresses, however, I was impressed by the relaxed atmosphere of the occasion and by the friendly way that some quite lively discussions took place on this piece of Haudenosaunee public land. The language used was English, but the mode of communication seemed to hold a key to something much more deeply seated in the people gathered that day. A couple of people sitting close to me in the audience became impatient when one of the speakers struggled with her notes. "If she knows her stuff, she shouldn't need to be reading," one commented to her friend—a good point, I thought ruefully, remembering how academics often simply read what they have prepared in advance. It is actually not that many generations since Indigenous people routinely remembered and passed on their history and cultural knowledge orally, and this is another skill that we lose as we become literate.

Postsecondary Education

Another movement that has been sweeping through areas with large Indigenous populations has been the introduction of postsecondary courses specifically designed to cater to their needs. Community colleges provide the language training mentioned above, especially for adults, but they also often offer subjects of cultural value and the preparation required for university and college entrance. One example is the Red Crow Community College in Cardston, Alberta, which claims that when its board of governors took control from the Kainai Board of Education in 1995 it became the first tribally controlled community college in Canada. Here students may take up to two years' worth of an arts and science program, with credits transferable to other public institutions. They may take courses in Traditional Land Use, including information about medicinal plant sites, burial sites, sacred sites, bison jumps, and the historical significance of places in their own vicinity. They may also take Kainai Studies, with or without transferable credits, that comprise seminars and workshops that focus on areas such as history, language, health, and the social and economic development of the Kainai people.

At universities, too, programs are offered in Indigenous Studies, Aboriginal Studies, or Native Studies, as well as the more specific Maori Studies in New Zealand. At McMaster University, for example, Indigenous Studies is offered in combination with one other subject for a Bachelor of Arts, and may also be taken as a minor. It offers a "unique and innovative approach to education by combining traditional knowledge with 'mainstream' scholarship, resulting in creative and interactive pedagogies" (promotional leaflet). Instructors include people qualified not only in the university system, but also within their Indigenous communities, so elders and clan mothers are valued alongside Native academics. In fact it was Trent University, in Peterborough, Ontario, that introduced this innovation, when they engaged Jake Thomas (whom we heard about in the last section) to set up Native Studies in 1973–1974. Courses again cover languages, but also include history, government, health education, land claims, environmental issues, and Indigenous human rights.

A Canadian University that administers a huge range of courses designed specifically for the Aboriginal Community is the University of Manitoba, which also started its Native Studies program back in the mid-1970s and operates a graduate program as well as three- and four-year undergraduate degrees. It now also offers an Aboriginal Business Education Programme, special access courses for the faculties of law, engineering, medicine, and social work, and participates in an off-campus First Nations' initiated National Environmental Education and Training Programme. Together with Keewatin Community College, it administers a Faculty of Nursing located in Norway House Cree Nation, a Faculty of Social Work in Thompson, Manitoba, and has a flourishing program of continuing education.

At the University of Auckland, the Department of Maori Studies, which split from the Anthropology Department in 1985, also has several disciplinary streams, including language and politics, but a section I found particularly interesting offered a hands-on engagement with material culture. I was shown around by Maureen Landers, who explained her teaching focus on knowledge recovery, so students spend time trying to replicate methods used by their ancestors. They must work from evidence acquired from archaeology, museums, or descriptions of the work, she explained, but they are then trying to experience the pain and toil of creating the artifacts that were used in their culture. Four students were working with flax as I went through, and the head of this department, Professor Dante, explained that sometimes they became quite emotional with this aspect of reclaiming their culture. They also found the work quite a spiritual experience, he said.

Support for Aboriginal students is widespread and generous. At the University of Auckland, there is a purpose-built *marae* or meeting house, *Tane-nui-a-rangi*, which features carvings, stained glass windows, and decorative weaving work to represent all the different *iwi* (tribes), as well as welcoming other Pacific peoples, and paying tribute to the wider society in which it is built. Here classes are taken, but it is also a place for ceremonial occasions, and a place to remember people associated with the department who have passed away. At the University of British Columbia, there is a magnificent longhouse called The First Nations House of Learning. It is said to serve as a "home away from home" for First Nations students, to provide a meeting place for a wide range of activities, and to make the university's wide resources more accessible to First Peoples. It also "enables First Nations to share their knowledge and cultures with one another, with the university community, and with the wider community" (brochure).

At Cornell University, which lies in the heart of the original Cayuga lands, there is a purpose-built hall of residence for Native students called Akwe:kon—a striking wooden building decorated to display the purple background of the beaded wampum, with windows representing each of the nations of the Haudenosaunee confederacy. It houses some 35 students, not exclusively Native, as well as faculty in residence, common rooms, a library, and the offices of the American Indian Program. In the city of Toronto, where students at the university may well be scattered for residential purposes, there is a First Nations House that offers a wide range of services summarized by the motto: "leadership, spiritual growth and academic excellence" (brochure). Programs include recruitment drives, academic and personal counseling, Native tuition, and financial assistance. There is also a Native Students Association and various cultural programs, including an elder-in-residence and a visiting elder, who comes in from different First Nations.

On the morning of the Summer Solstice in 2003, the day of the year designated as National Aboriginal Day in Canada, a ceremony to open the first purpose-built First Nations University (FNUC) was given detailed coverage on CBC Newsworld. Prince Edward was there, perhaps to mark the continuing relationship between First Nations in Canada and the Crown, and other dignitaries represented the City of Regina, the Province of Saskatchewan, and the all important Saskatchewan Indian Nations. Located on the spacious campus of Regina University, the splendid new building (see figure 4.1) had been designed by Douglas Cardinal with various features important to the people who would meet there. These apparently include a clear north/south axis, a close relationship with Mother Earth, and a tipi-shaped ceremonial room in the large central entrance hall. I happened to pass through Regina later in the year; and I drove by the FNUC just as daylight was fading over the swirling Cardinal curves (reminiscent of the Canadian Museum of Civilisations and the new Museum of the American Indian). As the electricity was switched on inside, the glass tipi became clearly visible from quite a distance, evidently affirming the importance of the spiritual core to this exciting new accomplishment.

On the Six Nations Reserve, I interviewed Rebecca Jamieson, who was in charge of the office that had been set up to advise young people about postsecondary educational possibilities. It was well stocked with brochures about universities and colleges, about the various

Figure 4.1 The First Nations University of Canada building in Regina, Saskatchewan, was designed, like the Canadian Museum of Civilisations in Ottawa, and the National Museum of the American Indian in Washington, DC by Douglas Cardinal.

courses they offered, and about the further support they could expect at each of the establishments featured. It provided information about the scholarships and bursaries available, and about the support to which students graduating from the schools on the reserve were entitled. Rebecca told me quite a bit about the recent movement for Indian controlled education. She said that the Maori "language nests" were one of "the first stakes driven into the ground to make own languages legitimate in the eyes of others," and they had led the way to the bicultural/bilingual movements that started in the 1970s. She described international gatherings such as the meeting in Calgary of the World Indigenous Peoples Conference on Education, which had established a "Global Consortium for Higher Education."

We also discussed "the world movement" to develop Indigenous Studies, and here Rebecca made an interesting point. She suggested that these courses had been largely designed to educate students who have come out of a strictly Western educational system and who have therefore come for the first time to a greater understanding of themselves and their Indigenous backgrounds. Children who have come through Mohawk or Cayuga immersion schools, or the trilingual

(Cree/French/English) education system that operates in the James Bay communities in northern Quebec, would not have the same need for this type of postsecondary education. They have their own language and culture from which to understand current issues. Indeed, she pointed out, culture centers themselves are a symbol of things that are at risk. Locally, at the Mohawk College in Hamilton and Brantford, Aboriginal students may choose to specialize in Aboriginal Technology and Business, or the two-year programs in Aboriginal Recreation and Tourism. Equally, and especially if they have a sound basic education in their own culture, they may choose any other subject that takes their fancy.

Educating the World

Another important aspect of education about Indigenous people mentioned by those with whom I spent time learning of these things is that it should be disseminated to members of the wider world. Indeed, members of this wider world probably need such education as much as anyone, for we are the ones who have retained (or even perpetuated) misleading ideas about how few Indigenous people remain and about how many have become assimilated into that world. Usually, representatives of the museums and culture centers I visited would explain that they give priority to their own people first to learn of themselves, but they also felt it important to rectify the erroneous history that continues to be taught through many Western textbooks and course curricula.

A particularly striking example of such education was introduced to me along with my first year anthropology students when a young anthropologist named Gemma Burford came with a Maasai companion named Lesikar Ole Ngila to speak about a nongovernmental organization (NGO) she had been involved in setting up in Tanzania. This organization is run primarily for the benefit of young tribal people living in and around the city of Arusha—to remind them of their cultural knowledge at the same time as introducing the Tanzanian national curriculum, and to give them the opportunity to sing, play music, and tell stories together (see figure 4.2). However, the organizers could see the wider value of the cultural knowledge they were passing on and have come up with the idea of offering it—at a price— to visitors from the outside world who wish to find out more about the peoples represented there. How much better, they reasoned, to turn this local knowledge into a commodity that could bring in an income than always to be asking Western nations to send young

Figure 4.2 Gemma Enolengila (nee Burford) and Lesikar Ole Ngila and students of the Aang Serian School in Arusha, Tanzania (Courtesy GE for Aang Serian).

people arrogantly to 'help out' in their schools and villages. Anthropologists would have to pay now for the knowledge they had formerly picked up so freely, but then the Maasai language has a word—*Oloipung'o*—to refer to people who travel away from home to find out about others, so perhaps that is how this idea was born.

Since that first talk, the organization in Arusha, known locally as *Aang Serian*, or House of Peace, has gone from strength to strength. It has increased the numbers of local participants, and raised money to build a community school in the Maasai area of Eluai, Monduli Juu, where regular lessons are taught in Indigenous knowledge, ethnobiology, and appropriate technology, alongside the national secondary curriculum. A course called "Peoples and Cultures," which started in January 2005, teaches local tribal peoples about other Indigenous societies around the world. This is partly financed by the International Summer School, which brings in fee-paying students to study anthropology with community elders and health care from traditional healers among Maasai pastoralists and Chagga farmers. The summer school also offers Swahili language tuition, drum, dance, and marimba lessons from a professional musician, walking tours, and day trips to see local wildlife (http://www.aangserian.org.uk).

Another interesting example I came across was when visiting an area that had been set up as a tourist venue on the island of Sentosa in Singapore. Entitled Asian Village, this was a large park where houses, gardens, and other features had been constructed to represent different countries of Asia. It was very quiet on the day of my visit, and although it was still early it seemed as though the place may have lost its ability to attract the passing public. In the Malaysia section, however, there was more of a buzz, and I found an office preparing none other than "educational tours." The young man in attendance—Ramli Bin Ibrahim—explained that the attraction had indeed begun to wear a little thin with the tourists, but they had had the new idea of introducing parties of school children to the Kampong way of life. A notice at the entrance proclaims that "this traditional type of Malay architecture reflects the people's strong sense of community spirit." The company—Kid's Kampong—was also in the process of building a pond stocked with fish so that children could experience the fun both of feeding and of catching them!

A serious educational program is operated out of the Woodland Cultural Centre, and it has two main parts. The first is to offer groups of school children and other visitors guided tours of the facilities, focusing on the museum of course, but sometimes also offering the chance to see more of the old Mohawk Institute. A period can be timetabled in for practical activities, perhaps to handle some of the objects in the collection, to play traditional games, or to use traditional materials and methods to make their own jewelry, tools, and pottery. Tara Froman, who runs this educational tour program, explained that 85 percent of the children who visit are non-Native so they need a lot more background information in preparation for their tour than those who live on the reserve do. She likes to remind them of the importance of women in the life of the First Nations, she explained. She also noted ruefully that many non-Native adults need much the same background preparation, so she tends to start at the beginning with them as she does with the children.

This is largely due to the lack of information about First Peoples in the school curriculum taught until very recently in Ontario, which was instead much oriented toward the settlement of the country by Europeans and their history back home. Now, there are two points in the primary curriculum that offer teachers a chance to rectify this oversight, and apparently they often timetable their visits to coincide with those. The first is in Year three, when there is a section about "Pioneers," and the second is in Year six under the heading "Aboriginal Peoples and European Explorers." Tara pointed out that the focus can still be on the settlers, and it rather depends on individual teachers how much they introduce about the Native occupants, but the new Year six section was only introduced in 2000 so they have at least made some progress. She also offers "teacher nights" for those who want to prepare for their class visits before they arrive.

The second part of the educational program is an outreach one, operated by Bernadette Wabie, the public education officer, who makes presentations at schools within an approximately two-hour drive radius of the center. She takes along an "Edukit," with objects including musical instruments to illustrate a Power Point presentation she has prepared, and the children enjoy passing them around, trying them out, and asking questions about them. She explained that she likes to make clear the contribution that Native peoples have made in food, land, technology, and medicines. I accompanied Bernie to visit a grade three class where she gave a presentation on the Contributions of Aboriginal Peoples to Society (see figure 4.3), and her talk was very powerful. There was a general introduction about the local First Nations, which included teaching the children greetings in Ojibwe, Algonquin, Mohawk, and Cayuga. Then she described how the

Figure 4.3 Bernadette Wabie, the Public Education Officer of the Woodland Cultural Centre, talks to a Grade 3 class about the contribution of the First Nations to their present lives (Courtesy of the Woodland Cultural Centre and BW).

ancestors of these same people had shown Europeans how to live in North America, how to build canoes fit to travel on their waterways, and how to find and follow the trails that had now become roads.

Seventy-nine new types of edible plants had been introduced to the Europeans, she explained, mentioning some examples that the children would surely enjoy, such as toasted corn flakes, peanuts, and maple syrup. Over 200 useful drug-yielding plants had been discovered and used by Aboriginal people, she continued, again giving examples that the children might recognize, such as cherry bark for coughs, witch hazel for sore muscles, and blackberry juice for diarrhea. She showed them beautiful containers made from wood, sweetgrass, birch bark, and porcupine quills, and she explained how the Algonquin birch bark canoes are light enough for people to carry as well as to ride in. She talked of the use of leather, fur, and cotton in clothes and moccasins and the way different styles of decorative beadwork were used by different peoples. Bernie also explained how the Haudenosaunee confederacy works, how it formed the basis of the government structures of the United States, and (like Tara) she mentioned the importance to this day of the clan mothers.

Turning to games and music, Bernie talked of Lacrosse, the Native game that is now Canada's national summer sport, and she explained how the bone and toggle game was good for developing the vital eye/hand coordination skills that would train people to be good hunters. She showed and explained different types of drums and rattles, the natural materials they were made from, and how they could be adjusted to produce different sounds. At this point, Bernie got the children to stand up and try an Iroquoian round dance that provided some fun, and then they got to pass around, and ask questions about, the objects she had on display. The children were enthralled by Bernie's presentation, and it seemed quite unclear to me why teachers weren't making use of this fascinating material all the time in their schools.

Bernie is also asked to attend school festivals and special days, and she responds to requests to design new presentations, such as the one about Maple Syrup for the Crawford Lake Conservation Authority's "Sweet Water Festival" (*Wadrihwa* 17,4/18,1: 9). Together with summer student Robyn Guest from Wilfred Laurier University, she made seven stand-alone presentations for a package of cross-cultural training courses entitled "Living Together, Understanding First Nations" (ibid. 10). In the summer of 2003, when I was visiting the center, she was working on a response to some requests from local high schools to offer something about Native spirituality for their World Religions courses.

In fact there are a number of courses about Aboriginal peoples available within the Ontario high school curriculum (Elijah 2003), and the Native Canadian Centre of Toronto has a Visiting Schools Programme that offers presentations about First Nations, Métis, and Inuit peoples (brochure). In Saskatoon, I came across a Treaty Awareness Speakers Bureau that seeks to offer an understanding to all residents of Saskatchewan of the treaties that underpin their residential arrangements. In the heart of Winnipeg, there is a beautiful new circular building called Thunderbird House that offers courses on drumming, 'rites of passage,' and holistic healing, which, according to the publicity, are open to "anyone, Native or non-Native, interested in experiencing traditional ceremonies and increasing their knowledge and understanding of Aboriginal ways." At the FNCCEC conference in Halifax, Herman Many Guns, a visitor from the Fort Museum of the North West Mounted Police, told me about week-long "cross-cultural awareness camps" they run for police, lawyers, justice people, judges, and prosecutors. The idea is to give them an insight into how Native people live—and how they lived in the past—so they put their trainees up six to a *tipi*, and they teach them hand games, singing, dancing, and ancient skills such as how to cut up meat.

Undoubtedly, courses such as these are being developed all over the world, as people begin to be aware of what they can learn from each other's cultural heritage. A last example, from Australia this time, is the Koorie Heritage Trust in Melbourne. Here a library, gallery, and two exhibition areas offer visitors the chance to learn as much or as little as they wish of the "continuous living culture, heritage and history" of the Koorie (or Aboriginal) people of South East Australia. According to the brochure, "staff of the Trust enjoy sharing our culture through talks, workshops and demonstrations, cross-cultural programmes, outreach visits and tours through the Centre." Through a program of the continually valued oral history, the center seeks "to restore family and cultural information to Koories and promote this unique and vibrant history to the wider Australian and international community."

Ultimately, however, Aboriginal people would like to see proper reference made to them and their history accurately portrayed throughout the mainstream curriculum and not just in culture centers and specialized Native Studies courses. Several people I have introduced throughout this book are working toward that aim, but one venture particularly relevant to this chapter is GoodMinds.com. Established by Jeff Burnham, this is a privately owned Native company that collects, vets, and sells books, videos, CD-ROMs, and audio-cassettes to ensure that appropriate materials are available that are at the same time "respectful of First Nations, Métis and Inuit people, their history and culture" (leaflet). Jeff identified a need for such material and had a growing list of around 2,000 titles (at the time of my going to press) for all educational levels, each carefully checked by his colleague Sheila Staats, who is an authority on Native books in Canada.

Sheila is trained to identify bias, stereotypes, and subtle discrimination. She insists that things be factually correct, and she discourages Jeff from stocking material that is sacred to particular peoples. "Writers should be sensitive to the people they are writing about," she explained. Sheila clearly knows the universities in the vicinity and the courses they run, so she can advise about useful materials to stock. She advocates strongly that the resources of GoodMinds.com should be used throughout the curriculum, and she has worked with Bernadette Wabie, at the Woodland Cultural Centre, to advise libraries and review books. In fact GoodMinds.com's reputation for disseminating accurate information about First Nations is continually increasing in the provincial education and library communities.

Jeff has produced a multimedia CD-ROM that works at three distinct levels of learning—primary, secondary, and higher education—to present a deep understanding of the culture and history of the Haudenosaunee people. It works through the examination of a triptych entitled "The Great Peace: the gathering of good minds" that depicts the crucial point in the history of the Haudenosaunee people when the Great Law was introduced (see above, and chapters 1 and 8). Jeff's choice of communicative medium would seem to be an excellent one for learning about an Indigenous people, for it takes advantage of contemporary technology to present through pictures and the spoken word stories that were originally passed on orally, at the same time as incorporating extensive subsequent writings and essays by Iroquois scholars. The project team enlisted U.S. and Canadian educators, historians, clan mothers, and chiefs, resulting in a rich collection of work by Six Nations authors at the same time as demonstrating the strengths of the previous oral communication system. The CD-ROM also points the user in the direction of further materials.

This medium is perhaps a little ahead of its time for old-style educators, who are still wedded to the written text, but it would seem clearly to be a way forward. Indigenous people in many parts of the world are using the Internet to put out excellent websites about themselves—just type a tribal name into a search engine, and they are likely to be there. In the National Museum of Kenya, in Nairobi, I encountered a team of people working on a Cultural African Network that is planned to offer electronic information interactively about the peoples of African countries—seven initially. We find out more about this network in the next chapter, where we examine several other ways in which First Peoples have harnessed new technologies to their processes of reclaiming their cultural identities. In chapter 8, we return to examine further general lessons we can learn from the world's Indigenous peoples.

References and Further Readings

Cook-Peters, Kaweienón:ni, 2003, Report on the Ahkwesáhsne Mohawk Board of Education Kanien'kéha Program, Developed for AMBE, MCA. SRCS, Kanien'kéha Education Parents, and the Ahkwesáhsne Community.

Elijah, Mary Joy, 2003, "First Nations Language and Culture in the Ontario Curriculum," presentation made at the Conference of the Sweetgrass First Nations Language Council, University of Western Ontario, October 2003.

Froman, Tara, 2003, "A History of the Mohawk Institute," *Wadrihwa*, 17(4) & 18(1 & 2): 2–7.

Graham, Elizabeth, 1997, *The Mush Hole: Life at Two Indian Residential Schools*, Waterloo: Heffle Publishing.

Harper, Ian, 2003, "The Protective Legislation Issue: Should Aboriginal Languages have a Bill 101, an Official Languages Act, or something else?," paper presented at the Conference of the Sweetgrass First Nations Language Council, University of Western Ontario, October 2003.

Peters, Kaweienon:ni (Margaret) and Bobby Jacobs, 2003, "Production of Language Resource Materials for Speakers and Non-Speakers," presentation made at the Conference of the Sweetgrass First Nations Language Council, University of Western Ontario, October 2003.

Peters, Tekahionhake (Theodore), 2003, "Music and Media in Language Teaching," presentation made at the Conference of the Sweetgrass First Nations Language Council, University of Western Ontario, October 2003.

Skutnabb-Kangas, Tove, 2003, "Revitalizing Indigenous and Minority Languages: Any Role for Linguistic Human Rights in Counteracting Linguistic Genocide?," keynote lecture presented at the Conference of the Sweetgrass First Nations Language Council, University of Western Ontario, October 2003.

Thomas, Chief Jacob and Terry Boyle, 1994, *Teachings from the Longhouse*, Toronto: Stoddart.

Chapter 5

Arts, Architecture, and Native Creativity

> Our art is like a bridge between non-Aboriginal and Aboriginal people, making them aware of our culture and stories.
> Inawinytji Williams, Desart Committee, Australia

Introduction

The quotation at the start of this chapter is a wonderfully optimistic view of the possibilities art holds for intercultural communication, and in this chapter I hope to show that it is at least to some extent justified. We have already seen in chapter 1 how displays of contemporary art are used in museums to demonstrate the continuing existence of the peoples whose ancient work is on show. In chapter 2 we discussed the ways travelers to different parts of the world seek examples of performing art to watch, and material objects to buy and bring back with them as souvenirs of their visit, thus depositing some of their external funds in the local economy. We have also seen how works of art are used as teaching aids, both for children to learn of their own cultural background, and for people of all ages to learn about each other. The quotation was taken from a brochure of Desart, the Association of Central Australian Aboriginal Art and Craft Centres, which lists no fewer than 31 centers in that so-called desert region of Australia, all Aboriginally owned and governed. Desart also helps the Aboriginal artists working at these centers to market and sell their work.

There have been a number of problems, however, and somewhat ironically, the worst ones potentially offer Indigenous artists the best income for their work. First, the classification of some people's creations as 'primitive art' lands them with a label that demeans their contemporary activities, and even though this term has now been revised to offer more acceptable descriptions, the world art market still insists on trying to freeze Indigenous artists at various points in their past. This is the same situation we discussed in chapter 2, about tourists seeking 'authenticity' in the objects they purchase and the shows they attend, but here the stakes may be much higher, for art collectors are willing to pay big money for the things they prize. This problem is of course compounded by the activities of some of the people who stand between the producers of artwork and the outlets where they are sold. These include dealers, both those who collect the work and others who offer it at the point of sale. Then there are the 'experts' who advise both dealers and purchasers which pieces to value and, at the same time, establish and confirm decisions about 'authenticity' and what it means.

There are also the problems of interpretation. If people are to learn of each other's "culture and stories" through the works of art they produce, then they may well actually need a lot of help. Australian Aboriginal art provides a perfect case to illustrate the point, as meanings embedded in the paintings are extremely deep and sophisticated. If an outsider is to take away more than an attractive design, then, he or she needs to be sure that the person doing the interpretation knows what they are talking about. Here is another level of authenticity to worry about especially if understanding culture and stories is the object of the exercise, which of course it may not be.

I don't intend to investigate the world art market, its aficionados, and their intentions in this chapter, but instead to look at some of the ways in which Indigenous people have responded to them. In many cases the tables are beginning to turn against the non-Aboriginal gatekeepers, who have for long imposed their own ideas on Native peoples as well as making money out of them. Collectors of art, and less well-off beings who buy souvenirs, provide a good source of income to Indigenous communities, and a substantial part of this increasingly finds it way down to the producers of the work, as we see later. We also look at some of the responses to pressures that abound to freeze people at a point in their past. The eventual and most important focus, however, is on the way that arts of various sorts, including architecture, theater, and broadcasting, have provided Indigenous people with a medium for the reclamation process, both in practice, and in providing funds for it. Artists have found some stunning ways of expressing their renewed sense of identity now that they have gained control of the work they create, and this chapter offers some examples of this revival and creativity.

Resistance and Renewal
In the South Pacific: The Jean-Marie Tjibaou Cultural Centre and Epeli Hau'ofa

New Caledonia is still a French colony, and the Jean-Marie Tjibaou Cultural Centre is not entirely a creation of the Native Kanak people, but it is a unique and extraordinary place that illustrates both the resistance and renewal that this section attempts to address. It was built to immortalize the Kanak man of that name who tried, ultimately in vain, to lead his people to independence from their colonial masters. One whole room in the center tells the story of Tjibaou, killed by a member of his own people for signing an agreement with the French to restore peace to his war-torn land, but whose philosophy lives on in the very essence of the cultural objects displayed:

> To live together today means recognising each other and accepting one another, accepting that we are of different cultures and promoting these different cultures both in school and in cultural events.

Emmanuel Kasarhérou, the Kanak cultural director of this largely French-funded project, explained the thinking behind the center. He explained, as I have already quoted in chapter 1, "The Pacific people need to be proud of what they are doing and not worried that they are not like their grandfathers were. The Centre . . . recognizes that culture changes and offers nothing less than a laboratory of creativity."

The result is a series of buildings like no others (figure 5.1), designed by the Italian architect, Renzo Piano, who won an international competition to secure the task. His proposal was to make the center modern, but "as Kanak as possible," and at the short-listing stage he consulted Kanak people and tried as he worked "to sense the smell of the sea and the trees, the strength of the wind" (catalogue). Three old style Kanak houses were constructed alongside the new buildings as they rose, and Piano tried to reflect their features, and the idea "that the construction was as important as the finished product." He tried therefore to leave the place looking unfinished, "architecture is a living being that evolves with time and use," he wrote, and he sought too to create a symbiosis with the surrounding vegetation. An important part of the display is outside, then, along the 'Kanak Path' that leads through native plants, illustrating some of their many uses and meanings, and expressing a passage of the people from their ancient myth of origin to a rebirth in their new world.

Inside the center, Kasarhérou explained that there are three domains. The first is devoted to visual arts, and the displays express an

Figure 5.1   The Jean-Marie Tjibaou Cultural Centre, Noumea, New Caledonia.

exciting blend of influences melding local heritage with the avant-garde from Europe. They also include materials from other parts of the Pacific, which enables an interesting comparative perspective. The second is an area for performing arts, which encourages dancers and musicians again to draw on their traditions while taking advantage of whatever new technologies might bring. The third section is one of documentation, and here a prized possession is the *mediateque*, which allows visitors to engage with facilities that make available sounds and images stored in all the latest media. An ongoing process of recording the rich oral traditions of the Kanak people in images and spoken memories demonstrates the advantages of digitalization and other multimedia for giving equal status to nonwritten forms of communication alongside the abundant collection of books, articles, and periodicals about them.

This center stands alone in illustrating clearly and forcibly what Indigenous cultural creativity can achieve, given the virtually limitless financial, technological, and artistic resources that French money provided. It also makes the important point that culture does not stand still. In discussing a new display of Kanak pieces at the Louvre in Paris, Kasarhérou pointed out that Europeans may be very proud of themselves, but they only want things prior to European contact. The Kanak people themselves need to find a new way, a new means of transforming themselves within their present circumstances. The Jean-Marie Tjibaou Cultural Centre would seem to have made an excellent start, and its local name, *Ngan Jila*, which means "house of riches" in Tjibaou's native language, nicely expresses the sentiment.

The sentiment expressed by Kasarhérou is practiced more widely in the South Pacific, as I heard from Epeli Hau'ofa, director of the Oceania Centre for Arts and Culture, whom I happened to meet in Port Vila shortly before visiting Noumea. Part of the University of the South Pacific, which is owned and controlled by 12 Pacific island nations, the center encourages "a combination of the influence of the ancestors with that of the contemporary world," he explained. According to Hau'ofa's website, the Oceania Centre "aims to promote the development of contemporary Oceanic visual and performing arts that transcend national and ethnic boundaries. In doing this the Oceania Centre is experimenting with creating an autonomous cultural space within the global system, a space that is ours, in which we breathe freely, and of which we have full control. We believe that it is only in such a space that we can be most creative in whatever we set our minds and passions on" (http://www.southproject.org/speakers/hauofa.htm). The center also offers financial support to the students selected to study there.

In Africa: Robino N'tila, the Kuona Trust, and the Cultural African Network

Outside funding has been injected into programs of African art as well, but the cases I discuss here illustrate considerable transfer of control at a local level, and several opportunities for tribal artists to flourish in their own media. The story starts in Dar-es-Salaam at the *Nyumba ya Sanaa* (House of Arts), an establishment set up in 1972 with Dutch funding to offer young, disabled Tanzanian artists a place to work and sell their art. The house is open to visitors, who come from many parts of the world, and they are able to buy directly things that are complete or put in orders for future supplies. The artists work in a variety of media, from batik and tie-dye, prints and papermaking, through jewelry, pottery, and other fine arts. Seventy artists are employed to work here, although there are also three-month-long training courses, and there is generally a cheerful atmosphere, especially among groups cooperating on some of the bigger projects.

I went to the *Nyumba ya Sanaa* to meet Robino N'tila, a local artist who had worked there for some 20 years, but who had now decided to set up on his own. He was a founding member of the center, he explained, he had been a coordinator for the last ten years, and he still used the center as a place to do business. He had been a member of the Tanzanian Arts Council for 12 years, he had founded several artistic associations, and he clearly knew everybody who was anybody in the world of arts in Tanzania and elsewhere. N'tila has also worked abroad, and he has exhibited in different countries around the world. When I visited him, he was in the process of setting up his own gallery, but in the meantime, he was also offering a kind of cultural brokering service whereby he would introduce me to some of the best artists in and around the capital city. He had a catalogue of their work, which he interpreted to my heart's content, and we made a plan to spend a day visiting a selection of my choice.

Had I been an art dealer, of really any origin, this would have been an excellent way to select a range of good quality work, and well worth the sum that Robino asked for his time. For me, too, it was a good, quick way to get a feel for some of the local artistic activities, and meet people who are making a living by selling their creative work. Robino assured me that artists in Tanzania are doing their own thing, and they are developing their own ideas, unlike those in neighboring Kenya, who simply made things for the tourists! We consider the case of Kenya shortly, but a couple of examples from the places Robino took me illustrates the way that individual artists are able to draw on the resources of their tribal origins at the same time as appealing to a global market.

Makonde artists are particularly well known in Tanzania for they are the ones with a license to work in ebony, and they produce beautiful human figures, as well as stubby tourist souvenirs such as Coca-Cola bottles. An intricate depiction of the "life tree" of generations of human relationships is one of their specialties, and the artist we visited, Emmanuel John Ukoti, had worked a similar depiction of *ujamaa*, the word for brotherhood chosen by Julius Nyerere to stand for Tanzania's socialist mix of people of many different backgrounds living harmoniously together. This shop was one of 50 to 60 shops in a row, a common destination for tourists, but Robino told me that he had picked out an artist "with an eye" for us to visit.

Another zone we visited also had a large number of individual artists, this time working in a distinctive, almost cartoon-like style devised by a Makua artist from the south of the country named Edward Said Tinga Tinga. He was shot by police, so the story goes, but not before gaining a copyright for his designs, and his style lives on in the work of some two to three hundred artists who have received permission to use it. Most are apparently from the same community of Nakapanya where Tinga Tinga himself was born, and they depict a huge range of messages in their work. One had chosen the Mozambique floods for a huge mural, complete with multiple hospital beds, another had decided to portray a single zebra in the Tinga Tinga style. Robino introduced me to a third artist, Mikidadi Bush, who had been invited to spend time in Japan, and he explained that this style appeals there, perhaps because it has some similarities with *manga*.

It wasn't until a few days later, when I was visiting the National Museum of Kenya, in Nairobi, that I realized how lucky I had been to have the benefit of Robino's guidance, for his name came up as a collaborator with local projects, and as a "very famous artist." By this time, I was seeking a program that had been mentioned in the speech of George Abungu, described at the beginning of chapter 1, about how the National Museum in Nairobi is opening up to local people. He had mentioned that one of the ideas they had had was to bring street children into the compound and give them the opportunity to develop skills as artists whose work could be on sale to tourists. I didn't find the street children, who had apparently proved a little too unruly for the museum compound, though they were doing an initial training elsewhere, but I did find several adult artists at work, and the offices of the Kuona Trust.

The program director, Judy Wanjiku Ogana, agreed to tell me about this organization, which she explained had been set up to promote contemporary art in Kenya but with links in Uganda and Tanzania (and of course Robino). They had been given the space in and around the old governor's house at the museum, and they had at first accepted any artist who wanted to work there, and who came with their work. In the first seven years, they had registered some 700 artists, and they were now full to capacity and looking for more studio spaces for them to work. Visitors are free to come and watch the artists working and to order the things they like. The project receives funding from various outside sources: through the Dutch Embassy, the Commonwealth, and the Ford Foundation, for example, and its trustees are quite international, but the three full-time employees are all Kenyan, as are the artists. There are also few limits imposed upon their work, so this is a great opportunity for innovation.

Working in an adjacent office were the designers of the Cultural African Network, mentioned briefly at the end of the last chapter. They explained that they were in the process of digitalizing cultural information, such as art, music, and architecture, as well as material objects, by filming it, editing it, and storing it in a database. Viewing of it is interactive, using a touch-screen process that they had designed, so that a student, or tourist, might start with a map of a country and then move through a series of options to learn about its cultural treasures. At the time of my visit seven other countries were involved: Ethiopia, Ghana, Mali, Mozambique, Somalia, South Africa, and Sudan, but if the project was successful, and the funding kept coming, it would be extended. Screens would be installed in museums, and the data would eventually be extended to include rituals and folk tales as well as material culture.

A great deal of African art is still exported to the United States and elsewhere through organizations such as African Heritage, which has a large outlet in Nairobi, as well as in Senegal, Nigeria, and Ghana. This enterprise is run by a Texan named Alan Donavan who had identified a market some 30 years before, and set it up in association with Joseph Murundi, the leader of the time, and his English wife, Sheila. I talked to some of the artists working in the shop, and they were clearly in a much less free situation. They were working to fill orders from Europe and the United States to designs mostly made by Alan. I also happened by chance to meet Alan, who was about to be presented with an award, and he explained how he had foreseen that a little input of capital could encourage weavers and other craftspeople to make things for an international market. Clearly this kind of venture brings a lot of work to Kenyans and other Africans, and it sells well in the United States, but it doesn't really qualify as an example of resistance or renewal.

The Maori Insistence on the Proper Treatment of Their *Taonga*

My third and last example of resistance is based entirely on two secondhand accounts of a Maori traveling exhibition entitled *Te Maori*. This collection of 174 huge Maori artifacts was taken to the United States in 1984, where it was put on display in New York, St. Louis, San Francisco, and Chicago before being returned to Aotearoa in 1986. Before any kind of agreement could be made for the packing to commence, however, the New York program administrator was summoned to New Zealand to hear the Maori conditions for the treatment of these important *taonga*. This is a Maori word that expresses the complex spiritual aspect of important cultural objects such as these carvings were. Carol O'Biso was the administrator and her book (O'Biso 1987) describes her own experience, moving from an initial skepticism about the whole venture to a profound respect for the value of the objects that spent some two years under her care.

These treasures were accompanied every step of the way by six Maori elders who ensured that Maori ceremonial conventions were observed and that the spiritual presence in the objects was properly respected. According to Arapata Hakiwai (1990: 35), this was the first time that the Maori people had been properly in charge of an international exhibition of their art and in control of the artistic heritage that it represented. "It was a momentous and historic occasion when our ancestors, as represented by these treasures, were freed from their dark and cold resting-places in the galleries and basements of our museums to experience, once again, the light of day," he wrote. This traveling exhibition laid the foundations for the future involvement of Maori elders in all displays of their artistic heritage, and the stunning results are exemplified in the New Zealand National Museum of Te Papa that we discussed in chapter 1.

Architecture as an Example of Aboriginal Creativity

We have already mentioned some cases of architecture as a form of Aboriginal self-expression and creativity. In the last chapter, for example, we discussed the First Nations House of Learning at the University of British Columbia, the *Akwe:kon* building at Cornell, and *Tane-nui-a-rangi*, the *marae* at the University of Auckland. All of these exhibit a combination of the features of building materials traditional to the people concerned, and innovations appropriate to their current use and situation. The *marae*, for example, uses stained glass windows as a tribute to the way they are valued in churches, and decorative carving and weaving represents all those who come to the university from different Maori tribes and other Pacific peoples. In chapter 1 we discussed the Canadian Museum of Civilisations in Ottawa, which was designed by Douglas Cardinal, an Aboriginal/Métis architect whose characteristic sweeping curves may also be found at the First Nations University in Regina (see figure 4.1), and the New Museum of the American Indian in Washington, DC.

The Great Hall at the Canadian Museum of Civilisations also boasts an impressive display of First Nations' architecture from the West Coast, which was commissioned from and constructed by members of local communities there. George McDonald was the director at the time and he told me how he worked with Bill McLennan to find leaders of communities who would be able to put up the necessary teams of builders. He explained that each one was a very individual contribution, and in one case, the Nachalnath, they held a competition within the community for an artist to design the threshold of their house. This turned out to form a wonderfully global symbol as it was made to accommodate the handprints of different peoples from all over the world. They also made videos about the construction in their own language, which can be accessed through the museum, and the Nishka people followed suit. The ceiling is again a Cardinal design, shaped to represent an enormous canoe, with its oars forming upright posts that line the perimeter of the hall, and are apparently a sign of peace.

The Dänojà Zho Cultural Centre in Dawson City, which we visited briefly in chapter 1 and on National Aboriginal Day in chapter 2, is another wonderful example of the use of architecture to express ideas important to a particular Aboriginal people. The design was commissioned from a non-Aboriginal company, Kobayashi and Zedda, when the Tr'ondëk Hwëch'in people were given the wherewithal to build a representation of themselves for the centenary of the Klondike Gold Rush. However, a local committee was set up to advise the company, and when I spoke to Jack Kobayashi, he confirmed the close involvement of the people. At one end, the most outstanding feature is a huge depiction of the fish racks (see figure 5.2) that the Tr'ondëk

Figure 5.2 The Dänojà Zho Cultural Centre in Dawson City, Yukon.

Hwëch'in used to set their salmon out to dry, and these are made of the birch wood that was always chosen for that purpose. The next section is a "gathering space" with long glass windows to fill the room with light, and represent the continual summer days, which in this part of the world reach 24 hours in length at the solstice. Wooden panels in this room represent the smokehouse that the fish were moved into once they were dry. At the other end of the building, a circular section that is completely closed in, except for a smoke hole in the roof, represents winter. The location of Dänojà Zho, on the bank of the Yukon River, was also crucial, for this is their highway, and through the glass at the side of the gathering place, they can see the village of Moosehide where many of them moved at the time of the Gold Rush.

Kobayashi and Zedda were also commissioned to build the Tlingit Heritage Centre in Teslin, which we visited in chapter 1, and this too has many important local features, such as a sunken area for shows, and an elders room. Out at the front it has a row of brightly painted carved poles representing the five clans of the Tlingit people, namely the Wolf, the Beaver, the Raven, the Eagle, and the Crow. In the last chapter, we also briefly discussed the design of the T'lisalagi'lakw School in Alert Bay, where the dance practice room has been made visible through glass panels that form part of the wall of the main vestibule. This was apparently a feature emphasized by members of the community when they were consulted about how they would like the school to be. The overall impression of the interior of the building is one of light and space, clearly made possible by the rows of large glass windows along each side, and a narrow second floor comprised of little more than rows of windows again. The building is constructed of local cedar, and it is decorated with a large whale at the front, and a thunderbird, one of the ancestral figures for the 'Namgis First Nation, on the roof.

An example of Aboriginal architectural creativity that I would like to examine in a little more detail is also a school, this time the Emily C. General School, on the Six Nations Reserve (see figure 5.3). This was picked out in an interview with its designer, local architect Brian Porter, as his "best work to date." "It is not a literal translation of a longhouse," he said, "but it references some of the same principles, and it embodies my philosophy of how you can manipulate materials and construction techniques to align with nature, and use what it offers you." Like some of the other buildings we have discussed, the light and the North/South (N/S) axis are important, and here Brian has incorporated a glass strip into his N/S roof, which admits the sun's

Figure 5.3 The Emily C. General School, Ohsweken, Ontario, was designed by Brian Porter.

rays onto a curved wall inside. This forms one end of a central hall of the school, in this case used for the library, and on a clear day the room is filled with cheerful sunshine. Moreover, the curved wall becomes a kind of natural sundial, so that people who use the place year round should be able to tell both the time of day and the season of year simply by looking at it, Brian pointed out.

Brian has installed a ground source heating system that takes advantage of the fact that the earth remains warm six feet under, even during winter, so he sends the cold water down that returns tempered, for some natural heating. He has also used a variety of different colors for the clay brick cladding so that the effect on the outside walls is to represent the strata of the earth. At the front of the school, he has left the steel superstructure completely exposed and had it painted a bright blue. He pointed out that the posts and beams holding up the porch also catch rainwater and bring it down into a basin at the base of the structure where it finds its way to a series of catch basins. "This makes a little music," he added, "and encourages the children to play with the raindrops as they fall." The teachers might not like it, he quipped, but it is fun for the kids, and it represents the simple conversion of something free. Brian has designed some other schools, but he has ideas for more ambitious projects in the future, and it is my guess that his name will become as well known as that of Douglas Cardinal with time. His company name, Two Row Architect, reflects the spirit and sentiment of the wampum treaty explained in chapter 1.

Performing Arts—Theater, Music, Dance, and Broadcasting

Another important and exciting medium for the reclamation process is to be found in various types of performing arts, including theater, dance, and singing, as well as in radio broadcasting, film, and television. Again, the choice of subject matter and style by peoples in different parts of the world displays a great range of possibilities, drawing both on local traditions, passed down physically, and in the many influences now more or less shared throughout the 'globalized' world. Thus, the concept of a theater production offers a medium for a great range of performance styles, as do the technical opportunities of film and television, while both allow Indigenous people to tell their stories. Likewise, meetings for making music can be as varied as the music itself, while young people all over the globe are attracted by the idea of making their individual creative work popular beyond their immediate circles. Another advantage to performance as a way of developing Indigenous arts is that it may well offer a source of income to support the artists as they pursue their creative activities.

Probably the most successful global illustrations of these points are the Indigenous films that have been distributed widely beyond their immediate location, for they have effectively carried the stories they reproduce around the world. In the last chapter, we talked of *Rabbit Proof Fence*, Doris Pilkington (or Nugi Garimara)'s tale of her mother's escape from residential school, which has made the world aware of the iniquities of the system. Another one did an excellent job of portraying the lives of Inuit people, and it was also the first Aboriginal-language Canadian feature movie, *Atanarjuat: The Fast Runner*, made by Zacharias Kunuk and a completely Inuit film crew. Niki Caro's production of *Whale Rider*, based on Sir Witi Ihimaera's story of the life of a Maori chief's daughter, has also been popular around the world, as well as having a Maori language version.

An older film that made another Maori story famous was *Once Were Warriors*, based on a novel by Alan Duff, and during a visit to Wellington, the capital of New Zealand, I coincided with a well-attended Maori stage production of the same story. This example illustrates well the value of cultural reclamation and renewal in a very modern context. It offers a heart-rending account of a dysfunctional Maori family in a tough urban neighborhood. The father drinks too much and becomes violent, the sons are out of control, and a daughter who shows signs of becoming a successful writer is raped by a family friend. One of the sons gets into trouble with the police and is sent to a reform institution where he regains some self-respect through taking part in a program that inculcates fundamental Maori values. Further tragedy befalls the daughter, but the thoroughly battered wife eventually returns to her community of origin, where she and the rest of the family benefit from a revival of more of the Maori values they had all lost.

A very practical example of cultural reclamation takes place daily at another House of Arts (*Nyumba ya Sanaa*), a performing arts school near Bagamoyo, in Tanzania. I called by when I was there, and, although I was not able to catch one of their bimonthly performances, a representative of the staff there told me about their activities. He explained that it was set up after Tanzanian independence to revitalize the tribal dances that had started to die out when the colonizers described the people as "undeveloped." Tanzania has 120 tribal peoples, however, so they are trying to create a Tanzanian identity by combining traditional dance and music with the use of Western instruments and technology. Around 500 young people apply for the 15 to 20 government-funded places here, but another source of income comes from short courses offered to (often foreign) paying students.

I'd like now to try and give a feel for the different dimensions of cultural renewal and self-expression concentrated in performing arts of this kind by looking, with a little more detail, at some of the activities of a group called *The Kanata Dance Theatre*. The group has its headquarters in the old Mohawk Institute at the Woodland Cultural Centre, and it puts on regular home performances there, so I had an opportunity to get to know some of the members and to see a couple of their shows. Naomi Powless and Brian General, both long-standing dancing members of the group who also do choreography for the shows, were often around, as was Carole Powless, who does the administration and fund-raising. All three were kind enough to give up some of their time one afternoon to tell me about the history of the group, the performances they do, and the background and training of the various members, both full-time and occasional.

As the title of the group would suggest, their type of performance uses dance [in an often quite spectacular way] to tell stories, enact themes, and sometimes to recount humorous skits. They draw on the heritage of Native peoples, though not limited to any particular group; indeed, some of their shows—like *The Journey* and *The Journey Continues*—make a point of traveling through different traditions, though always telling stories of their encounters with outsiders from the Native point of view. They also travel themselves, and they enjoy meeting other Indigenous people and sharing ideas about dance and performance. We look at some of these exchanges in chapter 7, for the group has a real international flavor, but suffice it to say here that the shows their agents arrange for them are often in schools and at public festivals. *People of the Land* is one title, described as a "pretty generic Native dance," another is *Legacy* in which they focus on Haudenosaunee dances and legends, and a third is *Spirit of a Nation* which is "geared to theatres and large venues."

In the early part of the December 2003, I was lucky enough to get tickets for *The Journey Continues*, a new dinner theater sell-out show they put on with the cooperative participation of members of the Woodland Cultural Centre. Dinner was served first, with local delicacies such as elk sausage, corn and pumpkin soup, salmon on a cedar plank, and wild rice with pine nuts. The show was a follow-up to *The Journey* (from east to west coasts) the previous year that had taken the theme of examining Native/non-Native contact from a Native point of view. This time the journey was from north to south, and included representations of Inuit, Métis, Sioux, Zuni, Seminole, and Aztec, always with amusing interactions with the non-Natives around them, and demonstrating a huge variety of different forms and dance styles, as well as singing and narrative. One particular item went down very well with the audience, and put me thoroughly in my place, for it was a hilarious depiction of a couple of researchers investigating through participation the activities of the people who were doing the dancing.

In fact, as we have seen in earlier chapters, dancing is a good way to revive, practice, and share cultural knowledge, and the Kanata Dance Theatre's performers had drilled their dancing toes for years at the annual powwows before they became professionals. The dances developed for these occasions, as well as the wonderful regalia worn by the competitors, are splendid examples of cultural creativity and ingenuity, for they display all and none of the symbols that marked out different tribes in the past. Several fixed dance styles have been agreed between the people who take part, and there are rules about how 'men's fancy', 'jingle dress', and 'smoke dance' performers should appear, but within the basic guidelines, they can still be stunningly inventive (see figure 2.3). *The Canadian Aboriginal Festival*, in Toronto, described briefly in chapter 2, brought together a huge celebration of powwow dancing, as well as offering many other artists and performers a chance to shine.

At the Sky Dome itself, there was an interesting fashion show, displaying the creations of several designers, and in one case, bringing the striking use of feathers into garments that could almost qualify as street wear. A tent on the site also ran a series of readings of their work by the Six Nations Writers literary group. The most spectacular event for live performers, however, was probably the previous evening's *Aboriginal Music Awards*, with entries for everything from Best Hand Drum and Best Powwow Albums to Best Blues and Best Rap or Hip Hop Albums. Hosted by a young, vibrant Jennifer Podemski, and a more sedate Tom King, who feigned a total lack of knowledge about things like "hip hop?," the show was also humorous and full of buzz. Phrases like "this is our time," and "Indian Time is now and forever," from Jennifer went down very well with the predominantly Aboriginal audience.

Despite the medium of their music, the names chosen by groups, and their mode of presentation, made no secret of their Aboriginal origins, indeed it celebrated them. The Best Blues album was won by a group of Six Nations brothers entitled Wolf Pack, and the Rap/Hip-Hop one was won by another Six Nations group called Tru Rez Crew. According to press reports, both groups are poised to make a name for themselves nationally, and chart-topping Inuit singer, Susan Aglukark, was there to cheer them on. These successes probably bring positive knowledge of Indigenous people to a wider, younger audience than any other medium, as the Ainu pop group, Moshiri (which is the Ainu word for their homeland) found in Japan. In that case, they made people aware of their very existence as a people seeking an identity. The Toronto Harbourfront festival Planet IndigenUS, running through a prime summer week of August 2004, undoubtedly had a similar effect.

Other presentations at the music awards went for a much more "traditional" sound, and sometimes they used their native languages for the title and lyrics. One entry for the Best Traditional Album Historical (as opposed to the Best Traditional Album *Contemporary*) was made by an Ojibwe group from Manatoulin Island and included Cynthia Bell, a woman I had met at the Sweetgrass conference organizing meetings, as well as at the First Nations Confederation of Cultural Education Centres (FNCCEC) conference in Halifax. It was a haunting song called *Anishnaabe Ngamwaasan*, and the CD was on sale with a number of other Ojibwe materials at the festival itself. Cynthia had made the recording with Ojibwe-speaking members of her family almost as a language exercise for herself as she was learning the language to keep up with her children who are in immersion programs. The song did not win an award, but it was certainly making a contribution to the importance of language as part and parcel of the revival process to have it chosen as a final nominee.

Another outlet for all this great variety of First Nations performing artists in Canada is the Aboriginal Peoples Television Network (APTN), which has its own channel and broadcasts throughout much of the later day and evening. This is a multilingual channel, with slots for Inuktitut, Cree, Ojibwe, and other language programs—such as an English-subtitled Maori film—but mostly the medium is actually English. It has a range of interesting shows. I got quite hooked on a 'soap' about people living in the Northwest Territories, but there are good documentaries and discussion programs, performances of music, poetry, and theater, and guest chat shows, such as a popular one called Buffalo Tracks. Between programs the channel identifier consists of two or three Aboriginal faces turning to smile and proclaim: "APTN: sharing our stories with all Canadians."

One reason contributing to the continuing success of APTN must be a broadcasting training program at the Manitoba Indian Cultural Education Centre in Winnipeg. I happened to come across this by chance, but Carol Beaulieu explained that it is a serious attempt to combine cultural material to insure the Aboriginal perspective with training in all aspects of television work. Tuition for the course is high, but the center provides a large classroom, there is equipment to practice with, and the instructors and guest speakers are well qualified. I don't know of another Indigenous people's network that is so widely active, though a Maori television channel was taking off in 2004, when I was visiting Aotearoa, and we have seen in chapter 3 how important television is as a medium of recording and sharing 'custom' in Vanuatu.

In many other parts of the world, as well as Canada, radio is used to keep local Indigenous people in touch with each other, and with local facilities, and it is also through these channels that language programs can be broadcast. We have heard already that there is a radio station in Kahnawake, chosen eventually in preference to television, which, though tried, turned out to be too expensive for the size of the community. This station broadcasts in both English and Mohawk, including a couple of DJs introducing popular music in Mohawk, which encourages graduates of immersion school to keep up their listening at least. In Scotland, there is a Gaelic channel on the west coast and some Gaelic programs on regular Radio Scotland as well.

Ohsweken, on the Six Nations, has a local radio station too, but the Mohawk and Cayuga broadcasts are still pretty limited, though Amos Key, who set it up, had been hoping for more. He was raised by a Mohawk mother and a Cayuga father, both of whom spoke four languages, so he has little time for those who complain about learning their own native language.

Amos Key has been ultimately responsible for many cultural programs. As well as the radio station in Ohsweken, set up in 1989, he was the one who founded the Six Nations Powwow in 1979–1980, with the cooperation of six families who made an initial investment of $500, now well returned as it has become the biggest in Ontario. He set up the immersion kindergarten in 1986 and the private high school in 1995, and we heard about its successes in the last chapter. He oversees the Aboriginal Language Initiative, also discussed there, and he was selected in 2003 to sit on the Task Force to look at future funding for language revival, as was mentioned. It will not be a surprise, then, if he is successful in his latest venture, which is to build a Performing Arts Centre at the Woodland Cultural Centre. When I was visiting, he had just resigned as executive director in order to devote himself to this "dream," a project he refers to as TNT, short for *The Northern Thunder*. Funding was almost complete for a feasibility study, and Amos explained his ideas.

Initially, these are to build partnerships with other local arts organizations, such as the Ontario Arts Council and the Arts Council of Canada, crucially important for funding, and with the Aboriginal Tourism Association of Southern Ontario, the Brantford Tourism Association, and the Six Nations Tourism Collective, for cooperative publicity. The Woodland Cultural Centre already has links with venues such as the Harbourfront in Toronto, with whom they organized Planet IndigenUS in the summer of 2004, and with the Royal Ontario Museum, through exhibitions such as the Dr. Oronhyatekha one that we discussed in chapter 1. Outlets such as the APTN and the Centre for Aboriginal Media in Toronto would also be important, Amos explained, and his chairmanship of the Aboriginal Music Awards seems likely to be valuable too.

The Woodland Culture Centre already draws on the support of highly skilled performers, such as members of the Kanata Dance Theatre and several other people who regularly take part in events there. *The Journey Continues*, for example, featured award-winning dancer Santee Smith, singer and songwriter Elizabeth Hill, TV and stage actors Lorne Cardinal and Cheri Maracle-Cardinal, and the multitalented Tom Hill in the role of narrator. Other events have drawn many other well-known performers, but at the moment the facilities are limited to a hall with a seating capacity of 150, whereas the TNT plan is to create a large, new theater and several studios for rehearsals and training. Amos would also like to set up internships for budding new performers and engage some of the immense talent around to help them epitomize the "excellence and integrity" that is the existing motto of the Woodland Cultural Centre. Ultimately his dream is to bring the same association of Brantford's name with Aboriginal Theatre as currently Stratford (Canada—and the United Kingdom) enjoys with Shakespeare, and Niagara on the Lake with Bernard Shaw.

There are several places offering training and practice to people of Aboriginal background in this area already. The Centre for Indigenous Theatre in Toronto, which, together with its predecessor the Native Theatre School, can claim a history of more than the 30-year focus of this book, offers a range of courses from two weeks to three years. Its graduates are apparently responsible for setting up no fewer than 11 Aboriginal theater companies throughout Canada (brochure). Somewhat more broadly, the New Orators Youth Project in Ohsweken builds on First Nations' reputation as good storytellers, and seeks to use a variety of insightful and humorous presentations (including the one made at the *Restoring Our Peace* conference mentioned in the last chapter) to build confidence and cultural understanding. The Northern Thunder project looks set to be all these things, and more, in the well-established avant-garde tradition of the Woodland Cultural Centre.

Art and Communication

In this last section, I want to come back to the issue raised at the start of the chapter by the quotation of Inawinytji Williams, taken from the brochure of Desart, the Association of Central Australian Aboriginal Art and Craft Centres. "Our art is like a bridge between non-Aboriginal and Aboriginal people," she said, "making them aware of our culture and stories." We have seen several examples of performing arts that would seem to illustrate this maxim, particularly film and theater, and at present Native themes are drawing an audience. In Canada alone, various theatrical groups advertise themselves by making reference to their Native performers. In Saskatoon, for example, I saw advertisements selling a group called the *Black Box Theatre* for this quality, and in Toronto, a group called *Native Earth* offers productions with titles such as "Tales of an Urban Indian" and "Storytelling and Feast Day."

The *Kahurangi Maori Dance Theatre of New Zealand* has been making a living in Canada and the United States under that name for several years.

All kinds of art made by Natives, or Aboriginal people from different parts of the world, are popular in North America, but other media probably don't have quite the same ability as films and theater to communicate stories directly. The examples of architecture mentioned above would have little to say standing alone, without the explanations of their designers or occupants, although they may be appreciated for their aesthetic qualities, clever harnessing of technology, and use of light. Paintings and sculpture may fall into much the same category, so that a "non-Aboriginal" might choose to buy a piece of work for its sheer beauty without understanding much in the way of its deeper meanings. Even more so, a potentially functional item such as a basket, a pot, or a piece of clothing may have all sorts of meaning for the maker that are quite lost on the eventual user of the object who many even have simply received it as a gift. The question I would like to consider here, then, is whether this lack of communication matters, and how it impacts on the process of reclamation and revival.

I'd like to examine examples of Australian Aboriginal art first, for these carry a prestige in their own right that some non-Aboriginal Australians seem still to find difficult to accord to their quite numerous creators. My experience in Australia has not been long, but I did spend a semester in 1994 at Melbourne University before I took up this study, and I was shocked by the curtailed stay in the city of an excellent Aboriginal film named *Blackfellas*. I was also disappointed at the general lack of reference to Aboriginal people in the southeast area, though I discover since visiting Bunjilaka (described in chapter 1) that they are rather numerous, and have an active Koorie Heritage Trust, which I described in the last chapter. I also discovered on my 2004 visit that various sites around the city have now been marked for their historical Aboriginal importance (Eidelson 1997). However, when I was picked up by taxi from Tandanya, the National Aboriginal Cultural Institute in not-too-distant Adelaide, the driver, who looked embarrassed at even having to enter such a place, quipped, "I hear that Aborigines are good at making pictures full of dots that fetch a lot of money." I won't repeat my response here!

Tandanya had actually been in Adelaide for 15 years by this time. It is run and governed by Aboriginal people, and it has a huge exhibition space that changes its shows every eight weeks. I was lucky enough to coincide with one that had been mounted by the new National Museum with displays of art from different parts of Aboriginal

Australia, some made for its opening festival in 2001. There was, therefore, a very contemporary air to the show, and the explanations of objects and paintings were all in the present tense. I learned a lot about different peoples and their customs and life styles just by touring the exhibition, and in the shop, an abundance of further material was available about the peoples whose work I had seen. This pedagogic element had apparently been part of the vision of the founders of Tandanya, and several Aboriginal employees were around too in case a visitor had more questions to ask.

One of them, an artist named Joel Birnie, said he was keen "to make visitors aware that not all Aboriginal people are black and wear spears." Although of mixed blood, he identified himself with his Tasmanian mother, and explained the influence that this identity had had on some of his work. In an exhibition entitled *Going Home*, for example, he had recreated in sandstone on canvas some of the images of petroglyphs found in caves in Tasmania, petroglyphs he felt were similar to, but a lot less well-known than those found in North America. In another series of pieces, he used sheepskin and clay to recreate a kind of jigsaw impression of scars elevated on the body.

During the day, there was a dance show by a Torres Straits Islander, who showed pictures of his land, and described some of the history of the area and its interactions with the outside world. A musician who was present gave an informal presentation with a *didjeridu*, again filling in much context about the instrument, how it developed, and where it is played. In the corner of one of the exhibition halls, there was a space marked "Artist in Residence" where presumably one could again have talked to the incumbent about their work—had it not been the artist's day off. In fact, some of the artists had put pictures and quotations by their work, and one, Ian Abdulla, from the Murray River region of South Australia had written, "If they don't paint, my children wouldn't know about their past. They need to know so that they can carry it on." Ian's work looked quite lifelike and recognizable to me, but I felt suddenly aware of how little I could possibly understand about its reference to the past of his people. As a notice at the door of the exhibition warns, "From traditions of the deepest past have come the artistic and cultural expressions of the present."

The announcement goes on to explain that these Aboriginal people have for many thousands of years passed down spiritual and cultural knowledge through music, dance, art, ceremony, and storytelling, and the twentieth century has seen them add film, literature, theater, and exhibitions to their repertoire of mediums for cultural expression.

"The communities and people featured in this exhibit welcome you to share their stories," it finishes up. So we can share, we can become *aware*, as the quotation at the start suggests, and we can even make a stab at understanding. We are encouraged with this at Tandanya, once we have paid our entrance fee, but ultimately we outsiders are not the ones for whom this knowledge is vital. To ensure its continuity, the Aboriginal children must learn, as Ian Abdulla made clear, children of the artists, and children of all other people who identify themselves with Aboriginal traditions. Tandanya helps with this process, both in the provision of education, free to Aboriginal people, and to the artists themselves, offering space to display their work, an outlet for it to be sold, and even materials for them to work with.

The South Australia Arts Council helps to support Tandanya, which also brings in an income from its shop, well stocked with the achievements of many excellent artists. In Australia more widely, Aboriginal art and culture centers have been supported by ATSIS, the national government's Aboriginal and Torres Strait Islander Services, a section that was closing down to be "mainstreamed" as I passed through in May 2004. I am not sure what the implications of this will be, but Sallie Anderson and Kathryn Wells, of the Arts and Culture Section, were kind enough to meet me in Canberra and tell me about some of its work to date. I was impressed, both to learn swiftly and efficiently about the enormous number of Aboriginal projects and programs that exist throughout the country and by the knowledge and enthusiasm these two (non-Aboriginal) government employees shared. I learned a lot from them, not least about Aboriginal views of the way their art can speak for them to the outside world, and they gave me a wealth of further material that has been collected about the arts and culture centers.

Apart from Desart, with whom we started this chapter, another major support agency is known as ANKAAA, the Association of Northern, Kimberley and Arnhem Aboriginal Artists, and their brochure lists 26 different centers. All these, and the 31 listed by Desart, are places where artists receive support of one kind or another and can display their wares. They are also places where outsiders can come and see the things that are being produced, learn about the people who made them, and pick up a little knowledge about the history and cultural treasure they hold. Kathryn Wells (2003) has edited a book about some of the wonderful creativity of a handful of artists working in the region between Tasmania and the south coast of Australia. It clearly demonstrates the value that both an Indigenous identity can bring to art, and the art to the continuity of that

Indigenous identity, particularly important in an area that many Australians think has no Indigenous people left!

In Lower Hutt, New Zealand, mentioned in the last chapter as the place where the preschool Maori "language nests" had been piloted, I also visited a gallery of Maori art called Maori Treasures where I met the proprietor Eleanor/Erenora Puketapu-Hetet. Her alternative names signify a dual heritage, but Erenora grew up in Lower Hutt where she acquired the skills of Maori weaving, which she now teaches and demonstrates to parties of tourists and other visitors. Her husband is a master carver who does the same. Erenora explained that the Maori learning techniques are quite different from Western ones, as very little is explained, and all skills are learned by careful observation and then by trying them out. She worked with other women to learn the weaving skills, and started by doing the least significant finishing tasks, and then gradually worked back to the more important earlier ones. Her husband had to look at a model, remember its detail, and then go away and work on his own.

Erenora has written a book about Maori weaving, where she begins to explain a little about the meaning of weaving in Maori thought and the "life force" of woven objects, another example of *taonga* we encountered above in the carved objects of the *Te Maori* exhibition. "Weaving is more than just a product of manual skills . . . [it] is endowed with the very essence of the spiritual values of Maori people. The ancient Polynesian belief is that the artist is a vehicle through whom the gods create" (1999: 2). In working on panels for the ceremonial house, the Waiwhetu Marae, also described in the last chapter, she discovered the complementarity of weaving and carving in these Maori acts of creativity. She writes, however, that the book "is merely a glimpse into the Maori world of weaving. To write about everything would be demeaning to the knowledge that is protected" (ibid. vi). She also concedes that no book can teach all that is required to become a Maori weaver, but justifies her decision to write one because "books can create an awareness" (ibid. 2).

The Woodland Cultural Centre mounts exhibitions of First Nations' Art two or three times a year. As with the performing arts described above, it can draw on the work of some of most accomplished artists in the area. Those who attend the openings are mostly First Nations people too, and I felt privileged to be present at the one in 2003 when a gallery was dedicated to the successful bone carver Stan Hill. Stan was there too, though he was clearly very frail, but he made his way to the stage and spoke about how he had come to take up carving in the first place. Son of a poor farmer, he had worked for many years developing manual skills in the dangerous Mohawk specialty of fitting the iron framework of skyscrapers. After a fall, and at the cost of a son to this work, he decided to give it up and try his hand at carving. "Half way through my life, I got together with the Creator," he said, "and after that, it was downhill all the way."

Stan's carvings sell for high prices now, and the pieces I have seen are exquisite works, symbolizing in some way or another aspects of his Indigenous background. A carved antler that stands in the entrance to the gallery named in his honor (see figure 5.4) may be understood in this way by examining the medium, the design, and the decoration, which is the Haudenosaunee Tree of Peace. Now that I have heard his talk, I can see further meaning in the technology and the source of his skill. Another non-Native visitor might understand part of what I see, a different Native might understand more, but I expect that only a Haudenosaunee would immediately grasp the full meaning of that symbolic tree. In chapter 3, I reported Judy Harris's account of the development of the exhibitions at the Woodland Cultural Centre, and she explained that they transmit different levels of information to different groups of people. Art works like that, doesn't it?

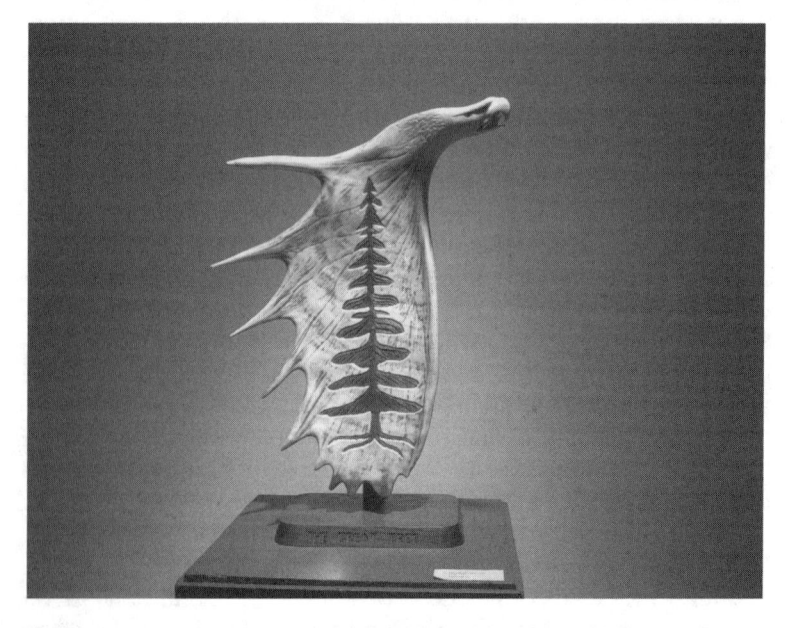

Figure 5.4 "The Great Tree," a moose antler carving by Stan Hill that greets the visitor to the gallery named after him at the Woodland Cultural Centre (Courtesy of the Woodland Cultural Centre).

References and Further Readings

Eidelson, Meyer, 1997, *The Melbourne Dreaming—A Guide to the Aboriginal Places of Melbourne*, Canberra: Aboriginal Studies Press.

Hakiwai, A., 1990, "Once Again the Light of Day? Museums and Maori Culture in New Zealand," *Museum* XLII(1): 35–38.

Kasarhérou, Emmanuel, 1991, "The New Caledonian Museum," in S.M. Eoe and P. Swadling (eds.), *Centres in the Pacific*, Port Moresby: Papua New Guinea National Museum.

Morphy, Howard, 1991, *Ancestral Connections: Art and an Aboriginal System of Knowledge*, Chicago and London: University of Chicago Press.

O'Biso, C., 1987, *First Light*, Auckland: Reed.

Puketapu-Hetet, Erenora, 1999, *Maori Weaving*, New Zealand: Pearson Education.

Wells, Kathryn (ed.), 2003, *Crossing the Strait, Tasmania to the South Coast*, Canberra: Aboriginal and Torres Strait's Islanders Commission.

Wright, Felicity (ed.), 1999, *The Art and Craft Centre Story: Volume One: Report*, Canberra: Aboriginal and Torres Strait's Islanders Commission.

Wright, Felicity and Frances Morphy (eds.), 2000, *The Art and Craft Centre Story: Volume Two: Summary and Recommendations*, Canberra: Aboriginal and Torres Strait's Islanders Commission.

Chapter 6

Land Claims, Archaeology, and New Communities

> Writing . . . it just came out a little while ago.
> — Johnny Sam, Tagé Cho Hudän Elder

Introduction

It was my contention at the start of this book that a people cannot proceed with any kind of land claim, or other legal process, until they have established an identity for themselves, and that a demonstration of their existence is primary to such further action. I argued that if museums, tourist facilities, books, and films present groups of people as if they no longer exist, then they may have a serious problem trying to convince others that they do. The case of the Ainu prefaced the book. The case of Australian Aboriginal groups, and especially Tasmanians, came up at the end of the last chapter, where we examined the importance of art, and especially performing arts, for sharing stories and for making outsiders *aware* of the existence of the people whose stories are being told. In previous chapters, we have seen how contemporary art is used in museums to make this point, and we have seen how the building and operating of a cultural center is a way for people to take control of making their identity clear.

For many Indigenous people, however, the issue of land lies at the heart of their reclamation process, and part of any statement of identity is also concerned with staking out the boundaries of the land they regard as their own. This is particularly true for those who live in relatively isolated places, who have managed to maintain at least a semblance of their old communities, and who continue to hand down

Land Claims, Archaeology, New Communities 157

environmental information from generation to generation. In such cases, the wider nation to which they belong has, of course, impinged on their lives. Its rulers may have deemed their habitat *terra nullis*, or 'wilderness,' and laid claim to daring 'discoveries' of it, but their very isolation has also protected them from the complete annihilation of all their old patterns of livelihood and the construction of alien cities on the lands of their ancestors.

Where the latter has happened, land issues may well be important too, but the solutions are likely to be different. It would be hard to hand back the land that is now Montreal to the inhabitants of Kahnawake, or the extensive campus of the University of British Columbia to the Musqueam people. In the first case, recognition of some demands and an injection of funding warded off a dispute that threatened to become quite nasty, in the second, discussions and negotiations are ongoing, but guests to the museum are soon made aware of the claim. On the other side of Vancouver, on the North Shore, the Squamish people have benefited greatly from several building developments, including a large shopping complex, on lands they have been acknowledged to own. They are paid rent by every developer, an income that in 2004 was said to have amounted to some 33 million Canadian dollars shared by a population of 3,300.

In New Zealand, during that same year, a big issue for Maori people was the disagreement between themselves and the government regarding ownership and property rights to the foreshore and seabed. It was being discussed during my visit in May, and in July I heard a paper on the subject at a conference in Europe, which argued that the issue had developed into a discourse on nationalism and nationhood that was polarizing the nation. The paper was presented by Ann Sullivan, a Maori political scientist who had made me welcome in Auckland, and she explained that although all political leaders argue that there is a single national identity, those on the center-right suggest that recognizing "difference" at all is racist while Maori argue that *failing* to recognize difference based on ethnicity is racist since Maori have a separate sense of nationhood with its origins founded on genealogical linkages (*whakapapa*). Clearly, issues relating to land, and in this case, the sea, touch on very fundamental differences of understanding.

In this chapter, we examine a few cases only. These are big issues and they have already been addressed by Indigenous and non-Indigenous scholars specializing in the relationship between a people and the land they claim as their own. The importance of land questions is too great to ignore in a book about revival and reclamation, however, as a crucial expression of Indigeneity is always through the long-term association with the environment of the ancestors, who passed on knowledge about its benefits and dangers. The naming of aspects of the landscape was also important to a people's worldview, and the first short example I consider is one of reclaiming names. After that, we look at a wider expression of care for the landscape, and also raise the importance of archaeology to contemporary Indigenous people. We then go on to examine the outcome in cultural terms of the success of the Inuit people in regaining control of their ancestral lands in the new territory of Nunavut, and glance briefly at the parallel case of Nunavik. The chapter closes by visiting a couple of innovative Indigenous communities in the Finger Lakes region of Upper New York State, the original territory of the Haudenosaunee.

Reclaiming Names

The quotation that introduces this chapter was made during a meeting at the offices of a Yukon people known officially as the Little Salmon Carmacks First Nation. They were discussing a project that formed an integral and important part of their land settlement, which was to make an Atlas demonstrating the agreement "in a way that everyone could understand." One part of the project involved putting back the ancient names for features of the region that had been renamed during the appropriation of this part of the world by explorers, gold seekers, and Yukon and Canadian government employees. The original names, in a language now called Northern Tutchone, marked many large and small features of the landscape, including places where people camped for fishing expeditions, where they met neighboring peoples for trade, and where they held annual gatherings to arrange marriages and other important events. Retrieving these land names, which had been passed down through the generations, would also reinforce stories about the land, the elder who was present explained.

For Indigenous people, renaming the land means reclaiming the way it was perceived by their ancestors, reasserting their relationship with it, and ensuring that the names are not forgotten. Through their names for features of the land, they can recreate their history, and make it clear to others who pass along that way. Another thing being discussed at the meeting in Carmacks was how the people of the community want the school to spend more time on local heritage. The children in the fourth grade are already learning some archaeology by looking for signs of the old fish camps, it was explained, and they are trained how to keep carefully the evidence they unearth. For Native land claims, archaeology is crucial, for it demonstrates to courts, or government authorities, the continuous use of the land in question by the people who claim it in a way that is also acceptable to the dominant society.

Names do this too for the people who know and own those places, so the reinstating of place names is an integral part of the *settlement* of a land issue, as I witnessed in this meeting. The Tr'ondëk Hwëch'in people we visited in chapter 2 had been called Dawson First Nation until 1995, when they reinstated their own name as part of an ongoing land claim (Dobrowolsky 2003: 108), and we encounter a parallel situation taking place in Nunavut in a later section of this chapter. For outsiders to accept these changes may take a little longer, so keen were pioneering travelers to deem land "wilderness" and name it for themselves and their exploratory zeal, so we examine a situation like this in the next section.

In a groundbreaking case in British Columbia known as Delgamuukw, after the Gitksan chief who brought it, *oral history* was also at last recognized as acceptable evidence for a land claim. Since then, the Western system imposed around the world has begun to acknowledge the value of this ancient way of transmitting knowledge from one generation to another. Indeed, the passing on of stories in all the new media at the disposal of Aboriginal and other peoples was demonstrated in the last chapter as a successful art form that makes the world realize why those names should be restored and the land (and human remains) returned. In this part of the world, as the elder pointed out, "writing . . . just came out a little while ago," and handing down stories that illustrate the link between a people and their land was a most effective way of ensuring their continuity.

Reclaiming the Landscape

Off the extreme west coast of Canada lies a group of some 150 islands, which many maps still call the Queen Charlottes, a name given to them in 1787 by George Dixon, British captain of a ship of the same name (Northwest Host Travel Guide 2003: 7). For the local people who lived there at the time, and whose descendants still live there, they are called the Haida Gwaii, or, quite simply, "Islands of the People" (ibid. 5). The Haida people are engaged in an ongoing court claim to regain complete control of these islands, which they have never formally given up, but in the meantime, they have achieved some considerable success toward that ultimate aim. The gradual use of the name for the islands by non-Haida local residents, by tourist brochures and by travelers, is one part of this. The reservation of the complete landscape of the southern third of these islands as the Gwaii Haanas National Park, accessible only by boat or plane, is another.

Before contact with the European sailors who brought disease to the Haida people, this part of the islands was home to several settlements, each of which has left ruins of the buildings they lived in, and the totem poles that marked important aspects of their lives. The populations were literally decimated by small pox, very possibly inflicted purposely through 'gifts' of infected blankets, and those few people who survived eventually moved north. Although they were distinct social groups with diverse ideas, they have now mostly settled in a single community in Old Massett, or perhaps the other Haida community in Skidegate, both of which we visited in chapter 3. The old ecosystem within which the Haida survived had been self-sustaining for millennia, the enormous cedar trees creating a canopy and support system for a huge diversity of plant and animal life within it. Because the Haida Gwaii are islands with a substantial sea passage separating them from the mainland, they had also sustained unique species, and minerals such as argelite, which is used by the Haida for wonderful shiny black carvings.

In other parts of the island, as in much of the rest of the province of British Columbia, commercial logging and fishing has seriously eroded that ancient ecosystem, and the so-called working forest created by the timber industry has changed much of the landscape forever. However, the insistence of the Haida, and wider conservation groups that have supported them, has resulted in the demarcation of 138 islands to be conserved as untouched as possible (see, e.g., www.spruceroots.org). Part of the land—at Ninstints—has also been designated as a UNESCO World Heritage Site. The official ownership of the Gwaii Haanas National Park remains under dispute, but its effective management is shared between the Haida Nation and Parks Canada, according to an agreement signed in 1993 (http://pc.gc.ca/pn-np/bc/gwaiihaanas/plan/plan2a_E.asp), and about half of the Parks Canada employees are Haida. All visitors need permission to visit the area, and they must receive orientation from an on-site "Haida Watchman" if they want to visit any of the historic villages. This is one of the services that will be provided by the new Qay'llnagaay Heritage Centre, which we discussed in chapter 3.

One more way in which Haida people have reclaimed their landscape is by repatriating the remains of their ancestors and those relatives who never had a chance to create descendants because of the scourge of the small pox. After the old villages were abandoned, physical anthropologists and other such 'scientists' collected many of the bones of people they thought were now a 'dying race' for their research. They were taken to museums, mostly in the United States and Canada, though probably also in Europe, and stashed away for this purpose. For the Haida people, as for many other people in the world, Indigenous or otherwise, they feel that their ancestors cannot rest in peace in such a situation, and they have therefore been engaged in negotiating their return. So far, they have been largely successful, and they have been able to proceed to the careful process of bringing them home. They do this by first placing them in properly constructed bent-wood boxes, carrying them back to the islands, according them all the appropriate burial rites, and burying them in their own landscape.

The process of reclaiming the landscape has been underway in different ways in many parts of the world. We spoke in chapter 3 about the return of masks to the Kwakwaka'wakw people at the U'Mista Cultural Centre, a place whose very name celebrates the return home of something (or someone) valuable. We mentioned above the claims of the Maori people for the right to use the seashore, and in Britain, New Age Druids have claimed with some success the right to worship at Stonehenge at sunrise on the Summer Solstice. Along the coast of Washington State, the Makah people literally reclaimed a part of their landscape when tidal erosion exposed a village submerged by a landslide some 500 years earlier that was demonstrated to have belonged to their ancestors. In order to justify and take control of this claim, several Makah set about learning the techniques of archaeological observation, and collected enough artifacts to open a tribal museum at Neah Bay.

An interesting aspect of the display, which I visited in 2003, was to show how the artifacts that were discovered confirmed the oral history of the people about their precontact fishing and whaling techniques. This had become an issue when the U.S. government granted them fishing rights and permission to practice whaling, but only as long as they used nothing but their traditional technology. These were another people decimated by contact with European disease, and the weakened survivors had not been able to convince the authorities that they could therefore use nets for their fishing until the excavation showed clearly that they were part of technology dating back to the fifteenth century! Another intriguing part of their technology was a drainage system constructed from whalebones. This case does demonstrate a way that anthropological research has actually been beneficial to Native people, but a crucial factor for the Makah has been their own involvement in the process.

A parallel case of literal land reclamation is taking place in the Yukon, where a recent aspect of climate change has been revealing many ancient sites of caribou hunting. Weapons found in ice patches uncovered as the long-term glacier recedes demonstrate use of the land dating back several thousand years, and the First Nations who live in the region have become thoroughly involved in investigating the past that this exposes (*Ice Patch* 2002). The caribou seek ice patches in the summer to avoid insects and the heat, apparently, and it is in their accumulated dung over this long period that the keys to the past of these peoples are stored. They are thus involved in archaeological research, of course, but also the transcription of oral history about the existence of caribou during living memory, the collection and preservation of the ancient artifacts that are being unearthed, and a strong program of education for their young people (ibid.).

One of the four First Nations involved is presently called the Champagne and Aishihik First Nation (CAFN), who have also recently settled a claim to a substantial part of an area known on Canadian maps as the Kluane National Park. This is a mountainous region that was still described as "unspoiled wilderness" in a film of orientation I saw in 2003 at the Park Canada Visitors Centre at Haines Junction, one of its access points. Indeed, the film made heroic noises about an Italian who was said bravely to have 'discovered' it, though the local First Nations had been hunting there for years before he arrived. Ann Landry, a Parks Canada representative I met in Whitehorse, explained that the CAFN has now been invited to mount their own display, so I went to their local offices to inquire about their plans. Diane Strand, the Heritage Officer, was kind enough to tell me about the situation.

She explained that they were still involved in the planning process, but they had been having a look at other such displays around the country to get some ideas. They were concerned to do the display themselves, rather than be represented by Parks Canada, so they wanted properly to educate their own people before they employed them to explain their history and culture to others. Diane gave me a paper entitled "Vision for Future Use and Management of Kluane National Park" summarizing the results of four workshops on the subject, which demonstrated that some of this "education" would be very practical. CAFN members needed first to undergo a healing process, reconnecting with the spiritual significance and natural splendor of the park, and they needed to reacquaint themselves with its land and resources after years of exclusion. They would need to rename, and renew their association with their old trails, cabins, campsites, and so forth, as well as matching them with the oral histories and knowledge of the elders (*Vision* 2000).

Once this was done, they could begin to devise educational programs about the archaeological sites, the CAFN history, and their traditional lifestyles, first for the young people of the CAFN, and then for outsiders. They had thought they might establish an "educational trapline" using an old campsite and trails for studying the animals that had been part of their lives, but they would also create static and interactive displays for the Visitor Centre at Haines Junction about their history, heritage, and wildlife management practices. They would show some of the artifacts that had been found under the receding glacier, and offer for sale arts, crafts, and services such as guiding, or storytelling. Promotional and informative materials would be prepared for CD-ROMs, pamphlets, posters, radio, film, and television, both for tourists and for school curricula. Generally, the CAFN was looking forward to playing a greater part in administering this park that was at last becoming their [reclaimed] land again (ibid.).

Retrieving Control: The Case of Nunavut (and Nunavik)

The examples we have considered so far demonstrate varying degrees of success by Indigenous people in regaining control over the lands they occupied prior to the arrival of settlers from distant worlds. They have been able to reclaim aspects of their culture in connection with that land, put back the names they had allocated to places, and retrieve their historical associations. In various ways they have been able to reclaim the landscape within which their heritage was formed, and through that renewed association, they can introduce the kinds of education they feel important to pass on to their children. The people we have considered so far still *share* control of that land, however, in some cases with Parks Canada, which can help to protect it from further development, and in all cases with the wider province or territory to which they now belong. The case of Nunavut, which is a new territory of Canada with 85 percent Inuit control—and this figure because they wanted their government accurately to reflect their population—offers a stage of success that goes one step further.

When people retrieve control of their own land to this extent, however, a situation arises which in some ways goes beyond the scope of this book, for their cultural identity is no longer in doubt. They are recognized as the people who are governing their own land, and their two languages, Inuktitut and Inuinnaqtun, are among the official four being used there (also including French and English). They have thus become less concerned with reclaiming their culture than with setting up and running the bureaucratic infrastructure of a national territory, with providing basic amenities such as health care, housing, and a formal system of education. Cultural identity is still a concern, as we shall see, and there is an interesting twist to how it is being displayed, but it can no longer be a top priority in the face of responding to the population's basic needs, retrieved along with the rest of the control. Several of the people I met when I traveled to Nunavut explained this to me, and although I did investigate the museum and a couple of cultural centers, I also followed local advice and found some examples of cultural display in places I had not anticipated. In this section, we take a brief look at both.

Iqaluit—formerly Frobisher Bay—is the capital of Nunavut, and it therefore houses the Legislative Assembly building, the Cathedral, the Nunavut Research Institute, the main campus of Arctic College, and the offices of Nunavut Tourism. The main museum is there, too, although there are other places in the vast territory of Nunavut that have, or plan to have, their own museums and cultural centers, and I visited a couple of those too. I was in this part of the world in the summer, when the pathways, such as they are, tend to be a little dusty and untidy, but the temperature was bearable—with a windproof coat! A snow covering and freezing temperatures are more usual, and this of course opens the whole terrain to travel by sledge or *qamutiiq*, skis, and skidoos, and a traditional economy perfected by the Inuit people. There is one tarmac-surfaced road in Iqaluit, named after Queen Elizabeth II who came to declare open the new Commonwealth territory, but certain other features of the city stand out. A "Sculpture Garden" collection of statuary and carved stone in front of the art department of Arctic College is one interesting feature, the white igloo-shaped cathedral is certainly another (see figure 6.1), and the blue Legislative Assembly building a third.

I did not at first imagine the extent to which the Legislative Assembly building would be a site of cultural display, but I could not have been more wrong. First, the basic architectural structure reflects both an understanding of the climate and a tried and tested Inuit decision-making process. Light enters through thick glass, with minimized exterior surface that protects it from cold, and the overall shape and seating arrangement is round. There are no political parties, and a division is found only between ministers and ordinary members. The gallery is open, to encourage public participation, and the sealskin covered seats are arranged to distinguish the valued elders, who sit on

Figure 6.1 Iqaluit cathedral has the circular shape preferred by its Inuit congregation, Nunavut Territory, Canada.

the same level as the Members. The symbol of authority carried in when the assembly is in session is a mace, on the British model, but constructed from a narwhal tusk and decorated with animals representing Inuit food sources. It is supported by a carved Inuit family representing values such as respect for the elders and equality of the sexes. It was made cooperatively by Inuit artists from across the region, as were other decorative features, such as hanging tapestries, prints, photographs, and a large carved rock.

In the center of the meeting hall lies a sledge known as a *qamutiiq*, tied up with sealskin ropes and set on whalebone runners, a gift from the airline that now flies between the scattered Nunavut communities. Laid out on it are some of the basic tools that sustained Inuit life and gave them light, heat, food, and shelter. Other important aspects of Inuit life, such as the Aurora Borealis, the North Star, and the Inukshuk stone landmark, have been incorporated into the Nunavut Coat of Arms, which hangs above the Speakers chair. A glass case contains beautiful carvings of the official animal, bird, and flower of Nunavut, again made by local artists. The different provinces of Canada have presented other splendid items of furniture in the Hall, among them a carved podium from the Yukon, birch wood bookcases from British Columbia, and a clock of bird's eye maple from Ontario. A pair of carved caribou antlers was presented by the Inuit people of northern Quebec (known as Nunavik), and a painting of a sea spirit "Sednaa" by the home rule government of Greenland.

The cathedral is another site of symbolic display (see figure 6.1), again circular in shape, and this time even more clearly representing the igloo influence because it is white, without windows. Inside, the middle pews are arranged in rows, but others encircle the area, and at the Inuktitut service I attended, they seemed to be rather popular. Behind the altar, large blue appliquéd hangings again displayed important elements of Inuit life such as animals and birds, garments made from skins, and families in igloos and kayaks. They are intermingled with Christian symbols, but the three officiants of the service were clearly Inuit, and some aspects of the procedure were quite different from any service I had ever attended before. Many people wandered in late, for example, and children were allowed to run around freely, not least to supply members of the congregation with samples of the tissues that sat in a box at the communion rail.

Other sites of cultural display in Iqaluit when I visited were the Unikkaarvik Visitor Centre and the Nunatta Sunakkaangit Museum, but interestingly for this study, both had been designed and put together by non-Inuit people, albeit with Inuit consultation. In the case of the first, literally "the place where stories are told," Nunavut Tourism had commissioned the arrangements from a specialist company, which had put together a combination of recreated Arctic scenery, a museum-like display about Inuit life, and a series of videos that could be selected for viewing. There were examples of contemporary Inuit art in the entrance, a desk where information could be requested (from non-Inuit staff), and the local library opened off the center offering further reading and Internet access. The whole place was being refurbished as I passed through, and as I saw members of the French Language Preservation Society carefully examining the bilingual Inuktitut/English signage, I suspect French will soon be added to the labels!

The museum, which has a fairly classic but beautifully displayed collection of tools, garments, carvings, and toys such as dolls, as well as a temporary display of Inuit art, already had all three languages on its labels, but it had also clearly been initially established by non-Inuit volunteers. Its history was displayed in the entrance hall, and although it had had Inuit directors in the past, Brian Lunger, the present non-Inuit manager/curator admitted to some difficulty in persuading local people, who thought of it as another place for visitors, that it had a role for them. He told me that he had been trying to organize events such as talks by elders, and openings of exhibitions of local art, to give it a community feel, but even the artists tended to think of it in economic terms, as an outlet for their work. Albums of old photographs were popular, though, and the Inuk assistant, Jimmy Ekho, who was there on the Sunday when I first called, seemed to have friends upstairs in the community area. He was very enthusiastic about the museum activities, and explained the background of items in the gift shop.

The Inuit are no strangers to museums, of course, and they are well aware of their importance for conserving evidence of their past. Nelson Graburn examined several examples that had appeared throughout the region occupied by the Inuit, including the area now known as Nunavik, during a process that he describes as "the emergence of the consciousness of cultural loss" (1998: 18). He classified them by date of founding, and according to the degree of involvement of the Inuit themselves, and he reported that the first cooperative one was set up in Cape Dorset as long ago as 1958 (ibid. 20). The importance of establishing facilities "for the conservation and management of a representative portion of the archaeological record" is also laid out in the Land Claims Agreement upon which Nunavut was established, and a body entitled the Inuit Heritage Trust (IHT— www.ihti.ca) was set up to oversee this task, in coordination with others (Agreement 1993: Article 33).

I made an appointment to see the executive director of this organization, William Beveridge, and he and his project manager, Ericka Chemko, explained that the situation was still in its infancy. Currently the three main stakeholders responsible for creating the museum, IHT, Nunavut Tunngavik Incorp (NTI), and the Nunavut government's Department of Culture, Language, Elders and Youth (GN-CLEY), are in discussions to access what has been done, where to go now, and what role each organization will play in the process. All parties want a museum, but ideally it should also include a space for performing arts, possibly a 360° movie theater, a children's hands-on gallery, and a small café. A model that William had seen and liked was Greenland's Cultural Centre, the Katuaq, which is also described on its website as "an active meeting place." The IHT share joint title of Inuit archaeological artifacts excavated from 1993 on with GN-CLEY. However, the presentation of Inuit heritage was at that time still under discussion with the above bodies as well as the many other heritage stakeholders around Nunavut that currently collect, document, or display Inuit cultural heritage. Various funding bodies such as Canadian Heritage, Parks Canada, Nunavut Tourism, GN-CLEY, and the regional Inuit business development organizations inject a good amount of money in Nunavut for various individual projects and community initiatives, they explained.

At the time when I visited, in 2003, three possible scenarios were being considered. One would be a full service heritage center for the whole of Nunavut, another would be a series of smaller centers in different locations (like the campuses of Arctic College), and a third would be a warehouse to store objects, but with a traveling exhibition to involve the smaller communities. The Legislative Assembly commissioned and tabled a feasibility study on creating a heritage center that favored the first, and as I go to press, Ericka reported that this is the favored model of all the major heritage stakeholders (NTI, IHT, GN-CLEY). The feasibility study rated various communities for a site, and Iqaluit came out highest, but it was anticipated that people in outlying communities with existing facilities might raise objections at the fund-raising stage. In the meantime, a version of the exhibit mentioned in the third scenario was being taken round Nunavut schools by IHT for educational purposes, and the now former assistant deputy minister of CLEY, Anthony Saez, who also agreed to talk to me, seemed to think that this outreach program would be further developed. He was keen to see sites where oral history could be shared as well.

While official bodies mull over the possibilities, there are still museums, arts centers, and heritage sites in several communities of Nunavut, and a report on a couple of these will add a ground level view of the Inuit reclamation process. The first one I went to was in Kimmirut, formerly Lake Harbour, a small community on the south of Baffin Island, which nevertheless gets an influx of tourists from time to time, not least from the occasional cruise ship that calls in. At a place called the Kimmirut Visitors Centre, Tommy Akavak explained that the displays were based on research done by the Department of Tourism and Sustainable Development and interviews with members of the community. There is a pretty comprehensive display about local life, about the "History of Change," and about the environmental surroundings, its flora and fauna, all illustrated with film and slides, as well as some recreated animals and scenery. Especially interesting in view of the Saez remarks above, however, was an abundance of quotations about the recent history of the community from local people, first in Inuktitut and then translated into English.

The center also had an air of great activity about it. People were coming and going, making and drinking cups of coffee, and generally enjoying the displays. Tommy had explained that local people use the center, although it was made for outsiders, and that they particularly like to look at the collections of old photographs. On the day I was there, most of the coming and going was about preparing for the school science trip that I mentioned in chapter 4. This was to be a five-day camp so that young people could experience living off the land that had sustained their elders, as well as learning about the plants and animals for their science lessons. This was a practical expression, then, of the quotation from a speech of a local MP Jack Anawak, which was displayed at the center under the heading *Asserting Control*,

> I want Canadians and Members of this House to understand that Nunavut exists now and has always existed in the minds and hearts of Inuit. We know that Nunavut is our land. What we have been seeking throughout the years is the acknowledgement by the Canadian government that this was and is our land, and that we have the right to control what happens to that land, our homeland.

The other place I visited was Pangnirtung, a community set in the stunning scenery of Cumberland Sound, where an Arts and Crafts Centre is witness to a successful project to replace the old sealing and whaling industries that became threatened by the activities of Green Peace and other environmentalists. Delicate prints on display at the museum in Iqaluit had been made here, as had a huge woven tapestry that hangs in the entrance to the Legislative Assembly building. Across the street from the Arts and Crafts Centre lies the Angmarlik Centre, which houses a public museum, a library, and an elders' room, and next to it there is a Visitor Centre operated by Parks Canada to orientate visitors to the Auyuittuq National Park. There is also a hotel here, for tourism is another industry that has been developed, though I stayed in an excellent B&B operated by an artist, Pudloo Kilabuk, who was in the process of carving intricate figures onto a narwhal tusk. The B&B was situated at a ten-minute walk from the airstrip, for this is a community of only 1,300 to 1,400!

Before I began my visits to all these places, I had an impromptu encounter with an interesting man in the Hamlet Office. I had called in on my way up from the airstrip, to seek the minister for Heritage, who happened to be the local member of the Legislative Assembly. He was not in his office, but I was passed to his brother, Bill Kilabuk, the Community Lands Administrator, who telephoned the minister for me. Unfortunately he was unwell, but Bill sat me down and regaled me with some of his ideas about heritage, though he gave me the strong impression that he would rather be out hunting geese than sitting in an office. "I don't really like us building walls around ourselves—for the betterment of human relations," he said. "We are all under one sky." He was clearly a contributor to this community of artists, for he showed me a poem that he had written, attached to a painting he had made of a local scene. It read:

> I do what I want to do, say what I want to say
> Am where I want to be and people are there,
> And to love not to be my own enemy,
> We will not regret the past,
> Nor wish to shut the door on it,
> No matter how far down the scale we have gone
> We will see how our experience can benefit others.

This is quite a sad comment, for like others throughout this "kerbside of the highway to North America" as Tommy Akavak had described Kimmirut, the Inuit people now residing in Pangnirtung had offered their knowledge and hospitality to a series of explorers and entrepreneurs. They came seeking Arctic fox fur, whale oil, and bones (for corsets, I seem to remember) and otherwise to exploit and take advantage of the benefits of the land the Inuit had made their home. All these encounters are presented in the museum section of the Angmarlik Centre, not always in a negative way; indeed the Scottish whalers seem to have hit it off rather well with the Inuit people, who acknowledge things like printmaking that they learned from them. However, disease and the mission activities did alter the lives of the people forever. Ooleepeeka Arnaqaq, manager of the center, gave me a tour of the display, which was fascinating because she explained details like the incredibly efficient use Inuit made of their resources, not least in the way that whale oil was converted into heating.

Sakiasie Sowdluapik, the renewable resource officer, was kind enough to give me an excellent account of the history and development of Pangnirtung, as described briefly above. Both he and Nancy Anilnilvak, who heads the Parks Canada Visitor Centre next door, emphasized how much the elders had been involved in the decision making about the various developments. In fact, the elders still meet regularly in the special room set aside for them in the Angmarlik Centre, though when I was visiting this was also being used temporarily for an IHT map-making project—the now familiar one of reinstating Inuit names to the various features in the area. Apart from educating the visiting public about Inuit culture, members of the community here are concerned to preserve their way of life as much as they can, and they seek especially to welcome visitors who will appreciate the land they have themselves fought to conserve, Sakiasie explained.

In the Parks Canada Visitors Centre, there is an abundance of information about the Auyuittuq Park, and here outsiders who wish to travel through it must pay a fee, and receive an orientation about public safety and emergency evacuation procedures. There is a polar bear watch, for example, and information posted about any that have been sited near the usual path. Visitors can also consult maps and hire a local guide if they are so inclined, and I met a man from Ottawa who had been impressed with the wildlife he had been shown by traveling with such a guide. Inuit can use the park free of charge, they can hunt to provide for their families, and a caribou skin drying on the fence outside one of the houses seemed to indicate evidence of this continuing practice. Nancy Anilnilvak explained that Parks Canada has always been very cooperative, and they offer good opportunities for local people, employing them, and training them for promotion, as had happened in her case. Of the staff working in the center, seven were already Inuit, three were not, and she hoped that in five years' time they would all be Inuit.

The Arts and Crafts Centre in Pangnirtung was still managed by a non-Inuit, Peter Wilson, but then there are so many new jobs in Nunavut that there are clearly not enough Inuit with the appropriate education to go around yet. Both Nancy and Sakiasie had emphasized the importance of education for the future of Nunavut, and I met one or two university students who were working in the facilities over the summer. Tommy, who was working in the Parks Canada Centre, for example, was taking Nunavut Studies in Ottawa, and he looked forward to a good career. Before this book went to press, the assistant deputy minister of CLEY responsible for heritage, Anthony Saez, whom I had interviewed, had been replaced by an Inuk man, David Akgeegok, but eventually the Inuit residents of Nunavut may choose not to do all the management and bureaucracy themselves. They may prefer to be out hunting, as Bill Kilabuk had mentioned. They probably employ too many non-Inuit people at the moment (some 15 percent of the population), and this is a bone of some contention, but the important thing to remember is that they are now the ones officially in control. *They* do the employing. *They* make the decisions. They actually don't need to do all the office work if they don't want to!

This crucial point about being in control was made again by Taqraliq Partridge, the only Inuk person I managed to meet for any length of time from the Quebec side of Inuit country, the area now known as Nunavik. Because of the strong divisions over the years between Quebec and the rest of Canada, their history has developed somewhat differently, but there is an Inuit-controlled political organization called the Makivik Corporation, which is active and respected. This was born out of the rapidly organized resistance in 1973 to a proposed hydroelectric project in James Bay, which also marshaled the Cree who live in that region, brought the developers and the local and federal government to a negotiating table, and eventually resulted in an agreement. Funding backed up the control over their own lands handed back to the Indigenous partners, and one of the results is the Avataq Cultural Institute (www.avataq.qc.ca), which has its headquarters in Montreal.

There I learned about the various plans for cultural display in Nunavik, which are mostly still at the discussion stage, although some building on earlier places described in Graburn's (1998) paper. Coordinator Sylvie Coté Chew made me welcome at the center, explained its role, and presented me with some of the beautifully illustrated materials about Nunavik that the center has prepared. She also introduced me to several of the people who work there, including Taqraliq Partridge, director of communications, who emphasized the importance to Inuit about being in control of their lands. She reiterated another point, made in chapter 1 of this book, "Museums have been so erroneous," she said, "because they try to display the past as the 'real Inuit'; but we have, and we *should* adapt. We are now greatly enjoying the use of GPS (global positioning systems), for example," she said, and she proceeded to explain to me (because I didn't know) how these clever devices work. Landscape reclaimed, and control retrieved!

New Communities

In this last section I briefly examine a movement relating to land that fits neither of the categories I set up at the outset. I made a distinction between people who are relatively isolated and can therefore contemplate regaining a fair degree of control over their lands, and those whose ancestral places have become completely caught up in contemporary cities. The movement I want to describe here is taking place in a part of North America that is still rather rural, which even looks (at least to me) like stereotypical 'Indian country'. However, it is at the same time easily accessible to one of the main hubs of the world, and has a scattering of old settler communities. Probably for these reasons, then, Native land claims are hotly contested, and I give an example of this situation. There are one or two less aggressive ways in which the original inhabitants of these lands are reclaiming links, however, so let us make a visit.

The area in question is located in Upper New York State, a region known locally as the Finger Lakes, for the fairly obvious reason once it is mapped that five long, narrow lakes resemble the digits of a splayed hand. These were the lands neatly divided between the Five Nations of the Haudenosaunee at the time of the arrival of the British in New England, and for a couple of centuries they agreed to share their abundant resources with the newcomers. During the eighteenth century there were an increasing number of skirmishes of various sorts, and the American War of Independence incited some sorry splits within the Haudenosaunee people, as well as among the settlers. The Mohawks sided with the British, as did many of their old allies, and they were subsequently settled on the banks of the Grand River, over the border in Canada. This is now the Reserve of the Six Nations, and the site of the Woodland Cultural Centre. Other Mohawk communities live in Kahnawake and Ahkwesáhsne, as we saw in chapter 4.

Upper New York State does still have the Haudenosaunee communities that took the side of the rebels, however, and in chapter 1 we visited the Seneca National Museum in Salamanca, which expresses resentment about the building of a dam that flooded the land they had previously occupied. In chapter 2, we visited Shako:wi, the Oneida cultural center that had been built with the proceeds of a successful casino, and this community has used its economic advantage to rebuild many public and private buildings. A third expression of Haudenosaunee occupation of New York State is to be found at the historic Seneca site of Ganondagan, where archaeological research has uncovered a huge settlement that was apparently sacked by French raiders in the seventeenth century. The Visitor Center welcomes tourists and school parties to demonstrate the former longhouse life of the Seneca people, but they also hold contemporary events such as an annual Native American Dance and Music Festival there, and the guide when I was there was a Seneca.

The Cayuga people, on the other hand, have retained none of their former lands, now the site of Cornell University, the associated town of Ithaca, and considerable space surrounding them. Many local names acknowledge this connection, there is historical evidence of the sacking of Cayuga communities there in 1779 for supporting the British, and the displaced Cayuga nation has an ongoing federal court case against New York State to reclaim some of that land (see, e.g., Hauptman 2003). This is the claim mentioned above that is hotly disputed by local homeowners, most of whom even seem to resist the idea of coexisting with the Cayuga on this abundant fertile land. They apparently fear a rise in taxes should such an eventuality occur, and they have set up an anti-land-claim group called the Upstate Citizens for Equality, which erects signs, demonstrates, and generally expresses its opposition to the claim.

Meanwhile, however, another smaller, but growing group of local people has launched a quiet resistance to this belligerent posture, and has formed an association to build bridges between the communities. Entitled SHARE, an acronym for Strengthening Haudenosaunee American Relations through Education, they operate from a 70-acre piece of land that was bought with the explicit intention that it should be returned to the Cayuga once the debt is paid off. To achieve this aim, an environmentally friendly organic farm is being run there, and the old Cayuga crops and medicines are at last thriving again on this ancient land. It is also a site of much meeting and merrymaking, and Natives and non-Natives travel from a wide area to see what is afoot, and learn of the Cayuga and their project.

Three anthropologists from Ithaca and Wells Colleges have become involved with this work, which they describe as "activist anthropology" (see Olsen et al. 2001) and they take students over, visit local schools to tell children about the venture, and volunteer to help out in many other ways. Brooke and Ernie Olsen are qualified in the relevant and useful skills of medical anthropology and conflict management respectively, and Jack Rossen is an archaeologist. He has worked in several South American countries, as well as the Caribbean, but he found evidence of a Cayuga longhouse in his own garden in Aurora, and he and his students now spend time unearthing artifacts very much closer to home! The Olsens, as well as Jack, traveled to McMaster to give a talk about SHARE when I was there, and they were clearly very enthusiastic.

Jack explained that the archaeological work he is doing there is very exciting because he always consults members of the Cayuga nation as he proceeds. They can help to identify the pieces that are being found, and they can warn him off sites that are still sacred to them. All the material adds to their understanding of their own history, and strengthens their land claim at the same time. For the students, it is a great opportunity to see the contemporary importance of archaeological research, indeed the whole SHARE project adds a practical dimension to their studies. Several were moved, for example, to witness Cayuga Clan Mother Bernadette (Birdie) Hill planting the "Three Sisters" of corn, beans, and squash there, with tears running down her cheeks. She said that it was the first time in 200 years that Cayuga corn had been planted on Cayuga land by Cayuga hands. Now the crops are thriving, and a medicine garden has also been planted. This has inspired a workshop on herbal remedies, and the site has become a central place for dialogue about environmental issues.

Other similar projects are undoubtedly taking place across the continent, and very possibly in other parts of the world. Andrew Martindale, an archaeologist whose room I shared when I was visiting McMaster, was working with the Tsimshian people in British Columbia to investigate their past (see, e.g., Martindale and Marsden 2003), and at the same time to bolster their claims to the land there. When I was traveling through the Cheyenne River Sioux tribal lands in South Dakota, I learned of an ambitious project to "Restore the Prairie" that supported their lives before the arrival of pioneers moving West. They already have a growing herd of buffalo in place, and they are working to restore and manage the populations of ferrets, prairie dogs, and deer. This project is also revitalizing the culture and spirituality of these Lakota people, according to their brochure, endorsed by the U.S. National Wildlife Federation (www.nwf.org).

One last exciting example is another community in Upper New York State, this time in an area still known as the Mohawk Valley, although the Mohawks, after whom it was named, moved north with the British over 200 years previously. The roadside abounds with notices proclaiming the sites of incidents that happened here during the war that established the United States of America, but one sign announces something a little different. This one makes it clear that there has at last been a return of Mohawk people to their eponymous valley, and that they are offering bed and breakfast to the passing public. Here is to be found an organic farm, a pasture for cows and horses, a walking trail among peaceful surroundings and the running water of a stream, and conference facilities offering lectures, workshops, socials, and meetings. A craft shop offers Native goods "from all over the country," and, if the visitor presses a little further, there is an archaeological site marking out the longhouse and the stockade poles of the Old Mohawk Turtle Clan Caughnawaga Village.

At the start of chapter 4, we met a man named Tom Porter, who jumped up after the speeches of the young people who had graduated from schools in their own Native tongues, and insisted that the elders in the audience shake their hands. This is the man—full name Tom Sakokwenionkwas Porter—who has founded the new Mohawk community in New York State, and reclaimed nearly 400 acres of Mohawk land for his people. At the Sweetgrass conference he was receiving an award for his contribution to the revival of the Mohawk language, for the Kanatsiohareke Mohawk Indian community is no mere token home in the old valley, it is the site of a veritable movement of reclamation and education. Founded in 1993, when Tom purchased the first 322 acres at auction, "the goal of re-establishment is to nourish and preserve Native language, traditions, culture and beliefs," states the brochure. It goes on to outline another dream they have to create a "reverse" boarding school that would "give back to Native people all that was taken: their language, their culture, their spirituality, their identity, their functional family practices" and "restore dignity among the Iroquois Nations. In the Millennium we have a chance to start again" it goes on, "this time with positive relationships. This is the goal of Kanatsiohareke."

For those who book a night's stay at the bed and breakfast, they are also offered "a collection of informative books and videos on various Native topics," and they are warned "discussions might occur during your stay regarding topics which focus on issues impacting Native Americans today, or on how historic cultural traditions have been kept alive." Participation is optional, the brochure makes clear, but if I find myself in the area again, I shall be particularly looking forward to hearing some of the stories that have kept alive such a strong and persistent sense of identity among a people who carried their history in a few prized objects. The Mohawks and other Haudenosaunee had few buildings to impress the outsiders who arrived expecting such marks of 'civilization', but their stories and their association with their lands have ensured a burgeoning recognition of those more subtle values. We will outline some of these in more detail in chapter 8.

When I was staying on the Six Nations Reserve in Ontario, I asked the elected chief of the time Roberta Jamieson, to talk to me about her role, and she agreed. She had been ombudsman for Ontario for ten years previously, so she had developed some skills in conciliation, and one of her dreams was to unite the old confederacy chiefs of her community with the council elected according to Canadian rules. During early contact with the new arrivals to our continent, we respected one another, she explained, and people knew who they were, but then the numbers grew large, values clashed, and greed took over. We almost lost our culture through the residential schools, she went on, and the settlers declared our land *terra nullis* and tried to 'civilize' us. But despite all this, our culture has survived, and now even people from abroad visit the Six Nations to learn how we do things. "It's easy to blame history for our problems, but the future is our responsibility and we need to take charge of it."

Through the process of reclaiming names, reestablishing the usage of and responsibility for traditional lands, and ensuring that stories are passed on effectively from one generation to another, members of

First Nations are able to do this "taking charge." For many years, they were frustrated in their efforts, but the recognition by the wider society of their oral histories, backed-up by the 'proof' of archaeological findings, is making it more and more possible. It seems likely that it was the 'evidence' of archaeology in the case of the site displayed at Head-Smashed-In that attracted my friends in Scotland, along of course with the wonderful name and story that are featured in the publicity. Names, land, and stories are important to everyone in one way or another, though archaeological research may have very differential value in backing up that importance.

References and Further Readings

Agreement between the Inuit of the Nunavut Settlement Area and Her Majesty the Queen in Right of Canada, 1993, Ottawa: Tunngavik Federation of Nunavut and Indian Affairs and Northern Development.

Dobrowolsky, Helene, 2003, *Hammerstones: A History of the Tr'ondëk Hwëch'in*, Dawson City, Yukon: Tr'ondëk Hwëch'in Publication.

Graburn, Nelson, 1998, "Weirs in the River of Time: The Development of Historical Consciousness among Canadian Inuit," *Museum Anthropology*, 22(1): 18–32.

Hauptman, Laurence, 2003, " 'Going Off the Reservation': A Memoir," *The Public Historian*, 25(4): 79–92.

Ice Patch, Spring 2002, newsletter of the Carcross-Tagish First Nation, Champagne and Aishihik First Nation, Kluane First Nation and Kwanlin Dün First Nation.

Martindale, Andrew and Susan Marsden, 2003, "Defining the Middle Period (3500 BP to 1500 BP) in Tsimshian History through a Comparison of Archaeological and Oral Records," *BC Studies*, 138: 13–50.

Neufeld, David, 2002, "The Commemoration of Northern Aboriginal Peoples by the Canadian Government," *The George Wright Forum*, 19(3): 22–33.

Northwest Host 2003 Travel Guide: Guide to Haida Gwaii, Queen Charlotte Islands: Haida Gwaii Travel Association.

Olsen, Brooke, Jack Rossen, and Ernest Olsen, 2001, "Helping the Cayuga Return to their Land," *Anthropology News*, 42(4): 19–20.

Sullivan, Ann, 2004, "We many peoples make one nation or are we all one nation?," paper presented at the Second International Conference on New Directions in the Humanities, Monash University Centre in Prato, Italy, July 20–23.

Vision for Future Use and Management of Kluane National Park: Highlights from Four Workshops, Spring 1999, Whitehorse, Yukon: Champagne and Aishihik First Nation.

Chapter 7

International Links, Cultural Exchange, and Personal Identity

> We are in touch with each other now, and we are all learning to feel pride in our ancestry again.
>
> Ainu woman, name unrecorded

Introduction

In chapter 2, reference was made to an interesting dinner-dance-show that can sometimes be attended up on Grouse Mountain, in West Vancouver. Visitors must book in advance, take the cable car to its upper terminal, and there meet a member of the Coast Salish group whose culture is to be explained and performed in the Hiwus Feast House. To arrive at the house, visitors follow their guide along a path through the woods, eventually to catch a glimpse of the decorated wooden building on the other side of a small lake. The path around the lake brings them to its entrance and on into the show. A similar journey must be made back down at the end of the show, and on the occasion that I attended this event, we were escorted by two of the girls who had been dancing for us.

An intriguing conversation took place on this return journey, for the girls asked us where we were from, and they chatted to us about their own travels as dancers. They had visited many countries, they said, including Japan, where they met members of the Ainu people. They loved these journeys because of all the new places they could see, the people they could meet, and because they offered the opportunity to engage in something they described as "cultural exchange." When I asked what this was like, they explained that it involved dancing, singing, and generally carrying on all night! Although the girls lived in Vancouver, performed the dances of the Coast Salish people, and had been learning the Coast Salish language since they were children, they said that they were both actually, by birth, Hawaiian.

This incident raises two issues that we have not so far considered in any detail about the process of cultural "reclamation," as we have been calling it, and together they form the chief focus of this chapter. The first concerns international links among and between Indigenous peoples and outsiders interested in Indigenous peoples, and we examine several examples and possibilities. By the end of the chapter we move to a more specific concern with "cultural exchange," and we offer a slightly broader (dare I say anthropological?) framework within which to place the activities of Indigenous peoples. The second issue is one of identity, and it raises the thorny question about how people qualify to be members of a particular ethnic, or Aboriginal group, and how much choice they have in presenting themselves as such. We look at a few cases as we examine the international links, which will raise a small sample of the issues that arise, and we summarize this aspect of our subject at the end of the chapter.

As for dancers who play the parts of other peoples, I don't think there can really be a major problem with this. When I was growing up, as an ex-pat Scot in the middle of England, members of my family and their Scottish friends used to make jokes about the English people who came to the meetings of our Scottish Society, dressed up in kilts, and even did displays of "our" dancing. "Who do they think they are?" fellow Scots would ask. However, these people were often much better at the dances than we were, and if they were doing them, and demonstrating them, the dances continued to exist, and to be performed. To me, it didn't really matter whose bodies were performing them, indeed, I would rather see a beautiful Scottish dance than know it was performed by Scot. Which is just as well, as it happens, for that society is now almost exclusively made up of English people, born and bred! But perhaps their grandparents were Scottish, and that can be very important.

INTERNATIONAL NETWORKS AND BIG ORGANIZATIONS

An original intention of this project was to trace the international links that had enabled people like the Ainu to hear about others who were fighting the same cause, and to see how they had come to learn to value their heritage again. I have used examples from many different countries to illustrate the various aspects of this process of reclamation, and although the most detailed cases have come from Canada, I have made a point of throwing in parallel illustrations from elsewhere. We have in fact visited all the continents of the world in this book, and I make no apology for this apparent eclecticism, for I am convinced that the movement I am describing is a truly global one. The reclamation of cultural forms by First Peoples who feel that they were robbed of their identity and their dignity is happening to a greater or lesser degree in all the former colonies and some other configurations, the resurgence in expressions of cultural difference is even more widespread.

How, then, has this come about? How do these big global movements spread, and why are people reviving their cultural diversity in spite of predictions of 'convergence' and similarity? How come small ethnic groups are working to immerse their children in languages that will serve them only within those groups, and to acquire skills that will be of benefit only among themselves? And why are people looking to their grandparents for ideas about dealing with the exigencies of the modern world? Are the ancient skills that they developed not out of date, or inappropriate in a society powered by gas and electricity, and going to war to secure supplies of fossil fuels? And when youngsters seek to be creative, to impress others with their individuality and their innovative ideas, why are they looking for inspiration in customs and traditions passed down through generations? Why are they rejecting cities for wide-open spaces and returning to land that seems inhospitable and undeveloped to the urbanites?

Global theorists might explain this movement by speaking of the new possibilities for communications in a world linked by cyberspace, and we have seen the popularity of websites among Indigenous people and the ways in which those in the most isolated communities are using advanced technology to "position" themselves. Certainly these have played a part, but the peoples we have visited are also reacting against shared forces that struck them long before the Internet appeared, before even the invention of telephones and telegraph. Indeed, the Woodland Cultural Centre shares a town with the Canadian home of Alexander Graham Bell, credited with having tried out the first telephone line there after emigrating from Scotland for the sake of his health. So we could perhaps turn to colonial theorists, then, who would offer explanations about how great powers subdued the peoples they found in the way of their advances, and detail some of the tactics they used to convince themselves they were bringing benefits to the lands they occupied. Social historians can add the reasons why vast populations of Europeans traveled the world to seek new homes and new lives for themselves, and at the same time, rudely displace the inhabitants who were living in those places already.

To understand the build up of the increasingly successful reaction of the Native peoples who were displaced in this way, one place to start is by looking at international movements that have been set up by, or that have supported, Indigenous peoples in one way or another. A standing committee at the United Nations has been meeting for decades, and it has submitted numerous cases for consideration to the Office of the High Commissioner for Humans Rights. Situations are compared here, resolutions are made, and this clearly provides a forum for the exchange of information. Further organizations such as the World Council of Indigenous Peoples and the World Heritage Indigenous Peoples Council of Experts have subsequently been established and offer opportunities for people to meet and exchange ideas (see http://www.unhchr.ch/Indigenous/groups-01.htm). These organizations all have websites, and their work has been documented and registered with the UNHCHR, as well as in other specific locations. When the delegates return to the countries where they live, there is no guarantee that these recommendations will be implemented, but at least they have put together their grievances.

Then there are the nongovernmental organizations (NGOs) that identify Indigenous peoples in need of support, make the wider world aware of their situations, and try to raise funds to help them in some way. Survival International is probably the best known such body and it is relentless in its search for cases of particularly bad treatment, and its aim is to summon support for resistance to the continuing despotic attitude of certain governments. Its main focus is to help "tribal peoples," and it announces that it stands for their right to decide their own future, while it helps them protect their lives, lands, and human rights. Hunters and gatherers are under particular threat, for the land that supports them is being gradually eroded, if they are encouraged to live off the land at all, which is not the case in Botswana, a country whose government seems to be operating as if in a past century.

My own research has been at a much more grass roots level, however, and in this chapter I present a few specific examples of links that would seem to be building and bolstering the movement of cooperation we have observed. Throughout my research I have asked people I was meeting about their connections with Indigenous people in other parts of the world, and how they learned of each other, and

I discovered a lot of interesting interaction. Any number of personal networks criss-cross the globe, linking individuals, families, and common interest groups in a veritable web of shared concerns and activities, and I decided in the end to make these the main focus of this chapter. This way I can continue to pursue the aim of privileging the voices of the people I have been working with and avoid the impersonal arena of organizations completely separated from their everyday lives. These personal networks also seemed to me to be more interesting than big meetings taking place in cities such as Geneva, New York, and Toronto, and these are also possibly more effective in influencing the lives of those we have been meeting and describing.

Dancing as Cultural Exchange

The first case I want to present is also probably quite effective in spreading the word about cultural revival and informing outside communities about the activities of Indigenous peoples. In chapter 5, we visited the Kanata Dance Theatre, which meets to practice, and sometimes to perform, at the Woodland Cultural Centre. This group in fact started life in consultation with another Aboriginal initiative because it was initially set up with the help of Maori dancer TeRangi Huata, a member of the Kahurangi Dance Theatre from New Zealand, also mentioned in chapter 5 as being based out of Niagara Falls. He had been involved with a group in Calgary called the Red Thunder Dance Theatre, into whose midst his sister had married, and Naomi Powless, the Kanata project manager, explained that they were inspired by this group to set up something similar. TeRangi took a year off at the expense of his own group to help the newly established Kanata group to create their own routines and to make them into a theatrical performance rather than just a dancing exhibition.

Now, the Kanata Dance Theatre trains dancers themselves, and spends a good part of the year traveling. They have regular contracts in the United States, in a series of schools in California, in New York City, at the Kennedy Center in Washington, DC, and in San Antonio, Texas. The group has also spent ten days performing at a martial arts festival in South Korea, and a group of 11 of them traveled to Italy to take part in a Sicilian festival. They have visited several other cities in Italy and schools and theaters in Germany, and Brian and Naomi went to Beijing to perform. Closer to home, they have worked in Newfoundland and Labrador. They also perform at powwows, where they make contact with members of other Native groups, and Brian mentioned in particular a Mexican group from Amecameca in southern Mexico. He had also had earlier contact with an Aztec group that danced at a venue called The Turtle, in Buffalo. Brian had made a point of learning their dances and was able to use them in *The Journey Continues* show that we described in chapter 5.

This group illustrates the principles that were outlined at the start of the chapter, then, namely that they have plenty of international links, and that they "exchange" dances with other peoples that they meet. In the show, *The Journey Continues*, they also did an Inuit dance with throat singing, they did some Plains dancing that anyway heavily influences the powwow scene, and they performed a dance that has been developed by the Métis and that looks to me pretty much like Scottish dancing. Dances have, no doubt, been exchanged in this way since time immemorial, and they are a great way for people to get along. Within the Kanata Dance Theatre itself, the long-term members claim allegiance to Mohawk, Cayuga, and Ojibwe ancestry, but over the years they have danced with Inu, Cree, Blackfoot, Métis, Mohican, Ojicree, Salish, and Tsimshian people, so that covers quite a range. As I mentioned in chapter 5, one of the shows they do for schools, *People of the Land*, was described as a "pretty generic Native dance."

To return briefly to the Grouse Mountain example given above, it is also worth considering the case of the leader and Master of Ceremonies on the evening I saw the show, for Bob Baker illustrates our two areas of focus for this chapter very neatly. His dance group, the S'pakwús Slúlum (Eagle Song Dancers), presents a series of Coast Salish dances and legends, though their nine members include the two Hawaiians we met earlier, a Nicaraguan with Cree relatives, and a person with forbears of Irish, Scottish, German, and Inuit descent. Bob made the important point, however, that people who are born and raised here regard themselves as Squamish (part of the Coast Salish group) even though they may also be deeply involved with their other relatives. Bob traces his own ancestry back on the one side to a well-known Squamish leader called Chief Joe Capilano, who passed away in 1908, and on the other, to an English mapmaker named John Baker who arrived in the area in the mid-nineteenth century and married a Squamish woman. Six hundred and fifty people in the local group now carry his name!

John Baker had a brother, an architect who is said to have jumped ship in Hawaii to marry a local princess. At that time, the Hudson Bay Company was bringing Hawaiians to work on the West Coast, and some stayed on, so there are plenty more of these intercultural links. As a young man, Bob traveled to Hawaii, "mainly for the surfing," but he learned the Hawaiian language and was adopted by a high-ranking Hawaiian family, both facts that impressed the other Hawaiian Natives he would meet there. He stayed for ten years, working in the American Indian Center, but maintaining his links with the Hawaiians, whom he would invite to the events at the Center, always making sure to acknowledge that they were on Hawaiian territory.

Bob is just one individual case, but there are many other stories of links such as these even only through an interest in dancing. The Nicaragua connection in his own group was apparently initiated on the occasion of the Aboriginal Olympics in Taiwan, and a marriage between their two peoples has engendered further exchange. Now the Squamish chiefs have apparently invited some South Americans to become part of their nation (just as Bob became a Hawaiian, perhaps). Diane Strand, of the Champagne Aishihik First Nation, whom we met in the last chapter speaking about the display they are preparing for visitors to the Kluane National Park, is also a dance teacher and she runs a big children's group. She took a party of them to Mexico to an event called the Yoreme Festival, a five-day occasion that brings together Aboriginal and Indigenous peoples from around the world to share dancing and other aspects of their cultural activities.

I mentioned in the prologue to this book that when helping to entertain a group of Ainu dancers who visited the Pitt Rivers Museum, I thereby learned not only of their continuing existence, but also of the pride they hold in their "first" identity. Masahiro Nomoto, whom I again mentioned in the acknowledgments, wrote to me for this section of the book as follows,

> I have been responsible for developing exchanges, which included dancing, with several indigenous cultures including the Maori, Nivkhi, Uilta, Sami, Cree/Blackfoot, Australian Aborigines and the indigenous cultures of Taiwan. Our performance art very often leads to the host indigenous groups visiting us, and it is very interesting to hear how they handle problems facing all indigenous peoples in the world such as discrimination and other social problems. This has helped the younger generation Ainu develop a new Ainu culture. This is still a new phenomenon but it has generated a new sense of pride in their Ainu heritage.

He also pointed out that this increase in cultural activities was aided by the passage of the "Law for the promotion of Ainu Culture" (Ainu *bunka shinkōhō*), which was enacted in 1997.

Writers Exchange Experiences

A parallel of cultural exchange of this sort was reported in the second issue of the newsletter of the Six Nations Writers, which had just established itself when I was staying in Ohsweken. L.M. VanEvery wrote that they had been pleased to distribute their new publication to authors from New Zealand and Australia who had been part of a tour called *Honouring Words* that visited Vancouver, Winnipeg, and Cape Croker in October 2002 (VanEvery 2003: 1). Organized by writer, spoken word artist, and publisher, Kateri Akiwenzie-Damm, the 16-strong group of international writers from New Zealand, Australia, and Canada "gave readings, discussed their work, and celebrated their similarities as Indigenous writers" (ibid.). Some of them had been moved to hear Jadah Milroy, an author from Australia, sharing songs written by her father about her grandmother's time in a residential school, an experience recognized by many Native people in North America too.

VanEvery wrote that the tour was "all about discovering connections and celebrating those similarities we all share as Indigenous people. We are all profoundly blessed that we have found our creative voice to write our stories and promote understanding" (ibid.). Later in the same year, I met Lisa VanEvery at the powwow in Chiefswood Park at Ohsweken where the Six Nations Writers had erected a tent with publicity about themselves. She reported that some of them had just returned from Australia where they had been on a return exchange for the *Honouring Words* tour of the previous year. It is ironic that these writers can now communicate with one another so well precisely because of a system that was immensely cruel and hurtful to their grandparents in the past. It is for reasons such as these that I proposed in the introduction to this book that the same Western world that created the need for cultural revival is also making it possible.

Another example of this paradox is to be found in the worldwide distribution of Aboriginal stories that have been made into successful films, as described in chapter 5. That medium makes it possible to portray graphically, and if necessary with subtitles, the point of view of Native people who have been forever affected by the unthinking expansion of the English-speaking world throughout the globe. The film, *Rabbit Proof Fence*, like the songs of Jadah Milroy, made Indigenous people in different countries aware of the background they shared, and the fact that they shared it has given them a common bond. The fact that they shared it has also given them a command of the English language, and access to the outlets of that English-speaking world. An interesting twist now, though, is that some of the films distributed through that world have been made in the original languages as part of the process of revival. *Whale Rider* is one such example, *Atanarjuat: The Fast Runner* is another.

Native newspapers are another outlet for the sharing of stories, and an interesting situation of influence was reported in a paper called *Windspeaker* that has been in print in North America since 1983. Paul Barnsley, a staff writer for the paper, had traveled to Vanuatu, where he discovered that a book by the Mohawk writer, Brian Maracle, had moved a local carver Pakon Bong Rodney to give up an addiction to drink and become an activist against the problems of alcohol. Having read Maracle's book, *Crazy Water*, a collection of interviews with First Nations people with alcohol problems, he turned to a local organization called the Lolihor Youth Awareness Team (LYAT) that "seeks to encourage young Indigenous people to embrace their culture and take pride in their heritage" (Barnsley 2003: 27).

In another article, Barnsley wrote about the success of the LYAT in the island of Ambrym, one of the Vanuatu group, where he had discovered people who were intent on resisting pressure from Western development policies to turn everyone into consumers and laborers (ibid. 26). Stanley Jack, the chairman of LYAT, had pointed out to him that people living on Ambrym are often still following their own, old ways of subsistence farming. They have land, houses, and work to grow their food, and they are also healthy, despite a lack of modern medical facilities. Poor people in the United States may have none of these things, and they are supposed to be "developed," he had pointed out. He was not against all change, but he wanted local people to value their own knowledge and skills, and not to buy unreservedly into the idea that all European ways are superior. Coca-Cola is marketed aggressively in the developing world as "smart and sophisticated," but does coconut milk give you tooth decay and diabetes, he had asked (ibid. 27).

The activists in Vanuatu had been pleased to meet three visiting journalists from Canada, to find that First Nations there shared many of their problems in dealing with the legacy of colonial masters, and struggling to survive as distinct peoples. The visit had been supported by the Victoria-based Pacific People's Partnership, another NGO that seeks to raise awareness about this part of the world, otherwise not given high priority in Canada (ibid. 26). Clearly inviting writers to share ideas and stories with other Indigenous peoples is a great way to disseminate ideas throughout the world.

Museum Initiatives

At the start of the book, we suggested that museums in the past had been particularly responsible for presenting people whose objects they have on display as if they had died out. In chapter 1, we discussed some of the changes that have taken place to rectify this problem, and we looked at the display of contemporary art, the use of Native voices, and the consultation of Native peoples as some of the activities that had been introduced. We have also seen that Indigenous people are themselves approaching museums for the return of their artifacts, and even more so, for the return of the remains of their ancestors. This last activity has had some positive side effects for the museums too, in that visits toward this end have helped to make the museum staff and their public aware of the continuing existence of the peoples whose names they have long known only from their collections.

Especially in Britain, where museums are often much less close to the peoples whose objects have been brought back for the displays, and where sometimes we anyway learn more about the travelers who brought them than the people who made them, Native visitors are playing this positive role. The visit of Ainu dancers to the Pitt Rivers Museum, raised again above, is one example, and the group had already been to the British Museum, where they had given a performance in one of the public halls. In chapter 1, I mentioned meeting Nokomis Paiz, who was visiting from Red Lake, an Ojibwe community in northern Minnesota, and who had been made physically sick by her visit. She had also been to the British Museum. In chapter 1 as well, I described the visit of Frank Weasel Head and Andy Black Water of the Mookaakin Cultural and Heritage Foundation of the Blood/Kainai people.

Frank and Andy were in the United Kingdom to take a traveling version of the Blackfoot exhibition they had been involved in mounting at the Glenbow Museum in Calgary to Manchester, and this kind of traveling version of displays is another way in which people interact. There is, for example, an ongoing exchange between the curator in charge of the Ainu collection in the Royal Scottish Museum in Edinburgh and various Ainu artists and exhibitors. Jane Wilkinson looks after a number of Ainu objects that were brought back to Scotland by Neil Munro who worked for many years as a medical doctor in Nibutani in Hokkaido in the nineteenth century. The Ainu visitors arranged not only to borrow some of these articles to display in Japan, but also to send carvers and weavers to study the items so that they could reproduce the old techniques. The people I visited there, as mentioned in chapter 4, had probably used these same models. Eventually an exhibition containing both the old items and their recent reproductions was held in Yokohama, near Tokyo, as well as in Sapporo, the main city in Hokkaido.

Actually, many of the places I visited in Canada had also received visits from Ainu people, and clearly the Japanese government support for their cultural activities, which became the law mentioned above, has enabled them to see what Indigenous people are doing in several other parts of the world. In the U'Mista Cultural Centre at Alert Bay, for example, there is a display of Ainu objects in the museum that were presented on the occasion of a visit, and in the 1996–1997 T'lisalagi'lakw School Book, there is a page of photographs of young people in Ainu garments. The Museum of Anthropology at the University of British Columbia in Vancouver had also received a visit from the Director Shigemasu Nabesawa and Assistant Executive Director Tokuhei Akibe of the Ainu political association, the *Utari Kyokai*.

This last museum, in its usual innovative way discussed already in chapter 1, is in the process of setting up a large collaborative project "to forge links among scholars, originating communities, and research museums" (A *Partnership of Peoples* 2001) through the creation of an electronic Reciprocal Research Network. This project, which is to link major museums in North America and Europe, will make available manipulable digital images of their collective vast collections, and it is billed as responding to a need to give originating communities "a major voice in shaping research questions" as well as to "benefit from the new knowledge that is produced" (ibid.). It will draw on "the power of cultural materials to trigger memory" as "an invaluable key to the recovery of orally transmitted information retained in originating communities" (ibid.), and expansion plans for the Museum of Anthropology in Vancouver include dedicated research space for members of First Nations communities. A Research Services Suite will also offer state-of-the-art oral history, language, and digital processing laboratories as well as the library and archives (ibid.).

Another aim of this project is to adapt its electronic tools "to culturally diverse traditions of knowledge management" (ibid.) following the museum's continuing efforts to overcome barriers between the traditional museum organization of artifacts and the conflicting ideas of Indigenous peoples that we discussed in chapter 1. In the last weeks of preparing this book for publication, I managed to visit Anthony Shelton, newly appointed director of the museum, whose long-term research with Native people of Mexico, as well as years in the museum world, has given him special insights into the importance of this plan. He explained another related opportunity that will be made possible with the reorganization associated with the expansion of the museum space, and that is to introduce Indigenous systems of classification for the display and (open-shelved) storage of the collections, according to consultation with the peoples concerned.

Relations with Native communities has also been an important part of the design and construction of the displays at the new Smithsonian site of the National Museum of the American Indian, which opened in Washington, DC in September 2004 with much critical acclaim. Each of the three major exhibitions features materials and explanations from eight specific communities, together covering the length and breadth of the American continent—from Alaska to Chile, and California to Amazonian Brazil. There is a real feel of hearing the voices of the continuing peoples whose ancestral treasure is featured, and an innovative multimedia presentation, projected onto sackcloth screens and a dome-shaped "mini-planetarium" ceiling, indeed introduces a variety of these peoples under the title, *Who We Are*. The exhibitions cover *Our Universes, Our Peoples*, and *Our Lives*, and a wonderful "inaugural book" offers a richly illustrated selection of those voices to mull over with more time than one museum visit can afford (McMaster and Trafzer 2004).

My visit to this great addition to the National Mall in Washington, DC was unfortunately brief, as it was made en route to a conference in San Francisco, and I did not even have time to spend a night in the U.S. capital. Due to the state of American security at the time, I could find nowhere to leave my luggage, so my delight at this evidence of reconciliation with their own continent's First Peoples was tempered somewhat by the way that the suitcase trundling after me symbolized the perceived threat from the latest enemies this rich but belligerent people has made. Some of the reviews of the new museum also reveal a continuing reluctance in their (non-Native) writers to accept how much this wealth of theirs deprived the people they displaced, for they griped about the cost of the beautiful art work on sale at the museum stores, and indeed, about the amount of space these stores took up in the building at all. Some also griped about the lack of an overall unifying theme. With the voices of peoples from such a vast area of the world, what did they expect? Thanks for bringing them together into a world of Western domination?

I was lucky enough to meet Gerald McMaster during my visit, coeditor of the inaugural book, and one of the designers and curators of the new museum, and he told me about some of the community exchanges that were made while the museum was being put together. These will continue over the years, for the peoples presently named in the displays represent only a fraction of those whose artifacts formed part of George Gustav Heye's original collection on which the museum was originally based, and members of other communities are already coming up with ideas for future exhibits. Gerald also described vividly the color and excitement of the Native celebrations at the time of the opening of the museum when much of the public space of Washington, DC, to say nothing of the hotels, guest houses, and friends' floors, was filled with the Indigenous people of the Americas, many splendid in their finest regalia.

Another project I encountered involves a partnership between the Royal Scottish Museum in Edinburgh and the Dogrib Treaty Eleven Council, which has just completed a land claim in the northwest territories of Canada. It seems that quite a collection of Dogrib and other Athapaskan objects was donated by ex-pat Scots who were living in the area in the 1850s, when the Scottish museum was being established, and the existence of these artifacts, made known in Canada through a more recent exhibit at the Canadian Museum of Civilisations, formed part of the Dogrib land claim. Records of their acquisition proved the existence of these people in that place at that time in a way acceptable to the Canadian government. Now a new exhibition, designed to display the aesthetics and craftsmanship of Dogrib tradition, is being planned for 2006 at the Prince of Wales Northern Heritage Centre in Yellowknife, a third partner in the agreement. The exhibition will also possibly tour communities where many of the Dogrib people live.

Chantal Knowles, at the Royal Scottish Museum end of the project, explained that these Dogrib representatives are happy to have this presence on the international stage, so they don't want to repatriate the objects as long as the partners can engage with each other. They see them as repositories of traditions that they are interested in reviving, so Dogrib elders will therefore come over to help choose the items for the exhibition and decide, with specialists from the Prince of Wales Northern Heritage Centre people, which ones are too fragile to travel. Everything is to be photographed and will subsequently be available on a website for viewing, and some of the images will tour as a poster exhibition. Eventually, when the objects return to Scotland they will be displayed with new items that the Dogrib intend to make and to send as a legacy for the next hundred years.

Some other activities in Britain are worth mentioning for the opportunity they threw open for cultural exchanges of this sort. One was the *Powwow* conference held at the British Museum in 2003, which was attended by delegates from various North American Native groups, as well as by local British people interested in the subject. It seems that there are people in Britain with no Native ancestry at all who love to dress up and do powwow dancing, and something similar happens in Germany. Beatrice Medicine, professor of anthropology and head of the Native Centre at the University of Calgary, had been to Sweden to do fieldwork with such a group, and she showed a film that she had made there. Members of the audience from North America found it quite amusing, just as members of my Scottish family found the dancing of their English partners, but I don't think they were entirely put out. Altogether, the conference was a great opportunity to make the wide international public visiting the British Museum aware of the continuing vitality of the Native Americans whose past objects they may well be examining inside.

A rather different example relates to the Horniman Museum, which has always sought a more locally based clientele, as the words carved in stone above its doorway pronounce: "For the recreation, instruction and enjoyment of the people of London." In the initial days, when the Horniman family presented its collection of artifacts from around the world to the local people, free of charge to visit, they wanted their relatively untraveled neighbors to learn of the creativity and richness of other peoples of the globe. Now, the population of its South London location itself includes a rich ethnic mix of well-traveled people whose families came to Britain from locations such as those that the Hornimans visited. The remit is therefore slightly different, and it so happens that Hassan Wario Arero, formerly of the National Museum of Kenya, who helped me during my visit to Tanzania and Kenya, is now keeper of anthropology at the Horniman. He told me about some of the community-based programs they have put in place to reach out to their changing public, and beyond them to make links with their heritage.

Since joining the museum in 2002, Hassan initiated an exhibition project based on the indigenous people of the Caribbean and South American mainland (especially Guyana). This, he explained, emanated from the need to show how multilayered identities such as that of the Caribbean are. "There had been very little critical assessment of the Caribbean identity—which most of the time was represented as homogenous—and through this exhibition one would be able to see the contribution of the Carib and Arawakan cultures to the constitution of the contemporary Caribbean culture. The continued consumption of cassava and the use of place names and other indigenous

Amerindian linguistic terms constantly remind us of how truly multi-layered the Caribbean person is."

"Museums such as the Horniman could benefit more by looking at these diasporic communities (Caribbean, in this case) as complex and interesting entities," Hassan continued.

> Cultures such as those of the Caribbean have come of age to be studied as entities unto themselves, not necessarily as appendices to "mother" cultures of Africa. Through the Caribbean Identities Community project, the museum has managed to gather a lot of interesting information and a better understanding of this group of people. What has clearly emerged is that among the Caribbean people (and people from mainland places such as Guyana) the contribution of the Indigenous people is accepted as part of their complex history. Most of the Caribbean people interviewed were of mixed extraction, some citing Indigenous links, others East Indian, Chinese, African and European descent. As the world becomes more "mixed" and cultures more "diasporic" in nature, museums have to try and reflect those universal phenomena. For the Horniman, starting with the Caribbean project, this is a way into a future of engaging more with the immediate community and the changing cultural landscape.

In this complex and exciting way, the Horniman is adopting some of the same principles I reported from George Abungu's speech in chapter 1, about the way African museums are working to be relevant to their local public. A future project for Hassan is to form links with museums in Kenya, which would be part of a larger partnership presently gathering funding between museums in Britain and Africa. Hassan's brief is not limited to Africa, however, and an exhibition he was working toward when we spoke was to focus on South America.

Issues of the Woodland Cultural Centre's newsletter *Wadrihwa* carry details regularly about visits to the museum, and journeys of its members to other parts of the world, under a heading "Coming and Going in the Museum." Many Native people from different First Nations around the world have visited the Woodland Cultural Centre over the years, and even within North America, there have been people from as far as Mexico and Bolivia. One write up tells of three Bolivian video-makers who brought stories about Quechuan elders, a man's greed in chasing after the *Cursed Gold*, and a sorry tale from Lake Titicaca about someone who loses respect for his Aymara traditions. Many of the visitors are artists, whose work is displayed in the gallery, and others come for conferences and workshops. Tom Hill is probably the most widely traveled member of the center, and trips he had made to a conference in Greece and a gallery exhibit in Germany were among those that appeared in recent issues when I was there. He also reported visits he had made to Rotorua and Wellington in New Zealand, and he had to turn down an invitation to visit Japan with a group of local artists during my stay because of conflicting engagements.

In 2004, it was reported that a Japanese PhD student at Queens University in Canada, Naohiro Nakamura, had spent time at the museum gathering material for his doctoral thesis. The aim of the project was to make a comparison of the activities of the Woodland Cultural Centre with those of the Nibutani Ainu Cultural Museum in Hokkaido, Japan. Nakamura was reported to have explained:

> I'm looking at how these two museums are taking a role in restoring, promoting, and spreading aboriginal cultures. I hope that the field work results will clarify that the cases of the museum can be generalized as an example of how aboriginal museums contribute to the preservation and promotion of aboriginal culture. (*Wadrihwa*, 19, 3/4: 12)

Wadrihwa (ibid.) also reports that Nakamura took part in many of the center's social activities. A project such as this must surely be an excellent way of sharing information between Aboriginal people in widely separated parts of the world.

INTERNATIONAL TOURISM

Tourism is of course another way that people learn of one another's activities, and a pullout section of the same issue of *Windspeaker* mentioned above gave much detail about venues within North America. All manner of festivals, concerts, powwows, storytelling, art exhibitions, and special projects were advertised in this "Guide to Indian Country," which it suggested the "Turtle Island" traveler pocket for the duration in order to "take in some Aboriginal culture." Even within southern Ontario, the Aboriginal Tourism Association (ATASO) has 40-member organizations that they help to market, and their advertising is designed to appeal to visitors from far and wide.

 Kim Porter, whom I met in the ATASO office in the summer of 2003, travels quite extensively to market Aboriginal tourism. She was one of the organizers of the Canadian Aboriginal Festival in the Sky Dome in Toronto, which we visited in chapters 2 and 5, so she has extensive contacts. Earlier that year she had been to a show in London called Spotlight Canada and at the International Tourism Exchange (ITB) in Berlin. The latter has no fewer than 10,000 exhibitors, apparently, and was an excellent opportunity to meet people and talk to the media, she said. Kim has plans to set up an Indigenous People's Exchange, and she had been able to talk to people she met at the ITB in Berlin about this. She was also expecting media writers from Italy and Germany to visit local places at the time when I met her.

Kim talked of another opportunity for people in Canada to learn about their counterparts elsewhere if an idea being planned for the Aboriginal Peoples Television Network (APTN) comes off. This is a project she attributes to her friend Trina Mather, who runs Aboriginal Experiences, the park in Ottawa we described in chapter 2. Trina is trying to raise the funding to make a series of programs about a variety of examples of Indigenous tourism from different parts or the world. Kim was hoping she might secure the position of host of this show, which sounds as though it would be a fun job! When I called Trina shortly before this book went to press, they were still seeking backing for the project, though they had secured the license with APTN. It may still have been a dream at that stage, then, but several years ago so was the idea of creating the Aboriginal tourist experience she runs on a prime piece of land in Ottawa!

Sharing Traditions . . . and Identity?

Not long after I returned to the United Kingdom from carrying out the research for this project, I was invited to give a couple of lectures to groups of British and Japanese artists who had been engaged in collaborative work. The first audience was largely made up of textile artists, the second photographers, and both included students as well as the professional artists who had in each case produced work for an exhibition. Prior to both occasions I was unsure what my role would be, and why they should have asked an anthropologist to address such a specialized group, but in each case I came away feeling not only that I had contributed appropriately to their event, but that I too had learned something new and exciting. My invitation was triggered by the work I had previously carried out in Japan, but full of a new enthusiasm for a broader view of the world, I asked if they would mind if I introduced some of this material as well.

On the first occasion, held at the Surrey Institute of Art and Design, the subject was Cultural Difference and the Creative Process, and I had proposed that I draw on my recent research to talk of the way that creativity is used by Indigenous people to express their cultural distinctions as part of a process of reclaiming their identity in a world that had tried to extinguish them. To my surprise, I was introduced as a controversial speaker who would argue against the idea that cultural differences are disappearing—which indeed, of course, I did, though I had not expected this to be such a controversy. As the day proceeded, however, I viewed the creations of partnerships between Japanese and British textile artists, always one young and one experienced, and I heard several other presentations. The world that these people of radically different backgrounds had created was an exciting one, they had produced beautiful work, but their sharing of traditions had indeed more or less extinguished their differences.

A parallel situation was to be found with the photographers, though this time the Japanese artists were working within a British context, and there was less exchange. It was still hard to isolate cultural distinctions in their art, but these organizers had asked me specifically to talk of my work in Japan, so I decided at the same time to try and unravel some of the preconceptions that seemed evident in the judgments of the British audience and present a more distinctive Japanese view. It seemed to work, up to a point, but I was reminded of the layers of meaning that I discussed in chapter 5 of this book, and how very often people do actually remain pretty much at their own level of understanding. It made sense, then, that the organizers of this event had invited not one anthropologist but three to help them with their interpretations, and I felt that we all had a useful role to play.

Ultimately, the British artists had clearly raised the funds to engage in exchanges with their Japanese counterparts because they find aspects of Japanese art interesting enough to pursue in this way, and although their collaborative work was producing some relatively culture-free creations, the differing background had somehow provided inspiration in each direction. As an anthropologist and not an artist, I could offer a middle ground of mutual interpretation, and because Japanese and British artists respect each other reasonably equally, there was no sense that I was trying to represent either side, or to take their knowledge and use it for my own benefit. In my work in Japan, I have always felt pretty much on an equal footing with my colleagues in Japanese universities, as well as with my 'informants' or perhaps 'collaborators' in the field.

This has, I think, been a good model for me in working with members of First Nations, for I simply carried over the same kind of respect for what they are doing that I accord the people I work with in Japan.

In the long run, I hope that all relationships between anthropologists and Indigenous people will be as mutually respectful and productive as the brief relationships established between the artists who invited us to the symposia described here. Cultural difference was the catalyst for the original mutual interest, just as cultural difference brings together dancers, writers, and people interested in material artifacts in the way we have described throughout this chapter. Cultural difference adds a spot of spice to the travel experience, and it no doubt contributes to the fun of the different kinds of dancing people choose to do whatever their own ethnic origins.

For the Indigenous people who have been the focus of this book, however, cultural characteristics are much more important than these rather trivial expressions of interest would suggest. To trace their cultural traditions, to build them into a blueprint for life and for the education of their children, and to draw on them in all kinds of creative ways is to reclaim an identity that had been severely threatened. If, at the same time, these people are willing to share their cultural treasures with the wider world, in their own way and at their own instigation, it can be to the benefit of both parties. As outsiders, we can learn many things—some of which I will review in the next chapter—and we, can be reassured that the people whom we might have thought extinct are alive, well and getting even stronger. As insiders, First Peoples can gain access to some of the resources they need to pursue the reclamation process and they can express with pride the identity that they sometimes almost lost.

We return at last to this question of identity, then, and one of the things I learned among the Japanese artists and photographers I met at British symposia was that some of them regarded themselves as rather British. Though usually born in Japan, some had been trained in the United Kingdom, at least one was married to a British person, and more than one had lived in Britain for several years. Although they all still spoke Japanese as a first language, and looked Japanese to their British hosts, their children may well have different options available to them when they come to think about their own identity. In the world more broadly, there are many people who can draw on various cultural traditions—through birth, marriage, and residence, as well as through lines of inheritance from their parents, and personal identity has been added to the things one may be able to choose in life.

First Nations rely on the argument that they were the First Peoples in an area, and they have over the years negotiated, and also been submitted to, treatment from the wider governments that administer the land they claim that differentiates them from later immigrants to that same land. That treatment was very often deeply disrespectful and detrimental, and many of their members succeeded in establishing an identity outside their communities, especially in subsequent generations when intermarriage blurred the differences. In recent years, it has become a matter of pride and sometimes advantage to be regarded as a member of a First Nation, as we considered briefly in chapter 2 when we looked at the financial benefits that have been brought by casinos to some Native groups. Exemption from tax may be another advantage, as may be access to the special educational facilities that we discussed in chapter 4, and artists can at last find outlets for their work that bring them a proper return for their investment in time and materials.

Small wonder then that some First Nations are guarding their boundaries a little, for to return to claim benefits after escaping the discrimination may seem hypocritical to those who stayed the course through thick and thin. Nevertheless, these boundaries are actually still quite porous, and people who demonstrate commitment to the Aboriginal group they claim to be part of do not necessarily need a full blood quotient to back up their choice of personal identity. Local laws vary from one country to another in terms of claiming tax and other benefits, but acceptance by a group is determined by other factors. In traveling to different nations, I have met many people with only one half, one quarter, or even less of a direct line of inheritance, working for the reclamation of that part of their cultural background. Their degrees of acceptance depend again on things like birth, parentage, marriage, and residence, but more than all that, a true commitment to the community and its aims makes a claim powerful.

A very readable account of one such situation is presented by Mary Crow Dog in her autobiography entitled *Lakota Woman*. As a half-caste child growing up on a reservation in South Dakota, but attending the establishments of the "white" education system, her story is chilling to say the least, but she rejects her own family's efforts to get her out of the society of "skins," and eventually marries a very traditional medicine man. Her choices were tied up with the rebellious activities of her generation, which included establishing the American Indian Movement in the 1960s, of which she became an active member. She also insisted on giving birth to her first child under siege at the site of the 1890 Wounded Knee massacre, and clearly found the claims of her Native companions much more convincing and supportive than the cruel and discriminatory treatment of the local "white" community.

Over the ensuing years, supporting her husband through an outrageous mistaken arrest and nearly two years of imprisonment, as well as raising several children in a small home besieged with fellow Natives seeking help from her husband and his family, she at times hankers after the life of the "white people" who offered her a home as a high profile Native wife. She even runs away on one occasion, but her total commitment to the practices of her husband and the Lakota people from whom she draws as much blood, bring her back, and make her—eventually—a highly valued member of the group herself.

Ultimately, as we have seen throughout this chapter, individuals have a certain amount of choice about their personal identity, and in these days of easy global communication and mobility, their interests and attachments may influence this choice almost as much as their place and circumstances of birth. The anthropologist Gordon Mathews (2000) has written about this subject from the perspective of a man of American birth living in Hong Kong who has worked with musicians in Japan. Many of his students in Hong Kong are seeking an identity that goes beyond their unchangeable attachment to the nation-state—China—that now administers the land where they were born. In quite different but strangely parallel ways, increasingly large numbers of people in other nation-states are seeking to foster a First Nations identity that they might in previous generations have tried to deny. This book has attempted to address this phenomenon, and in the next and last chapter I offer some possible concluding explanations for this change of heart.

References and Further Readings

A Partnership of Peoples: A New Infrastructure for Collaborative Research, UBC Museum of Anthropology, Canadian Foundation for Innovation Summary, June 2001.
Barnsley, Paul, 2003, "Mohawk Writer Changes Activist's Life," *Windspeaker*, 21(3): 27.
Crow Dog, Mary, 1991, *Lakota Woman*, New York: Harper Perennial.
McMaster, Gerald and Clifford E. Trafzer (eds.), 2004, *Native Universe: Voices of Indian America*, National Museum of the American Indian, Smithsonian Institution, in association with National Geographic, Washington, DC.
Mathews, Gordon, 2000, *Global Culture/Individual Identity: Searching for Home in the Cultural Supermarket*, London and New York: Routledge.
Shelton, Anthony A., 2000, "Curating African Worlds," *Journal of Museum Ethnography*, 12: 5–20.

United Nations High Commission on Human Rights website http://www.unhchr.ch/Indigenous/groups-01.htm.

VanEvery, L.M., 2003, "Six Nations Writers Attend Honouring Words Tour," *Kawennahia:ton*, 1(2): 1.

Wadrihwa, Quarterly Newsletter of the Woodland Cultural Centre, Brantford, Ontario.

Chapter 8

Conclusions: What We Can Learn

> Contrary to popular belief, mankind was not made to rule and have dominion over nature and her children. Remember the earth can live without us; that is how unimportant we are.
>
> Cree speaker, Royal Saskatchewan Museum
>
> Indigenous people have the key to planetary survival.
>
> Tove Skutnabb-Kangas, Sweetgrass conference

Introduction: 'Sharing'

'Sharing' is one of the words I have learned to use in new contexts during the course of this research. Working largely within my own native tongue has been unusual for me, as an anthropologist brought up in the tradition of learning through translating from foreign languages, but that training didn't stop, and I have delighted in ways that I have relearned English among Indigenous peoples. That training has me always looking beyond words, for the implications of those words, and for the value they hold for their users. As outlined in the last chapter, Aboriginal peoples in different parts of the world have been *sharing* their experiences, *sharing* their (mostly) colonial heritage, and they have formulated some *shared* views, and some *shared* ideas about how to rebuild their confidence and reclaim their threatened identities. I started out on this venture by trying to trace a new discourse it seemed that they had created, and persuading people to *share* it with me (Hendry 2003).

Once I was confident about the existence of this discourse, I began to examine it in more detail, and the results of my examination form what I have presented in this book. I was lucky that the people I have worked with were willing to *share* their ideas with me, for in my appearance at least, I immediately represented the 'white aggressor' group that brought about their *shared* situation. But they did *share*, and that, for me, is one of the reasons I like the way this word is being used. Sharing has an optional quality . . . people ask one another if they are willing to share, and parents teach their children to share, but with an implication that it would be a good thing to do, rather than as an order about how to behave. The people I've been working with had nothing compelling them to share things with me, rather they had every right to keep their ideas to themselves, and to put me through the same kind of exclusion that they have experienced—and I describe a case or two of this shortly.

Most of them didn't, however, and the wisdom that I have observed, both in their ideas and in their individual decisions to *share* those ideas with me, is the quality I want to *share* with you the reader in this final chapter. People whose ancestors have been made to suffer in the past have at least three choices in the way they react to the descendants of their aggressors. They can try to become part of the society of their aggressors, they can seek to take revenge, or they can try to heal the rifts. The first has been the reaction of many subordinates over the millennia of aggression between peoples, including not a few of those who now call themselves First Nations. Indeed, this would undoubtedly account for the whereabouts of many of the Ainu I was failing to find in the prologue to this book. To suffer all kinds of discrimination as an individual is bad enough, but purposely to bring the same kinds of anguish on one's children is a tough decision to make if a road lies open to avoid it. The "lost generation" of adults who don't know their native languages are able to make choices about their identity precisely because their parents took the road that they saw as easier for their children.

To seek revenge for the misdemeanors of past generations is an option that has been chosen by many over the years as well, and at the time of this writing, the followers of such a path are perpetuating the most atrocious world situations. The deaths of hundreds of innocent children and their caretakers in the first days of a new school year in Beslen, Russia, have been just one awful consequence of a series of such decisions. Examples of cruel genocide in different regions of Africa provide others, and the support of many American people for the unprovoked invasion of Iraq in 2003 boiled down in many cases to a continuing sense of revengeful outrage at the attack on their system that they refer to as 9–11. The attack itself can of course be analyzed in this way too.

The third reaction, the one about trying to heal the rifts, may sound at first a little weak, but ultimately I think it must be the most powerful of all. If people whose ancestral villages have been sacked, whose forebears have been massacred, and whose languages and cultures have been derided and destroyed, can renew their integrity, then why would they want to have it destroyed again? Somewhere in the persistence of a people who are able to do this, who are able without compromising their own history to heal the wounds of the past, lies a deep wisdom that is worth examining. In practice, it is almost certainly within that history that the basis of this wisdom grew, and the efforts being made to reclaim thousands of years of history and culture by Indigenous peoples around the world express recognition of the value of the wisdom their ancestors accumulated. The detail of the ancestral knowledge and wisdom is of course varied, and appropriate to different contexts and situations, but the wisdom of reclaiming it is something that is shared.

In this last chapter, then, I draw together, and "share," some of the learning that I have done while working with people who claim a primary connection with the land on which they live. I want to share it with 'educated' museum-buffs who think the people who made the objects they admire have died out, with anthropologists and film makers who work to 'salvage disappearing worlds', and with the tourists and the art collectors who concern themselves about authenticity. I want to reassure you about the continuing existence of the people you had consigned to the past, and about their abilities. Moreover, I want to suggest that those of us who were born and brought up in societies that presented themselves as superior, and that sought to impose our 'civilized' systems on peoples we dominated, might actually have some important lessons to learn from those very peoples we saw as inferior. No one will deny that the world at large has problems. I would like to suggest that we might here find one or two solutions.

Discrimination

This section will not contain lessons for all of my readers, indeed it may not be new to many, but by chance of my birth I have lived an extraordinarily privileged life, and I had not really suffered much negative discrimination before I started on this project. As mentioned earlier, most of the people I have worked with were kind enough to talk to me, but they often didn't do it without grilling me first about my intentions, and in one case, I was actually shown the door. I was quite happy to be grilled. I have always thought that the situations anthropologists put themselves in are interfering, to say the least, and it is perfectly reasonable for any people anywhere to want to know why someone is asking questions about them. As one of my young sons once put it to me, "you anthropologists . . . you're just nosy Parker's, aren't you?"

Being shown the door was different. It had a physical effect on me, and I felt so thoroughly demeaned that I could not continue with my planned activities for several hours. I was sorry that it happened in the place where it happened because I was in a shop where a young man behind the counter had been particularly helpful, and had been chatting to me about his life and his plans for the future. I had explained to him that I was doing research about cultural revival, and he had said that he was working for just that same end, so he was actually quite keen to tell me about his ideas. It was an older person who came in with a snack for him who turned the tide. Perhaps if I had said nothing to her, she might have withdrawn, and my encounter with the boy would have continued uninterrupted, but I made the mistake of volunteering information about my presence at this point as well.

While the boy was briefly out of the public area, this woman asked me whether I had the permission of the local Band Council to do this research. Now, as it happened, I had applied for such permission several weeks before leaving the United Kingdom, I had received the forms some time after arriving in the area, completed them, and returned them to the Band Council as soon as I could. I had heard nothing, and my phone calls of inquiry had elicited only promises that things were in hand. Since my time in the area was limited by the extent of my leave, I had asked various people about how to proceed, and had mostly received the same reaction—that each individual I was consulting would act on their own initiative. The Woodland Cultural Centre had given me permission to work there, and in any case, my inquiries were largely confined to public places.

This shop was ostensibly a public place, though as the notice outside was in a native language, it was not encouraging to outside visitors, as other shops in the area clearly were. Anyway, when I explained my situation in response to the question, I was literally shown to the door, which was opened for me to leave, and I had little option but to make an exit. I did return briefly to ascertain the name of my interlocutor, since I decided to go immediately to the Band Office and inquire about my status, and at that moment the young man returned, telling me as he came in about someone else he thought I should contact. He was cut short by his companion, who handed me the name cards on the counter, which did not incidentally include her name, and I was dispatched again.

It was slightly therapeutic under these circumstances to have somewhere to go, and I headed straight off to the Band Office to inquire about my status. The person with whom I had made all previous inquiries was on holiday, but her replacement cheerfully consulted the files and pronounced my application to be among those that had been approved. [This turned out later to be incorrect, but I didn't know that for several weeks.] Armed with this information, I suppose I could have returned to the shop, but in practice, I did not. Now, looking back, I am not sure why I did not. I am not usually deterred by setbacks in my research, but this one was somehow different, and I simply could not take myself back to that place. Instead, I drove home to my lodgings, and I recounted my experience to Phyllis. She guessed who the individual in question was, and explained personal reasons why she thought she had behaved in such a way, but these details are not really the point of the story. Rather, it was my reaction at being treated in this way.

I encountered a lesser version of the same experience at many of the events I attended while I was doing this research because I clearly stood out by my appearance as a nonmember of the local societies where they were held. I was used to this, for I stand out in Japan, where I have done much research, but in Japan I am usually welcomed, and receive pleasant, if curious, inquiries. On the Six Nations Reserve, the situation was different, and I was regarded with suspicion, if I was noticed at all, so I felt out of place, unwelcome, and alone, unless and until I saw a familiar face. At the *Restoring Our Peace* conference I described in chapter 4, the discrimination was made explicit in addresses that referred to 'we Native people' or 'all Indigenous Peoples', for I was clearly not recognized as part of those categories. On these occasions, I felt alienated, and I understood that feeling, but I was also aware of reasons for the rhetoric, and I simply took notes!

So that was my first lesson. I find it impossible in writing to transfer quite that experience of being discriminated against to anyone else, though I daresay some might recognize the type of situation, and many might have much worse experiences to their name. I mention this lesson here because I felt it was good for me to experience some of the negative feeling—or simply indifference—that the people who were excluding me expressed. They were involved in rebuilding their own lives, lives that had been grossly interfered with by people who looked pretty much like me, and it was really none of my business to be there at all. Fortunately for me, and for this project, most of the individuals I met were a lot kinder than the woman I mentioned above, and they were wise enough to know that perpetuating discrimination and exclusion solves nothing.

The Value of Elders

My second lesson was again partly a personal one, but potentially it has much wider and more important implications. I'll start with an anecdote about an event that took place one Saturday afternoon, when I joined several members of my host Phyllis's family around the pool at the home of her elder daughter. I had been working on my application to the Band Council on Mary's computer, and as I got up for a break, they offered me a cold drink, so I sat down with a group that also included two more of Phyllis's daughters, and several grandchildren and great grandchildren. Someone asked me about my family, and I mentioned that I had a lively mother of 92. "How wonderful," they exclaimed, and possibly, "how lucky!" I do, of course, love my mother dearly, but she can also be difficult, and I made a retort that would probably have simply caused a smile of understanding among people in the United Kingdom, and likely more widely in the Western world. I said something like "well, yes, most of the time."

The reaction was a palpable silence, and I don't think I am being paranoid if I say that the whole atmosphere toward me cooled considerably after that. I had clearly misjudged the audience if I expected to raise a laugh by appealing to an imagined empathy about coping with difficult mothers. Phyllis was not difficult, indeed she was a positive help to everyone in the family, but she is almost a generation younger than my mother who had also been helpful at an earlier age. My mother is not particularly difficult either, actually. At the time, she was still taking care of herself, with the support of friends and neighbors, and she remains a loved member of the community where she lives. I am sure that there are elderly people on the Six Nations Reserve who need much more care and concern from their offspring than my mother did at that time. I was simply drawing on a collective idea in many English-speaking societies where elderly relatives are often represented as a burden.

In Indigenous communities, elderly people may practically be a burden as well, but they are also recognized as the valuable source of knowledge and wisdom that their accumulated years have given them, and it was clearly not appropriate to complain about the first, rather than value the second. I thought a lot about that moment afterwards, especially as I observed the important role that 'elders' play in societies where they are valued. Of course, the situation is crucial in places where the language is threatened, and where the elders are the only ones who remember the traditional stories and place names, and these things we have discussed. However, respect for elders is a much more profound part of the way of thinking of many peoples of the world. Not to respect and value elders is a characteristic of the so-called modern English-speaking worlds where rushing about to earn 'loads of money' and 'make progress' are somehow seen as more important than learning directly from our forbears about times we have classified as 'old fashioned', or 'out of date'.

The reasons for our mistaken disdain for age and its wisdom are not the subject matter of this book, but the fact of its existence might be worth presenting in a little more detail, in case there are doubters among you, my readers, that this is what we have done. As I write, my mother is living in a care home for "older people," where she is helped with practical tasks that have become difficult for her, and served meals at regular times of day. The carers are kind, and my brothers and I feel that she is lucky, but they are much better at dressing her and giving her hugs (as though she were a baby) than they are at listening to her quite innovative ideas about how to improve all their lives. I expect her suggestions are regarded as 'interference' in their carefully controlled world of 'coping with the elderly', and valuing the knowledge and wisdom that my mother has acquired over her years as a nurse and mother are not part of that remit. Her sister, my aunt, who had been a teacher, a local councilor, and an avid traveler, had motor neuron disease for some years before she died, and despite her still excellent mental faculties, she was given even less personal respect.

Of course, it could be pointed out that relatives should be caring for their seniors, and that I, as daughter, have the responsibility to look after my mother. However, I am not advocating that we return to a time when women were expected to carry out all kinds of undifferentiated roles largely under the rubric of 'care', simply because they were women. That was another reasonably recent invention, anyway. My proposal is quite the reverse, actually, because my mother was a professional 'carer', so she could conceivably be valued in a caring context for the knowledge she has acquired over the years. She could also be valued in all kinds of other ways (and I have been trying, myself, to appreciate that value ever since). Unfortunately for our elders, we have imbued our fast-moving contemporary thinking with the idea that all that they know is old-fashioned, and irrelevant to the modern world.

A nice example of the foolishness of this thinking was being discussed in the British media as I was writing this book. It relates to the increasing prevalence of MRSA (Multiple Resistant Stephalylococcus Aureus), a disease induced by a hospital stay, rather than alleviated by it, and it is said to be caused by insufficient care to the cleanliness of the place. My mother and many other old school nurses have been commenting on the drop in standards for years, and my mother grew particularly anxious when she accompanied my father during hospital stays in the latter part of his life. No one would listen to the 'old dear', of course, and I have to admit that even I tried to reassure her that they would know what they were doing. Ironic then that the National Health Service in Britain—or, at least, the press on their behalf—has decided at last that they need to reinstate some of the old standards of hygiene that were common practice before the discovery of antibiotics made everyone far too relaxed about spreading germs. My 'old dear' Mum and her age mates were there and practiced them!

It is particularly in areas relating to health that the wider world has gradually become aware of the great body of useful knowledge that Indigenous people have conserved and transmitted through the generations. In my part of the world we were brought up to think of our grannies' warnings about health to be 'old wives' tales', and the potions and powder that they conserved to be little more than palliative at most. Now, the movement among many has been to seek again the 'natural' cures that we have almost lost, and more and more to value the so-called alternatives to the chemicals that we are prescribed by medical practitioners. Pharmaceutical giants are sending researchers out to rain forests in South America and New Guinea, among other places, to plunder the knowledge of the Native peoples about their plants, and other companies with an eye to profit continually try to take advantage of remedies that work for local people.

In Vanuatu, for example, visitors from Germany and the United States are seeking to extract products from *kava*, a Native plant used to make a drink offered to guests in welcome, but which also has powerful properties of intoxication. The head of the museum there, Ralph Regenvanu, worried about the dangers of this "bioprospecting." Drunk in moderation, *kava* can induce pleasant experiences, but like alcohol and any number of other intoxicants, it can also cause people to pass out, and even to become ill and die. In any case, Regenvanu explained, knowledge about this and many other local herbs has been acquired over thousands of years, and it is passed down differentially to those individuals who earn the right to hold it. This knowledge goes with the responsibility to use it wisely, and should not be taken for granted, as the bioprospectors expect. Vanuatu is also the place I mentioned where anthropologists were excluded for several years, and where some people are rejecting the brash Western world of television.

In Tanzania, on the other hand, while I was visiting Maasai country, I discovered that these are a people whose treatments for ill health are valued widely in the area, and whose experts are able to make a good living by offering a range of herbal cures and remedies. Before the conference I attended in Arusha, mentioned at the start of chapter 1, some of us were taken by a couple of anthropologists to visit a Maasai community. While we were there, we quizzed the anthropologists, and through them our Maasai hosts, about what they did for protection against malaria when living in the area on a long-term basis. For those of us who had agonized about the various possible prophylactics and their side effects, their answer was quite galling, for they replied simply: "We get it anyway, but the Maasai have a cure. For them it is treated rather like a cold!"

Environmental Concerns

The efficacy of herbal remedies known to Indigenous peoples in different parts of the world is only a part of their tried and tested systems of knowledge that also include an understanding of how to live in harmony with their local ecosystem. Those who hunt animals, catch fish and sea mammals, and gather wild roots, fruits, and berries are well aware of the seasonality of their food supplies, and they know how to conserve them. They are careful not to kill spawning fish or pregnant animals, and they ensure that they harvest fruits and vegetables in such a way that the plants continue to thrive. Very often they give thanks to their Creator (see below) for their daily supplies, and some people have ways of recognizing animals "giving themselves up" for their consumption.

In places where people planted crops before they were colonized, they had often developed systems over the centuries that were more efficient and effective in their own environment than those that were subsequently imposed upon them by the so-called developers. A good example of this is the practice among the Six Nations of planting their three staple crops—the Three Sisters (sometimes called Three Sustainers)—of maize, beans, and squash in the same compound. Each helps the other to thrive, apparently, by the way the leaves of one protect another from too much sunshine, a second conserves the moisture in the soil, and the third keeps the soil fertile. A patch planted in this way is thriving in the First Nations section of the Botanical Gardens in Montreal, alongside an explanation, as are several other examples of successful native environmental usage, now on display for the visiting public to learn about.

In the rain forest of South America, an indigenous agricultural practice called slash and burn cultivation allows the forest continually to regenerate itself. This works because a patch cleared by this method is only cultivated for a few years before it is abandoned and a new one sought. By moving continually in this way, people for thousands of years conserved the forest and all its qualities at the same time as making space for themselves to grow crops. Unfortunately, big ranchers and industrialists have not used the same intelligent conservation techniques in the vast areas that have been 'developed' in this area and the ecosystem has not only been irrevocably damaged on site, but its alterations are causing long-term negative effects on the world climate.

We have already heard in chapter 6 about the arts and crafts that were encouraged in Pangnirtung in the new Inuit territory of Nunavut to help people overcome a slump in the market for sealskin and whale products because of the activities of Green Peace. Part of the problem was that these traditional activities of theirs had been overtaken by big industrial concerns, to which Green Peace rightly objected, but there were also some fundamental misunderstandings about the careful way in which they had always conserved their own supplies. In typical fashion, people who thought they knew better made assumptions about the situation, and worse, they made decisions about the use of land on the part of those who actually knew it a lot better than they did. The deep knowledge of the Inuit who had lived in the area for generations was simply ignored by 'environmentalists' and 'conservationists' who came to count polar bears and other animals and apply their scientific principles to matters that the Inuit already knew well.

This situation is changing now in Nunavut, thankfully, and in other parts of the world too, those who are concerned about the damage that large enterprises are doing to the climate and the environment are beginning to consult local people and to value their knowledge. There are other places where this has still to happen, and some environmental organizations are still so concerned to conserve animals, such as nonhuman primates, that the human beings who live in close proximity are suffering from excessive crop-raiding and other problems over which they have lost control. Other organizations are making the world at large aware of the issues. We mentioned Survival International in the last chapter. Others include the New Internationalist (http://www.newint.org) and the Forest Peoples Project (http://www.forestpeoples.gn.apc.org). I think it is true to say that more and more people are becoming aware of the vast knowledge of the environment that First Peoples hold, and we are learning from our past arrogance.

Spirituality

Spirituality is probably one of the areas of Indigenous life that remains most varied among different peoples, for ideas of the spiritual world are deeply ingrained and not easily displaced, though Christianity has in many cases been successfully introduced. From the point of view of the missionaries who brought the Christian faith, they may believe it has replaced previous convictions, but in practice on the ground, my anthropological experience and training would suggest that prior ideas may be lurking not too far beneath the surface. Whether the people I have been working with embrace Christianity or not, they have usually been exposed to it, so they share that association, but some Indigenous people presented another set of ideas to me that I think could provide a useful lesson to the wider world. I made only a limited attempt to investigate this subject, however, so I offer it only rather tentatively.

There are two parts to this learning. The first is extracted from the language used by most, if not all of the people whose words I recorded, and it may indeed have its origins in the dual education they received in the English tongue and in Christian faith. The part I want to explain here, however, is a little different from the doctrine that most theologians would expound, though I incorporate the words of one Native Christian practitioner. I am mostly going to quote from the words of people who have rejected that Christian teaching and who have turned back to ideas they perceive of as having been prior to the introduction of this new faith. In other words, they are drawing on the teachings of their elders, holders of the wisdom they are seeking to reinstate. The second part comes directly from one example of such a prior system.

The first part, the language I am concerned with here, makes reference to the links with the land that characterize the indigeneity of the people, and the crucial shared idea is that it was given to them by a being they call the Creator. The land was theirs to use, and to care for. It provided all they needed to sustain them, and as long as they were careful in their use of it, and regularly gave thanks to their Creator for that gift, it would continue to meet their needs. Different peoples may have any number of other ideas about the spirit world, and their relationship to it, but a profound respect for the Creator of their land underpins their links with it and their concern about it having been misappropriated. The lesson here, however, is that the people who talked to me about these matters also seemed to share a respect for other variations on their basic theme.

The first such person we actually met briefly in chapter 1, a man named Travis, who was working with the characteristic red pipestone found in an area of Minnesota now designated in the United States as a national monument. The museum introduces the background to this area, which it explains has always been considered sacred to Native people for preparing the "pipes of peace" they smoke to resolve disagreements, among other things. Travis was carving the stone into pipes, but he drew our attention to a small "altar" of sacred articles that he explained were to be used in ceremonies. They comprised a buffalo skull, with some tobacco, sweetgrass, wild sage, and cedar laid out in front of it. He burns these when he wants to pray, he said, which he does before and after he collects the red stone for his pipes. Interesting here, however, is that he went on to volunteer his conviction that "the spiritual" is the same whatever we call it. Whether people go to church or to Native ceremonies, "We are all praying to the One Creator," he said.

A similar view was expressed by the Native employee who came to talk to us at the Akta Lakota Museum in Chamberlain, South Dakota. He was Lakota, he said, but he preferred not to make distinctions between the Lakota, Dakota, and Nakota. "We are all Sioux," he said, and he went on to express a similar view about churches. "There are too many of them. If people looked into it," he said, "they'd find that while Jesus came to one part of the world, the same God, the Creator, sent the Peacemaker to North America, the Buddha to India, and appropriate prophets to all other people." The gist of his view was that there could only be one Creator, and the Creator of course recognized that different peoples needed different messengers. He added that recognition of this fact would solve all sorts of world problems. He mentioned Palestine and Northern Ireland in particular.

In Fiji, there are several culture centers, where Fijian life prior to the arrival of the Christian missionaries is explained, although most Fijians now proclaim themselves to be Christian, and the guides make no secret about their own beliefs in their explanations. In reconstructed villages, there is usually a tall building known as a *burekalon*, which it is explained was the focus of ritual activity and the priest's temple and residence before the arrival of Christianity. Guides make much of the fact that human sacrifice was part of their so-called heathen rituals, apparently to shock the audience, and they explain that the bodies of virile young men were buried under the corner posts of the chief's house to give him power—until the missionaries told them that this was wrong. Whether or not this was true is disputed, but I had the distinct impression that the guides were expecting approval of their Christian commitment. One thanked us for our attendance, and terminated his speech with the words, "in this little country, we believe we are all one in the eyes of the Almighty God."

On the Six Nations Reserve, there are some 17 churches of a variety of different denominations, but many people choose to attend Haudenosaunee ceremonies that have become known as "Longhouse" instead. One Anglican churchgoer told me ruefully that you can't fit in if you try to go to a Longhouse meeting, but the churches are half-empty. There are five Anglican churches, but the congregations have diminished so much recently that they hold a service in four of them once a month, and in the Chapel of the Mohawks only in the summer and for special functions such as weddings and funerals. The local priest, Father Norman Casey, does the rounds, as do some of the congregation, and a group of people go to breakfast together after the Sunday morning service. Father Norman talked to me about his views on the subject, and he affirmed that most of the people who attend church are old or middle-aged because young people prefer Longhouse.

He is himself from the Mi'kmac First Nation, so he has grown up with the different possibilities, and he told me that he was trying to get members of the separate groups to see that there are many similarities in their ideas. If we don't move closer together, the Church won't survive, he explained, but there are problems on both sides. People in the Longhouse tradition have been told for 200 years that their spirituality is bad, and wrong, so it is hardly surprising if they spurn the new Anglican policy to seek reconciliation. On the Christian side, those who attend are very conservative, "almost Catholic," he said, so they are not interested in sharing anything with the Longhouse. The Anglican policy is called *A New Agape* and is an attempt to use local customs and symbols as part of a program of healing, he explained, but it may be too late, especially while they are dealing with claims of abuse in the residential schools they administered.

This brings me to the second part of my learning, for according to Tara Fromen, the education officer at the Woodland Cultural Centre, the "traditional" people in the Longhouse have a rather special view of different religions. It is not unlike that expressed by the Lakota people I quoted earlier, though a little more exclusive. They apparently think that the Creator made different religions for different peoples, and that you need to be born into the Longhouse tradition to espouse theirs. They have great respect for other ways of doing things, but they want no interference from the outside in their ways, just as was expressed in the two-row wampum agreement. Tara went further, and suggested that the Mohawks became Christians "for gain," and because it reinforced a class system among the Six Nations. I didn't do any further research on this subject, so I cannot back up this idea, but in the next section I outline a great lesson that the world could learn from these "Longhouse people" if we offered them an opportunity to share it with us.

Peace

This lesson was presented very clearly at a temporary exhibition of Iroquoian beadwork at the Woodland Cultural Centre that was described briefly in chapter 1. It was called *Ska-ni-Kwat*, which means "the power of a good mind," and the principles of that power were laid out alongside the material exhibits that were designed and made to illustrate it. These principles are embodied in the Great Law, passed down among the Haudenosaunee people as the rationale for their alliance of first five, and then six nations, brought to them by an ancestor they call the Peacemaker who, in turn, is recorded as having been sent by the Creator. The message is said to extend to "all nations on earth," and "to shed the light of understanding upon the minds of all people," and the colorful examples of beadwork were made through the collaboration of "people of all ages from a wide variety of ethnic and national identities."

Boards in the exhibition explain that the three main principles of the Great Law brought by the Peacemaker are Peace, Power, and Righteousness. Peace is the first and foremost, and this requires cultivating good feelings of Love, Honor, and Friendship among one another. Weapons of war were to be buried under the Great Tree of Peace, and their power was to be replaced by the Power of Equity and Justice, the power of a society in which people treat all others as equals and respect their rights. "When people believe in peace and act to perpetuate it, they will become healthier in spirit," it goes on, and it continues that a soundness of mind, body, and spirit creates a unity of thoughts and actions, which brings True Power. The third principle, that of Righteousness, is brought about by the cultivation of the Good Mind of the title of the exhibition, and requires one "to promote self righteousness, shape personal conduct and foster mutual resolutions not to foster resentment, hatred or envy."

It is by these principles, then, that the Six Nations of the Haudenosaunee have continued to live reasonably harmoniously as one people, despite divergences of opinion about the leadership imposed on them by the Canadian government, and the severe divisions enforced at the time of the American wars of independence. The scattering of members of these six nations across the Canada/United States border was a strong incentive for the negotiation of an agreement called the Jay Treaty which should (in theory) allow them to cross unhindered. The elected chief of the Six Nations of the Grand River when I was staying, Roberta Jamieson, explained to me that the concept of having a Good Mind means to be constructive, open, and willing precisely to accommodate difference. This concept underpinned her aim, mentioned in chapter 6, to build bridges with the old confederacy chiefs as part of a larger plan for a Haudenosaunee future entitled: "seven undertakings for the seventh generation"—the future generations are valued as well as the elders.

In accordance with the advice of the Haudenosaunee Peacemaker, the principles they share could and should also apply to all nations of the earth. The mounting of an exhibition of beadwork that brought together 'over 500 people from at least 25 countries' to use techniques and designs passed down through generations of Iroquois people is testimony to a sharing of these principles as well as the skills. Sam Thomas and Lorna Thomas-Hill, co-curators of this exhibition, explained at the opening of the show that they had held workshops in several locations of the United States and Canada to pass on the practical skills of decorating the rich colorful velvet with beadwork. The resulting garments on display are testimony to their success, both in fostering beautiful work, and, undoubtedly, in the joy of sharing of this collaboration.

As I mentioned in chapter 1, the principles presented here offer a wonderful blueprint for world peace. Although there would seem to be little chance at the time of my writing that they be adopted by leaders of "all the nations of the earth," there are plenty of occupants of those nations who have demonstrated visibly for a more just and equitable world. The concepts of a Good Mind would seem to be excellent ones for us all to think about in reference to respecting each other's differences, and more so, in seeking to foster mutual resolutions rather than resentment, hatred, or envy. The good news at the time of my writing is that Indigenous people in many different countries are working together, perhaps through a sharing of past iniquities, to heal their wounds, and to make a better world for themselves and their peoples.

In the keynote speech that George Abungu gave in Arusha, referred to at the start of chapter 1, he proposed that museums offer neutral spaces for the peaceful expression of difference, especially important in the war-torn countries of the African continent that we occupied at the time. They also empower people to own their own heritage and express their own identity, he pointed out. We have seen an abundance of examples from around the world to bear out his argument, and if we take the trouble to visit each other's displays, and learn there about our differences, we may well be reluctant to condemn people for things they do that seem strange. I started out by criticizing museums, and some tourist shows, and this was largely because of the way that they had appropriated the "wrappings" of people they had dominated. In the last chapter, we saw the efforts several museums are making to open an ongoing dialogue with those same people. If those who are displayed are actually in charge of their own representations and can choose their own ways of doing that representing, then public cultural display would seem indeed to offer a path to that elusive notion of world peace.

Conclusion

Objects have a tremendous power for communication, though as we saw in chapter 5, they may communicate different things to different people. In societies that relied on oral history to transmit important cultural knowledge through the generations, objects were also often used like contracts, or as mnemonic devices, and we saw that wampum belts played this role for the Haudenosaunee. The two-row wampum that we have referred to several times represented a serious agreement that was broken when the Canadian and U.S. governments instructed schools to punish Haudenosaunee children for using their own languages. The appropriation by any colonial power of objects that had significance for a people was demeaning, but when those objects carry the very history of those same people, it may be seen as nothing less than an attempt to take over the basis of their identity.

In this book, we have observed many examples of Indigenous peoples retrieving their history and reclaiming control of their identity by agreeing among themselves how objects and other cultural paraphernalia should be made and displayed. We have seen people repatriating the remains of their ancestors, and bringing home the objects that those ancestors made. We have seen them reoccupying their land, and returning to the places of significance the names that they were long ago given. We have also seen them rekindling their languages, and using their creative skills to make art that both expresses allegiance to their own traditions and impresses the wider world. In this implicit way, they have announced their continuing existence to that wider world, and in some cases, they offer to share a selection of their treasures to tourists and other visitors.

This expression of cultural difference is part of a movement that pervades the contemporary world, and there are many people throughout that world who are ready to enjoy those treasures, and to listen to the wisdom that comes alongside them. There are unfortunately still some who ignore them, however, who seek to emphasize a perceived superiority, who feel the need to resort to big, ugly weapons to preserve their imagined special identity. There are many others—like the people introduced in chapter 2 who sought out Head-Smashed-in to visit—who need the reassurance of 'history' and archaeological investigations to persuade them to include a site of cultural interest in their itinerary, even if they find themselves lured there by a compelling story, and its name!

This is a book that should end optimistically, however, for in my experience it is the younger people of our contemporary world who are beginning to see the sense of the long-held wisdom developed by our ancestors—those 'Native' ones who knew how to live in harmony with the land, who could find food and medicine in the environment around them, and others more widely who, if we would listen, could tell us how to live at peace with one another. During my studies, I found the greatest zeal for all these ideas among youthful Aboriginal people who have many years to develop them and to disseminate them.

First, there was Nokomis, whom we met in chapter 1. It could almost be said that she inspired the whole project! Then there was a schoolgirl named Cindy, who offered David Neufeld and me a "six-hour tour" of a rather small Tagé Cho Hudän Interpretive Centre at Little Salmon Carmacks so enthusiastic was she about her cultural heritage. The four young people speaking about their language whom we met at the start of chapter 4 brought tears to the eyes of their audience so determined were they to persist with what they had started, and Jamie-Lee in Kahnawake, whom we met in chapters 3 and 4, also reassured me that she would pass on the beautiful language she had learned to her children. Finally, I would like to mention the young boy barely introduced in the section above on discrimination, for his enthusiasm about ideas of cultural revival was matched only by his open and friendly attitude.

These are a few examples only, but they stand out from my research, and if they should they prove to inspire others, we can surely look to a positive future for cultural reclamation and all the healing that goes with it.

References and Further Readings

Ghimire, K.B. and M.P. Pimbert (eds.), 1997, *Social Change and Conservation*, London: Earthscan Publications Ltd.

Hendry, Joy, 2003, "An Ethnographer in the Global Arena: Globography Perhaps?," *Global Networks*, 3, 4.

Voss, A., 2004, "Preventing the Spread of MRSA," *British Medical Journal*, 329: 521–533.

Epilogue

In May 2004, as the last snowy patches of the winter were receding in northeastern Hokkaido, and this book was planned out and partially written, I traveled back to the Ainu 'village' I had visited some 33 years before. The place was transformed. The tourist part was still just one street, but it was neatly paved and lined with newly built shops, each offering an array of goods marked in some way as Ainu. At the top, a large building with an Ainu name advertised performances of dance and theater at intervals through the day. There was still one old Ainu-style house, though in much better condition than those I had seen in 1971, and inside were laid out a reconstructed hearth and a tidy display of objects that had been used in the past. There were no living bears in sight, though there were still several carved ones of various sizes, some with salmon in their mouths. There were also carvers working in some of the shops, but there were no people wandering around in Ainu 'costumes', and no students from Tokyo.

In some ways, the place at first looked less appealing than it had 30 years before. To a seasoned traveler, it looked like a tourist trap rather than a cultural 'village', and the car parking down the middle of the street detracted from the overall atmosphere—until darkness fell and the cheerful lights directed attention to the buildings. The architecture was a mishmash of different styles, with no particular coordination, and there was no sense at all of recreating the past for the benefits of tourists. This 'strip' was very much a place of the present, though bristling with intriguing symbols of something quite different to the surrounding Japanese style, and inviting for someone with time to wander.

This time, people offering goods for sale in the shops were happy to describe themselves as Ainu, as were the carvers, and one I met—Akibe Hideo—chatted about a cultural exchange visit he had made to Vancouver some years before. A local café had an array of books and magazines about other Indigenous (and oppressed) peoples around the world, and a young man serving there regaled us with details of the Ainu pedigree of several members of his family, though he himself had married in. Inside the reconstructed Ainu house (for the *real* ones anyway needed replacing regularly), a friendly woman in an Ainu appliquéd jacket not only proudly proclaimed herself Ainu, but also invited us to sit down around the hearth and pass the time of day.

Teshi Sigiko was 73, and she had been born and brought up in Akanko. She had thus been there 33 years before, when I visited, and she explained that none of the local people wanted to come out and meet visitors because of the discrimination they suffered. So the local authority had decided to hire students to work in the 'village' while the descendants of the Ainu people they were representing got on with their own lives just a block or so away. Dancing was practiced, and for some time displayed, but other Ainu apparently bullied those who did it for making themselves into a show and accepting money for it. None of her contemporaries spoke the Ainu language because their grandparents had been punished for using it so they didn't teach their children. The one old man I had met was probably their last speaker.

Now life is different, Sigiko explained. The theater and all the shops are Ainu owned and operated, only Ainu (and their spouses) can live in their hamlet, and she has traveled extensively to dance and play the mouth harp. She recounted tales of "exchange visits" to Europe, Taiwan, and Alaska, and expressed a wish to make her next trip to Mongolia, noting that in the past the Ainu used to walk huge distances to China and back. Sigiko talked of the past as she showed us the objects and garments hanging up around the room. She was clearly a holder of valuable cultural knowledge, and the new world that has grown up around her at last appreciates that.

Later we saw the dance show, which was a splendid display, presented as a creation of this local Ainu community of 200 people. In the evening, we were able to watch a striking theatrical production named *Yukar* that was a highly symbolic, but gorgeously costumed depiction of the plight of the Ainu people, and their return to some family contentment. The highlight of my visit, however, was an after-show meeting with Akanko's star dancer, Hirasawa Ryūji, who invited us round to his home, just a few steps away in the next street. His wife turned out to pour the beer, and we spent a happy couple of hours hearing their stories, their accounts of the revival movement taking place, and their plans for their future.

I had been given his name by Nomoto Masahiro, from Shiraoi, but Ryūji was keen to point out that Akanko was different from the "museum" they have built there for it closes down at night and is basically a place of preservation. Here people have homes above the shops, he explained, this is a living community, and we are able to practice an Ainu life. They had yet to relearn their language, though plans are afoot for this too, but in the theater they can draw on their colorful, creative history, and ensure that their children will grow up knowing their cultural background. Ryūji had been six years old when I had first visited this place, and he thinks that the old man I met was probably his grandfather, who used to travel to Shiraoi to dance and to keep up their traditions. In this family, the new generation looks able to be proud of them as well.

INDEX

Aang Serian school, 124
Abdulla, Ian, 151–2
Aboriginal
  businesses, 93, 123
  contributions to society, 19, 126–7, 193
  Healing Foundation, 118
  Language Initiative, 115, 148
  Music Awards, 75, 146, 148
  Olympics, 184
  People's Television Network (APTN), 147, 148, 194
  status, ix
  Studies, 119; support for, 120–4
  theatre companies, 149
Abungu, George, 17, 28–9, 40, 44, 137, 192, 215
academic standards, 12, 112
acknowledgements, 9, 10, 12–27, 38, 68, 82, 87, 90, 184
actors, 25, 61, 71–2, 148
Adamson, Joy, 30
Adelaide, 25, 150
Africa, 17, 44, 67–8, 111, 130, 135–8, 192, 201, 215
  scholars in, 28
African Heritage, 138
Aglukark, Sue, 146
Ahkwesáhsne, 173
  Freedom School, 106, 112, 113; report from, 113
Ainu, x–xi, 1, 12, 24, 156, 178–80, 184, 187–8, 201
  appliqué work, 117, 219
  on display, 6
  language, 219–20
  museums, xi, 220
  pop group, Moshiri, 146
  'village', x, 24, 218–20
Ak-chin Indian Community, 46
Akavak, Tommy, 168, 170
Akiwenzie-Damm, Kateri, 185
Akta Lakota Museum, 33, 211
Alaska, 69, 219
  Highway, 69
Alberta, 58, 98
  Red Crow Community College, 119
Alcatraz, 10, 110
alcohol abuse, 94, 144, 186, 207
Alert Bay, 37, 46, 95–6, 116
  T'lisalagi'lakw School, 116, 141, 188
Algonquin
  birch bark, 127
  language, 126
  Mississauga people, 74
American
  Indian: Movement, 197–8; Program, 121
  Revolution, 9, 74, 173, 214
  security, 189
Ames, Michael, 21
ancestors, 34, 40, 72, 83
  influence of, 135, 201–2
  learning from, 11, 41, 120, 127
  supposed, 79
ancestral
  connections, 141, 183–4
  creations, 51
  knowledge, 66, 202, 216
  remains, 11, 50–1, 100, 102, 160–1, 187, 216
Anderson, David, 26

Anderson, Marcia, 14
Anderson, Sallie, 25, 152
Anilnilvak, Nancy, 170–1
animals, 57–8, 113, 124, 160, 163, 209
  bear, x, 218; ceremony, xi
  caribou, 162, 171
  polar bears, 171, 209
  products as symbols, 164–6
Anishnaabe, 91, 146
anthropologists, 12, 20, 38, 96, 124, 174, 194–5, 202
  biological/physical, 50, 160–1
  exclusion of, 85–6, 208
  and Indigenous people, 196
anthropology
  "activist," 174
  conference, x, xi, 59
  department, 18, 120
  research, 161, 203
  studying, 2, 124, 200
  of tourism, 63
Aotearoa, 25, 64, 87, 111, 138–9, 147
archaeology
  evidence, 57, 78–9, 120, 173, 174, 177, 216
  importance of, 158–9, 161–3, 174–5
  specimens, 32, 45, 167, 175
architecture, 11, 19, 131–4, 150, 218
  as e.g. of Aboriginal creativity, 139–43
  as living being, 133
  Malay, 125
  monumental, 29–31
  period, 69
  as reminder, 110, 164–5
archive, 50, 82–3, 188
Arctic, 23
  cruise visitors, 22
Arero, Hassan Wario, 17, 191–2
argelite, 160
Arizona, 46
Arnaqaq, Ooleepeeka, 170

art
  Aboriginal, 11, 131–2, 150–4
  collectors, 132, 202
  and communication, 131, 149, 185
  contemporary, 32, 131, 137, 151, 156, 166, 187
  dealers, 132, 136
  display of, 51–2, 96
  First Nations, 25, 91, 197;
    teachers' training, 96
  Indian, 62, 91
  market, 132, 138, 189;
    global, 136
  meaning of, 132, 150, 154, 195
  'primitive', 132
  schools, 101
  shows, 91, 151, 193
  work for tourists, 44, 131, 153
artists, 30, 85, 169–70, 192
  in house, 36–7, 151
  local, 101, 166, 193
  Native, 40, 77
  support for, 152
  textile; Japanese/British partnership, 194–5
  as vehicle for gods, 153
  workshops, 100–1, 192
arts, 131–55
  and crafts, x, 48, 50, 58, 77, 95, 138, 163; play, 102
  performing, 131, 134–5, 184:
    center, 20, 135, 144; plans, 92, 102, 167; shows, 58, 141
  traditional, 84, 190
  visual, 133–5
assimilation, x, 59, 62
  policies of, 8, 106–10; rationale for, 107
  programs, 11, 92
ATASO, 74
Athapaskan, 22, 190
Auckland, 157
  Museum, 16, 30
  University, 16, 120
audience interaction, 73, 137

Index

Australia, 25, 86, 106–7, 128, 153, 185
   Aboriginal: art, 150–3; ANKAAA, 152; Desart, 131, 149, 152; dancing, 184; and Torres Strait Islander Services, 152
   National Museum, 25, 38, 150 South; Arts Council, 152
authenticity, 56–62, 65, 75, 79, 132, 202
Avataq Cultural Institute, 23, 172
Awan, Rabia, 18
Aztec dancers, 183

Baker
   Bob, 21, 183–4
Bancroft, Anne, 61
Banff, 91
Barnsley, Paul, 186
beadwork, 41, 62, 84, 117, 127, 213–14
Beaulieu, Carol, 147
Beaulieu, Jody, 14, 83–4, 110
Beijing, 183
Bell, Alexander Graham, 74, 180
Bell, Cynthia, 146–7
bentwood boxes, 100–1, 161
Berlin
   International Tourism Exchange, 194
Beveridge, William, 167
Bierling, Gerald, 18
bioprospecting, 207–8
Birnie, Joel, 151
bison, *see* buffalo
Black Hills, 33
Black Water, Andy, 49, 187
Blackfoot/feet people, 35, 49, 58, 183, 184, 187
   Mookaakin Cultural and Heritage Foundation, 49, 187
blood quotient, 117, 197–8
Bolivia, 192
Bolt, Glenda, 22
Bolton, Frances, 21, 37
Bolton, Lissant, 49

Bomberry, Vince, 105, 109
books, 116
   collections of, 82–3, 96, 134, 176
   Native vetting of, 129
   for sale, 75, 76, 118, 128–9, 219
Botswana, 181
Bracho, Mary Louise, 14, 26, 33, 57
brand
   design, 5
   names, 3
Brant, Joseph, 74, 78
Brantford, 8, 74, 87, 89, 123, 149
   Tourism Association, 148
   White Pine Native Centre, 75
Bread and Cheese Day, 19
Brewster, Patti, 15
Brigham Young University, 64
British, 9, 19, 74, 78, 101, 173
   artists, 194–5
   legacy, 29, 65, 159
   Museum, 51, 187; Powwow conference, 191
   National Health Service, 207
British Columbia, 160, 165, 175; history of, 71–2, 159
Brown, Naomi (and Alan), 21
Buddha, 211
buffalo, 33, 57–8, 74, 119, 211
   restoration project, 175
Buffalo
   The Turtle, 183
Buffalo Bill, 61–2
   Historical Centre; Plains Indian Museum, 24, 33
Bunjilaka, 25, 38–9, 150
burial, 31, 50, 100, 119, 161
Burford, Gemma, 17, 123–4
Burnham, Jeff, 128
Bush, Mikidadi, 137

calendars, 96, 116, 118
Calgary, 24, 35, 49, 51, 56–7, 98–9, 122, 187
   Red Thunder Dance Theatre, 182
   University Native Centre, 190

California, 85, 182
  Anaheim, 70, 99
  San Francisco Bay, 10
Camarena Ocampo, Cuauhtémoc, 45–6
camoflauge, 89
Canada, 5, 9, 18, 20, 87–98, 107, 150, 161, 180
  Arts Council of, 148
  Auyuittuq National Park, 169–71
  government, 18, 37, 40, 62–3, 115, 158, 214: Cultural and Education Centres program, 89, 93–4; evaluation of, 93, 115; Indian control of, 94; departments, 20; of Heritage, 20, 68, 94, 97, 167; lobbying, 70; negotiating with, 172; Indian (and Northern) Affairs, 89, 97
  Kluane National Park, 162, 184
  Museum of Civilisations, 20, 38, 52, 99, 121–2, 139, 190: Aboriginal Training Course, 22; First Nations Hall, 38; Great Hall, 38, 43, 139
  Museums Association of, 52, 92
  National Aboriginal Day, 68–9, 121, 140
  prairies, 15, 57
  Queens University, 193
  West Coast, 21: First Nations, 38, 72; houses, 99, 139; North West Coast peoples, 36
Canberra, 25, 152
canoes, 38, 64, 71, 89, 127, 100, 140
Cape Mudge, 37, 46
Capilano, Chief Joe, 183
Caplan, Pat, 17
Cardinal, Douglas, 121–2, 139–40, 143
care, 124, 158, 164, 205–7, 210
  home, 206

Caribbean Identities Community project, 191–2
Carr, Emily, 101
Cartier, Jacques, 97
carving, x, 34, 36–7, 154, 186, 211
  Ainu, 187–8, 218
  Haida, 70, 99–101
  Inuit, 166, 169
  Maori, 117, 120, 138–9, 153
Casey, Dawn, 38
Casey, Father Norman, 212
casinos, 47, 77–9, 197
Cayuga, 183
  lands, 121, 173–5
  language, 105–6, 115, 126: broadcasting, 148; immersion through high school, 112, 115, 122, 148
ceremon(y)ial, 71, 102, 106, 116–17, 128, 139, 151, 211
  grade-taking, 86
  memorial, 37, 51
  objects, 35, 49, 50
  pipes, 34, 50, 211
  space, 40, 100, 118, 120, 121, 153
  welcome, 66, 73, 97
Chagga, 124
Champagne and Aishihik First Nation, 22, 162, 184
Chemko, Erika, 26, 167–8
Chew, Sylvie Coté, 23, 172
chiefs, 19, 35, 46, 65, 66, 96, 129, 176
children, 40, 44, 46, 66, 68, 108–9, 151–2, 166, 201
  activities for, 91, 102, 125, 167
  band of, 84
  dancing, 184
  and language, 85, 111, 147, 216
  rebellious, 87, 109, 197
  school, 65, 75, 87–9, 106–7, 125–7, 174
  street, 137
China, 198
Christianity, 210–13

Index

church, 139, 211–12
  Anglican, 87, 89, 109, 212;
    Policy: *A New Agape*, 212
  of Jesus Christ of Latter Day
    Saints, 64
  Roman Catholic, 110
clans, 48, 116, 141
  mothers, 119, 127, 129, 174
clothes, x, xi, 30, 69, 150,
  166, 219
  as 'wrapping', 6, 8, 14
Cody, Wyoming, 33
collaboration, 49, 102, 213–14
collectors, 29, 31, 202
  ignorance of, 31, 132
Collison
  Nika, x, 21, 101–2
  Vince, 21, 99–100
Commanda, Claudette, 21
commemoration, 68
Commonwealth, 29, 137, 164
  Studies, 18
community(ies), 29, 36, 40, 67,
  85, 96, 102, 197, 220
  diasporic, 192
  new, 172–7
  old, 156
  schools/colleges, 110,
    119–20, 124
  values, 113, 125
Conaty, Gerald, 24, 35, 49
Connecticut, 78
conservation, 28, 39, 46, 208–10
  human/wildlife conflict, 209
consultation, 5, 32, 35, 36, 44, 84,
  101, 187
  lack of, 51, 209
continuity, 32, 33, 84, 131, 152,
  159, 216
control
  reclaiming, 81–102, 116, 122,
    159–61, 163–72
  transfer of, 67–72, 132, 135
Cooper, Matt, 18
cooperation, 5, 12, 43, 92, 95, 102,
  181–2

Cornell University, 173
  Akwe:kon, 121, 139
counseling, 121
courts, 159, 173
Coutts, Lorraine, 25
Cranmer-Webster, Gloria, 43, 95
creativity, 11, 131–55, 180, 185,
  194–5
Creator, the, 42, 72, 154, 208,
  210–11, 213
Cree, 35, 74, 120, 172, 183, 184
  languages, 96, 110, 115, 116,
    123, 147, 200
  of Lubicon Lake, Alberta,
    51–2
Crow Dog, Mary, 197–8
Crow tribe, 34–5
Crown, the, 36, 121
  Prince Edward, 121
  Queen Elizabeth II, 164
  Queen Victoria, 19, 41
Cultural African Network, 129,
  137–8
cultural
  awareness camps, 128
  broker, 41, 136
  difference, 180, 194–6, 215–16
  display, 4: economic value of,
    63–7; Indigenous forms of,
    81–7, 166; political
    associations of, 81, 83, 165;
    power of, 5, 180, 215
  education, 116–30, 152, 170,
    176, 196
  messages: contradictory, 108
  skills, 116–19
culture, x, 12, 63, 70, 95, 117,
  128, 133
  appropriation of, 8
  centers, xi, 4, 11, 12, 50, 82,
    128, 156, 164: associated
    with casinos, 78–9;
    confederacy of, 93–8; future
    projects, 98–102;
  definition of, 4, 82
  dying-out, 59, 161

culture—*continued*
 exchange, 9, 178–9, 182–99,
  218–19: dancing as, 182–4;
  writing as, 185–56
 healing power of, 4, 94, 202, 212
 living, 128; celebration of, 101,
  185, 190
 as wealth, 11
 as 'wrapping', 6–8, 13
Curtis, Tony, 61
Curve Lake First Nation, 77

dance(s), 44, 69, 84, 102, 123,
  127, 128
 classes, 116–17, 124, 144, 184
 competitions, 76, 116, 145–6
 disapproval of, 219
 keeping alive, 90, 144, 151
 performance, 48, 64–5, 70–1, 75,
  77, 98, 99, 118, 179, 187,
  218–19
 screen, 43
 space, 116, 141
dancers, x, 24, 134, 144–6, 178–9,
  182–4, 187, 196
 Hirasawa Ryūji, 24, 219–20
 Santee Smith, 148
Dänojà Zho Cultural Centre, 69,
  75, **140**
Dar-es-Salaam, 30, 44
 Nyumba ya Sanaa, 135–6
Dawson City, 22, 48, 69–70, 140
de Costa, Ravi, 18
de Lisle, Andrew, 10, 23, 62
Delgamuukw, 159
delinquency, 94
democracy, 97
diabetes, 186
digitalization, 134, 137–8, 188
discourse, 3, 4, 157, 200–1
'discovery', 8, 9, 68, 157, 162
 boxes, 102
discrimination, 129, 184, 197, 201,
  202–5, 219
disease, 36, 160, 161, 170, 207

display
 'interactive', 43–4
 of peoples, 7, 60, 61
 see also 'cultural'
diversity, 1, 2, 4, 39, 58, 64,
  95, 180
Dobrowolsky, Helene, 69
Dogrib Treaty Eleven Council, 190
Doxtator, Deborah, 1
dreams, 34
drug
 abuse, 94
 yielding plants, 127, 207–8
drumming, 28, 65, 76, 124, 127,
  128, 146
Dugay-Grist, Mark, 25

ecomuseum project, 46
ecosystem, 160, 208
education, 20, 40, 49, 91, 152
 of children, 2, 4, 37, 164, 196
 Christian, 110, 166
 inappropriate, 94, 107, 197
 Indian control of, 122
 of non-Native people, 8
 outreach, 20, 91–2, 126, 128
 postsecondary, 115, 119–23, 171
 programme, 37, 57, 78, 95, 101,
  162–3; Aboriginal, 113,
  119–20, 163, 196
 'Western', 46
'edukit', 126
Ekho, Jimmy, 23, 166–7
elders, 35, 101, 106, 111, 139,
  156, 190
 access to, 50, 74, 111, 121, 170
 meeting place for, 48, 141,
  169, 170
 passing on knowledge, 66, 83,
  113, 119, 124, 158, 163
 program for, 96, 164, 166
 respect for, 165, 205–6
 teaching of, 210
 the value of, 205–8, 214
Enlightenment, the, 3

environment, 70, 71, 100, 158, 168, 208–10
  teaching related to, 113, 120, 157, 175, 216
environmentalists, 169
ethics, 52
ethnobiology, 124
ethnographers, 2–3
  African, 45
Ettawageshik, Frank, 62
Europe, 3, 6, 30–2, 61–2, 114, 134, 138, 161, 219
  avant-garde from, 134
Europeans, 9, 125, 181
  arrival of, 57, 72, 99, 127, 160
evolution
  ideas of, 3, 7
exhibition(s), 8, 20, 150–1, 154, 166, 193
  EXPO 67, 9; *Indians of Canada* pavilion, 62
  Fluff and Feathers, 8, 56, 60–1
  Great, 6, 7, 9
  of photographs, 41, 43, 63
  Ska-ni-Kwat (the power of a good mind), 213–14
  Te Maori, 138–9, 153
  The Spirit Sings, 52
exploration, 6, 7, 8, 31, 51, 59, 89, 100
explorers, 5, 30, 125, 158, 170
extinction, x, xi, 10, 11, 156

family, 19, 71, 77, 128, 144, 182, 219, 220
  separation, 107, 197–8
  values, 165, 176, 205
farming, 124, 153, 174, 175, 186
fashion show, 146
feasability study, 89–90, 100, 148, 168
feasts, 14, 70–1
  community house, 100, 116
feathers, 33, 56, 60, 62, 70, 146

festivals, 45, 65, 127, 145, 151, 173, 182, 193
  Canadian Aboriginal, 75, 145–6, 193
  Toronto Harbourfront, 146
  Yoreme, 184
FNCCEC, 21, 22, 93–8, 110, 115, 128
  annual conference, 94–8, 146
field
  researchers, 91
  workers, 86, 193
Fiji, 15, 64–5, 211–12
  National Museum of, 16
  Pacific Harbour Cultural Centre, 16, 65
  Suva, 30
film, 32, 33, 38, 44, 46, 57, 137, 149–51, 163
  collection, 82, 85–6, 90, 96, 168
  feature, 143–4, 185: *Atanarjuat: The Fast Runner*, 143, 186; *Blackfellas*, 150; *Once Were Warriors*, 143; *Rabbit Proof Fence*, 106–7, 143, 185; *Whale Rider*, 143, 186
  IMAX, 64
  makers, 2–3, 61, 86, 143, 192, 202
  promotional, 67, 95
First Nations, ix, 186, 195, 196–8
  Canadian Assembly of, 51–3, 115
  Confederation of Cultural Education Centres, 21, 93–8
  exhibitions, 8, 128, 213–14
  galleries, 35, 77, 95, 96, 97, 101, 128
  museums, 20, 39–44
  'Namgis, 95, 141
  and renewal, 9, 133–9, 180
  research, 36, 188
  Siksika, 98–9
  training, 22, 119, 127, 135, 182
  University, 121–2, 139
Fisher, Kyra, 24

fishing, 109, 125, 158, 160, 161, 208
food, 44, 57, 64, 66, 71, 87, 101, 118, 167, 216
　gathering, 100, 208
　Native, 73, 75, 77, 145; "three sisters," 174, 208
　produce, 108, 165, 186
　to sustain early settlers, 89, 126–7
Ford Foundation, 137
forest, rain, 66, 100, 207
　slash and burn cultivation, 209
Forest Peoples Project, 210
Forth, Terry, 23
Frankfurt, 91
French, 46, 48, 133–5, 173
　language, 96–8, 115–16, 164, 166
Froman, Tara, 20, 91, 125–6, 212–13
Fuller, Nancy, 26, 46
fund distribution, 78, 94, 115
fund-raising, 33, 81, 92, 102, 123, 144, 168, 181, 194–5
funding, 51–2, 90–1, 97, 100, 111, 122, 135
　Dutch, 135, 137

games, 44, 64, 102, 125, 128
　lacrosse, 127
gaming halls, 47
gender roles, 109, 125, 127, 165
General, Brian, 144–5, 182–3
Geneva, 182
genocide, 11, 130, 201
George, Leonard, 25, 71–**2**
Germany, 182, 183, 190, 192, 194
gifts, 6, 8, 75, 89, 160
Gilbert, Trimble, 69
Gitksan people, 48, 159
glaciers, 162–3
Glaeser, Gunter, 22
Glasgow
　People's Palace, 46
glass
　cases, 30, 32, 38, 46, 49, 165

　panels, 116, 141
　windows, 141, 164; stained, 108, 120, 139
Glenbow Museum, 24, 35, 49, 51–2, 187
Global Consortium for Higher Education, 122
global
　fieldwork, 12
　movement, 180–1, 10, 38, 51, 114, 119, 122, 180–1, 216
　positioning systems (GPS), 172, 180
　theorists, 180
globalization, 10, 18, 143, 180
Goldsmith, Mike, 16, 38
good mind, power of, 129, 213–14
Good Minds.com, 76, 128–9
Goodstriker, Lorraine, 58
Gosden, Chris, 14
government
　colonial, 106–7; legacy, 186
　policies, 7, 87; resistance to, 110, 181
　portraying own system of, 63
　self-, 70
　teaching about, 120
　tribal offices, 78, 83
Graburn, Nelson, 23–4, 167, 172
Greece, 193
Green Peace, 169, 209
Green, Sonja, 18, 20
Greenbird, Joan, 20, 91
Greenland, 165, 167
guides, 13, 16, 17, 18, 37, 68, 117
　Aboriginal, 38, 58, 163, 178
　English-speaking, 67, 68
　Indigenous, 65, 171, 212
Guillaume, Danny, 25, 71
Guyana, 191–2

Haida, x, 100, 160
　Gwaii, 21, 99–102, 159–61; Haanas National Park, 160
　Museum, 21, 101
　Ninstints, 160

Old Massett, 21, 99, 160; Kluu
    Laanas Cultural
    Development Project,
    99–100
  Skidegate, 21, 100–2, 160;
    Qay'llnagay Heritage Centre,
    xi, 21, 99–102, 160
  watchmen, 99, 160
hair, 108–9
Hakiwai, Arapata, 139
Halifax, 21, 94, 98
Hanson, Emma, 24, 33
Haram, Liv, 17
Harris, Judy, 91, 154
Haudenosaunee, 9, 41, 60, 113,
    145, 154, 158, 212–14
  confederacy, 121, 127, 176, 214
  history, 43, 118–19, 129, 173–5
  see also law *and* Six Nations
Hau'ofa, Epeli, 16, 133, 135
Hawaii, 30, 64–5, 183–4
  Bernice P. Bishop Museum, 70
  Native people, 179, 183
Head-Smashed-in Buffalo Jump,
    57–8, 79, 177, 216
headdresses, 34, 60, 62, 84
Headstart Aboriginal program, 116
healing, 65, 66, 83, 86, 124, 128,
    162, 215, 217
health, 78, 164, 186, 207, 208, 213
  education, 119, 120, 124
Hendry, Beatrice, 26
Hendry, Charles, 89, 103, 109
Henshall, Ken, 16
Hepburn, Audrey, 61
herbs, 65, 66, 89, 174, 207, 208
heritage, 82, 102, 128, 134, 158,
    191, 200
  celebrating, 76, 145
  in control of, 139, 163, 169, 171,
    215, 218–19
  loss, 2, 117
  place of, 29, 44, 46, 100
  preservation of, 90, 93, 103, 185
  reclamation success, 93, 116,
    179–80

Herle, Anita, 21
Heye, George Gustav, 190
Hill, Bernadette, 174
Hill, Darlene, 20
Hill, Jessica, 20
Hill, Stan, 153–4
Hill, Tom, 10, 20, 25, 39, 52, 56,
    89, 107, 118, 149, 192
Hillerman, Tony, 83
Historical Xperiences, 72
history, 5, 7, 22, 45, 47, 113, 166,
    202, 216
  colonial, 31, 65, 180–1, 200
  of First Peoples, 52, 68; telling of
    own, 63, 72, 78, 100–1,
    162–3, 174, 215
  as it relates to future, 33, 44, 48,
    103, 176, 214, 220
  Indians' contribution to, 90, 103,
    126–7
  local, 47, 68, 78, 168, 170, 173
  natural, 29–30, 32
  in objects, 176, 215
  oral, 36, 43, 83, 119, 128, 159,
    161, 163, 168; recognition
    of, 177
  record of, 30, 82–4; setting right,
    103, 123, 158
  teaching of, 113, 119–20, 128
Hiwus Feast House, 21, 70, 178
Hokkaido, x–xi, 24
  Akanko, 218–20
  Nibutani, 25, 117, 187–8; Ainu
    Cultural Museum, 193
  Sapporo, 188
  Shiraoi, 24, 219–20
Holland, 52
Hong Kong, 198
houses, x, 38, 186
  of arts and culture, 46, 82,
    84–5, 135–6
  Big, 46, 95
  as exhibits, 44, 68, 133,
    139–40
  Haida, 70, 99–102, 160
  Kanak, 133

houses—*continued*
  'keeping', 50, 96
  reconstructed, 65, 218–19
Hudson Bay Company, 183
Hudson, Rock, 61
human
  remains, 14, 31, 50–2
  rights, 120, 181, 213
  sacrifice, 212
hunters and gatherers, 181
hunting, 66, 109, 113, 127, 162, 169, 171, 208
  for sport, 57
Hurricane Juan, 98

identity, 10, 81
  (re)building, 4, 89–90, 98, 144, 176, 200
  choice of, 179, 196–8, 201
  cultural, 1, 4, 90, 103, 111, 163–4
  multilayered, 191–2
  reclaiming, 1, 11, 130, 152–3, 195–6, 215–16
  representing, 29, 132, 156–7, 194, 215
  self-, 12, 94–5, 108, 178–9, 194–9
igloo-shape, 164–6
images, 2, 9, 30, 134, 188, 190
  misappropriation of, 5
  false, 8
  power of, 9
imprisonment, 198
independence, 86, 100, 133, 144, 173, 214
India, 211
'Indians', 1, 9, 36, 40, 56, 61
  country, 193
Indigenous Studies, 18, 119, 122
Ingold, Tim, 26
Inoue, Laura, 26
Instituto Nacional de Antropolgia e Historia (INAH), 15, 45, 84
international links, 92, 178–99
Internet, 129–30, 166, 180

interpretive center, 57–8, 98–9, 100
Inu, 183
Inuit, 128, 129, 143, 145, 158, 209
  control, 163–4, 169, 171
  Heritage Trust, 167
  Languages: Inuktitut, 110, 115, 147, 163–4, 166;
    Inuinnaqtun, 163–4
  people, 115, 164–72, 183
Iqaluit, 23, 164
  Cathedral, 164–**5**
  Nunatta Sunakkaangit Museum, 23, 166–7
  Unikkaarvik Visitor Centre, 166
Iraq, 201
Irish, 183
ironworkers, 40, 42, 154
Iroquoian, 43, 62, 97, 117, 129, 176, 214
  see also Haudenosaunee
Iroquois and Allied Indians, Association of, 89
Irrapmwe, 38
Italy, 5, 182, 194

Jack, Stanley, 186
Jakarta, 30
Jake Thomas Learning Centre, 76, 117
James Bay, 110, 123, 171
Jamieson
  Cathy, 19, 113
  Connie, 19
  Keith, 19, 41, 43, 82, 87–**8**, 92
  Linda, 19
  Mark, 19
  Mary, 19, 81, 205
  Rebecca, 19, 121–3
  Roberta, 19, 176, 214
Janes, Tony, 17
Japan, x–xi, 37, 117, 137, 146, 178, 193, 195, 198, 204
  as exhibitor of Ainu, 6, 187–8
  as "late developer," 3
  National Museum of Ethnology, 32, 51

Index

Japanese
  artists, 194–6
  first, xi
  government, 188
  student, 193
Jean-Marie Tjibaou Cultural Centre, 48–9, 87, 133–5
Jesus, 211
Johnson, E. Pauline, 74
Jones, Simeon, 26
Jordan, Rosita, 18

Kahnawake, 23, 62, 147, 157, 173, 216
  Cultural centre, 96–7
  Declaration of Languages, 114, 116
  Language Centre, 114
  Mohawk immersion school, 97, 106, 112, 113, 122
Kainai people, 119
Kanata Dance Theatre, 144–6, 148, 182–3
Kanak people, 48, 133–5
Kanata Village, 74, 75
Kanatakta, 23, 96–7
Kanonwiioustha (Jamie-Lee), 23, 97, 113–14, 216
Kasarhérou, Emmanuel, 16, 48, 133–5
Kayano, Shigeru, xi
'keepers', 49, 97, 191
Kenya, 111, 136, 191–2
  government, 29
  National Museum of, 17, 28–30, 137–8, 191–2
Key, Amos, 20, 93, 114–15, 148
Keye, Lottie, 105
Kilabuk, Bill, 169, 171
Kilabuk, Pudloo, 24, 169
Kimmirut, 24, 113, 168–9, 170
  Visitors Centre, 168
King, Tom, 146
Kjipuktuk (the Great Harbour), 94, 98
Klondike Gold Rush, 69, 140–1

Knotts Berry Farm, 70, 99
knowledge, 2, 14, 17, 18, 38, 43, 63, 188
  cultural, 83, 113, 119, 120: denying, 109; passing down, 151–2, 158, 159, 207, 214; sharing of, 66, 101, 120, 145, 170; value of, 67, 123, 186, 219
  esoteric, 86, 153, 208
  Indigenous, 124, 188–9, 202, 207, 210; plundering, 207–8
  local, 18, 22, 23, 86; as a commodity, 123
Knowles, Chantal, 14, 190
Kobayashi, Jack, 140–1
Kuala Lumpur, 30
Kuona Trust, 135, 137
Kwakw<u>a</u>ka'wakw
  art, 95
  dance, 116
  people, 37, 43, 161

La Foret, Andrea, 20, 43
Labrador, 182
Lakota people, 33, 47, 96, 110, 175, 198, 211, 213
land, ix, 8, 10, 74, 126, 158, 177
  ancestral, 11, 157–9
  appreciate, 72, 101, 113, 186
  claims, 120, 156–77: agreement, 69, 158–9, 190; contested, 172–4
  continuous use of, 159
  loss, 114, 117
  reclamation, 69, 78, 99, 156, 158, 162, 175, 216
  relationship with, 158, 210
  respect for, 35, 100, 211
  traditional, 97, 113, 176, 196–7
Landers, Maureen, 16, 120
language, 7, 11, 17, 29, 105–16, 210–11, 216
  Basque, 114
  Blood/Kainai, 49, 119
  broadcasting, x, 132

language—*continued*
  Catalán, 114
  classes for adults, x, 106, 110–16
  computer software for, 96
  continuity awards, 98, 110
  Cornish, 114
  Creole, 85
  Dene, 96
  displays about, 35, 110
  elimination of, 7, 109, 202
  English, 185–6, 200, 210
  Gaelic, 114; broadcasting, 147
  and identity, 106
  Japanese, x–xi
  Kiswahili, 111, 124
  Kootenai, 111
  Kwak'wala, 37, 95; classes, 95
  learning, 105–6, 113, 119,
    146–7, 153, 200
  manipulation, 7
  'nests', *kohangareo*, 111, 122, 153
  Northern Tutchone, 158
  punishment for using, 11, 107,
    109, 215, 219
  revival, x, 11, 92, 97, 110–11,
    114–16, 147, 175–6, 186,
    216: history of, 114–15;
    proposals, 89–90, 148
  Sauteaux, 96
  teaching, 100, 124: aids, 116;
    remuneration for, 115–16
  under threat, 206
  unwritten, 6, 119
  Welsh, 114
  Woiwurrung, 38
laws, 114, 197
  Canadian, 63; Indian Act, 63
  gambling, 77
  Haudenosaunee: Great Law,
    41–2, 117, 129, 213–14
  Japanese: for the promotion of
    Ainu Culture, 184, 188
  U.S., 34, 51–2, 77, 83; Dawes
    Allotment Act, 83
lawyers, 108, 128
Lee Strasbourg Theater Institute, 72

Legat, Allice, 26
Leverhulme Study Abroad
  Fellowship, 18, 24
libraries, 82–3, 96, 97, 129
  see also Woodland Cultural
    Centre
Lickers
  Kathy, 19
  Keith, 9, 18–19, 25, 26, 62,
    89–90, 108
  Norman, 108
  Phyllis, 9, 18–19, 25, 204, 205
Little Salmon Carmacks First
  Nation, 156, 158–9, 216
Lock, Margaret and Richard, 23
logo, 5, 10, 51
London
  Horniman Museum, 191
  Spotlight Canada, 194
Longfellow's Hiawatha, 61
longhouse, ix, 70, 71, 75, 97, 115,
  120, 173–5
  ceremonial Longhouse, 40, 118,
    212–13
  influence, 141
'lost generation', 109, 201
Lower Hutt, 16, 111, 153
Lunger, Brian, 166

MRSA, 207
Maasai, 17, 67, 123–4, 208
  Oloipung'o, 124
Mackey, Eva, 18
McDonald, George, 23, 139
McFarlane, Nathalie, 21, 101–2
McLennan, Bill, 139
McLeod, Georgette, 22, 37
McMaster, Gerald, 189–90
McMaster University, 18, 119,
  174, 175
Makah, 161
  Cultural Centre, 23
Makivik Corporation, 171–2
Makonde artists, 136
Malaysia, 16, 87, 125
Manchester, 187

INDEX

Manitoba
  Indian Cultural Education
    Centre, 147
  Museum of Man and Nature, 24,
    36, 44, 50
  University of, 120
Maori, 38, 64–5, 73, 138–9,
  143–4, 153
  dancing, 184: *Kahurangi Maori
    Dance Theatre*, 150, 182;
    TeRangi Huata, 182
  language, 38, 120, 143; preschool
    immersion, 111, 122, 153
  rights to foreshore, 157, 161
  Studies, 16, 119–20
  Treasures, 153
maps, 84, 96, 138, 158, 170–1, 173
Maracle, Brian, 186
marae, 73, 117
  Tane-nui-a-rangi, 120, 139
  Waiwhetu, 111, 153
marriage, 158, 184, 196–7, 219
Marsden, Susan, 21
Martin, Ian, 26, 115
Martin, Lindsey, 21
Martin, Peter, 41
Martin-Hill, Dawn, 18
Martindale, Andrew, 18, 175
Mashantucket Pequot, 78–9
masks, 37, 43, 46, 48, 95, 117, 161
material culture, 12, 14, 39, 43,
  60–1, 99, 102, 120, 138, 196
Mather, Trina, 194
Mathews, Gordon, 198
medicine
  bundles, 35, 50, 96
  man, 197–8
  plants, 119, 126–7, 174–5,
    207, 216
Medicine, Beatrice, 26, 191
Melbourne
  Aboriginal places, 25, 150
  Koorie Heritage Trust, 128, 150
  Museum, 25, 30, 38
  University of, 16, 150
Melbourne, Hirini, 16

memories, 29, 44, 48, 134
methodology, 10, 12–27
Métis, 36, 128, 129, 139, 145, 183
Mexico, 10, 15, 30, 45–6, 84–5,
  188–9, 192
  Amecameca, 182–3
  government, 84
  Mixtec Highlands, 45
  National Museum of
    Anthropology, 45
Michigan, 62
Mi'kmac, 94, 98, 212
Milroy, Jadah, 185
Minnesota, 14, 31, 82, 187, 211
  Historical Society, 14, 83–4
  St. Paul, 14
missionaries, 70, 84, 107, 170, 210,
  211–12
mneumonic devices, 6, 8, 215
  as historical record, 8, 43
Mohawk, 41, 62, 74, 97, 154,
  175, 183
  College, 123
  community, 23, 113, 175;
    Kanatsiohareke, 175–6
  Her Majesty's Chapel of the, 74,
    108, 212
  history, 113, 173, 175, 213
  Institute, 87–9, 107, 125, 144;
    history of, 108, 109
  language, 74, 96–7, 105, 108,
    147, 175: broadcasting, 116,
    148; in school, 112, 113,
    116, 126
Mohican, 183
Montana
  Billings: Chief Plenty Coups State
    Park, 34
  Bozeman: Museum of the
    Rockies, 33, 44
  Pablo: People's Center, 111
Montreal, 9, 23, 62, 91, 97, 157, 172
  First Nations Botanical Garden, 209
Monture
  Angie, 20
  Janis, 20, 92–3

Morales, Teresa, 15, 45–6, 84
Morantz, Toby, 23
Morman church, 64
Morphy, Howard and Frances, 25
Mother Earth, 49, 121
movie
    industry, 61
    theater, 167
Munro, Neil, 187
museum(s), 2, 12, 28–55, 138, 161, 167, 169, 172
    advisory board, 32, 33
    alternatives to, 81–7
    audiences, 28–30
    "bicultural," 38
    buffs, 59, 202
    changing face of, 32–8, 156, 187
    collections, 8, 31, 52, 91, 188–9
    community, 45–7
    curators, 2–3, 29, 189–90, 214
    as 'death lodge', 49
    defunct, 100
    Indigenous view of, 47–50
    International Council of, 46
    labels, 32, 86
    "living," 65, 100
    and nation-building, 5–6, 8, 30
    open-air, 59
    opening up to community, 28, 36, 40, 44, 46, 137–8, 191–2
    as platform for dialogue, 44, 187–93, 215
    state-of-the-art, 78, 188
music, 102, 116, 123, 124, 127, 142, 143, 151
    awards, 146
    broadcasting, 147
    collection of, 84–5
    digitalizing, 137
musical instruments, 126, 144
    didjeridu, 151
musicians, 134, 151, 198
Musqueam, 36, 37, 157
myths, 50, 133

NAGPRA, 50–1
NGOs, 123, 181, 186
Nairobi, 17, 28–30, 137–8
Nakamura Naohiro, 193
name(s), ix, 13, 58, 97, 116, 177, 216
    for identity, 11, 83, 158
    reclaiming, 158–9, 162, 170, 176, 206, 216
naming ceremony, 71
National Museum of the American Indian, 26, 32, 121–2, 139, 189–90
Nationalism, 30, 157
Native(s)
    American Dance and Music Festival, 173
    status, ix, 197–8
    Studies, 119–20, 128
Navajo, 83
Netherlands Development Organisation (SNV), 67
networks, 9, 17, 182
Neufeld, David, 22, 68, 216
New Age
    Druids, 161
New Guinea, 207
New Caledonia, 48, 86–7, 133–5
New Internationalist, 210
New York, 91, 182
    State, 78, 158, 173: Albany, 30; Finger Lakes, 158, 172–4; Ithaca, 173; College, 174; Mohawk Valley, 175–6; Salamanca, 47, 78; Upstate Citizens for Equality, 173–4
New Zealand, 16, 73, 107, 117, 119, 153, 182, 185
    government, 157
    Te Papa Museum, 38, 139
    Waikato University, 16
    see also Aotearoa
Newfoundland, 182
news reporting, 121, 146
newsletters, 67, 91
    Wadrihwa, 91, 92, 108, 192–3

Index

newspaper
 clipping, 91
 Native, 186; *Windspeaker*, 186, 193
Niagara Falls, 43, 62, 182
Nicaragua, 183–4
Nicks, John, 18
Nicks, Trudy, 18, 20, 43, 52, 62
Nisga'a, 22
Nivkhi, 184
Nomoto, Masahiro, xi, 24, 184, 219
Northwest Territories, 115, 147, 190
Nova Scotia, 94
N'tila, Robino, 17, 135–7
Nuffield Foundation, 17
Nunavik, 158, 163, 165, 167, 171–2
Nunavut, 23, 113, 115, 158, 159, 163–71, 209
 Arctic College, 164, 168
 government, 167
 Land Claims Agreement, 167
 Legislative Assembly, 168, 169; Building, 164–5
 Research Institute, 23, 164
 Studies, 171
 Tourism, 164, 166, 167
 Tunngavik Incorp (NTI), 167

Oaxaca, 15, 45
 Santa Ana del Valle, 15, 84–5
O'Biso, Carol, 138
Oceania Centre for Arts and Culture, 16, 135
Ohsweken, 112, 142, 148, 185
 New Orators Youth Project, 149
Ojibwe, 14, 82, 183
 language, 36, 116, 126, 146, 147
 people, 60
 reservation, 31, 187
Ojicree, 183
Ole Ngila, Lesikar, 17, 105, 123–4
Ole-Sikar, Tom, 17, 67
Olsen, Brooke and Ernie, 174
Oneida, 78, 173
 Shako:wi Culture Center, 78, 173
Ongoongotau, Mele, 64

Ontario, 8, 89, 125, 142, 148, 165, 176
 Arts Council, 92, 148
 Ministry of Education, 9
 Royal Ontario Museum, 43, 52, 90, 148
 Southern: Aboriginal Tourism Association of, 74, 148, 193; Tourism Association, 74
oral
 traditions, 63, 134, 215
 transmission, 6, 112, 119, 129, 188
Oronhyatekha, Dr., 41, 43, 148
Ottawa, 20, 22, 30, 38, 52, 62, 77, 139, 171, 194
Oxford, x–xi, 14, 24, 31, 41, 82, 99

Pacific
 islands, 64–7
 peoples, 120, 133–4, 139
paintings, 30, 32, 40, 170
 interpretation of, 132, 150–1
Paiz, Nokomis, 14, 31–2, 82, 187, 216
Pakeha, 38
pan-Indianism, 62
Pangnirtung, 24, 169–71, 209
 Angmarlik Centre, 169–70
 Arts and Crafts Centre, 169, 171
parades, 6–7, 19, 22, 69
Paris, 10
 the Louvre, 134
Parks Canada, 22, 23, 68–9, 101, 160, 163, 167, 169
 Visitor Centres, 162, 169–71
Patridge, Taqraliq, 23, 171–2
patronage, 39
Patterson, Mary, 16
Pawnee, 33
peace, 44, 133, 140, 216
 blueprint for, 41, 213–15
 Great Tree of, 97, 154, 213
 pipes of, 211
Peacemaker, the, 42, 97, 211, 213–14
Peers, Laura, 14

Pelly-Landrie, Linda, 50, 96
Perez, German, 15
Peters, Margaret and Teddy, 116
petroglyphs, 151
Pettipas, Katherine, 24, 36
photographers, 194–5
photographs, 82, 111, 165, 166, 168, 188, 190
Piano, Renzo, 133–4
Pickford, Mary, 61
Pine Ridge reservation, 47
pioneers, 68, 125, 175
Pipestone (U.S.) National Park, 34, 211
Pitt Rivers Museum, xi, 13–14, 18, 22, 31, 49, 99, 100, 184, 187
Planet IndigenUS, 146, 148
play, 123, 125, 142
Podemski, Jennifer, 146
poles, 36, 48, 141
  totem, 62, 70, 99–102, 160
political
  activities, 10, 11, 83, 157
  situations, 92
  systems, 40, 97, 164–5
politics courses, 120
Polynesian
  belief about art, 153
  Cultural Centre, 64–5
  Studies, 65
Pope, Rob, 26
Porter, Brian, 19, 141–3
  Two-Row-Architect, 143
Porter, Kim, 193–4
Porter, Tom, 106, 175–6
potlatch, 37, 43, 53, 95, 100
Powless
  Bill, 40
  Carole, 144
  Naomi, 144–5, 182–3
powwows, 76, 145–6, 148, 182, 193
prayers, 211
  of thanksgiving, 117–18, 211
Presley, Elvis, 61
pride, 79, 109, 186, 196, 220

in ancestry, 1, 178, 197
rekindling, ix, 10, 46, 184
Prince Rupert, 21–2
  Museum of Northern British Columbia, 21
  Sea Fest, 22
protest, 51–2
Puketapu, Patsy, 16, 111
Puketapu-Hetet, Erenora, 16, 153

Quebec, 96–7, 115–16, 123, 165, 171–2
Quechuan stories, 192
Queen Charlotte Islands, 159
  see also Haida Gwaii

radio, x, 97, 115, 116, 143, 147–8, 163
Rapid City
  Journey Museum, 33
recordings (audio and video), 86, 90, 115, 117–18, 124, 146, 128–9, 134, 140, 176
  CD-ROM, 129, 163
recycling, 49
Red Lake Nation, 14, 31, 187
  Tribal Information Center, 14, 82–4, 110
regalia, 7, 11, 14, 76, 116, 145–6, 190
Regenvanu, Ralph, 16, 48, 66, 86, 207–8
Regina, 121–2, 139
  Royal Sasakatchewan Museum, 35, 200
  University, 121
Reid, Bill
  School of Art, 101
religion, 34, 127, 210–13
  respect for others, 211
Rendille, 17
renewal
  cultural, 2, 9, 10, 33, 48, 133–9, 143–4
repatriation, 8, 11, 46, 49, 50–3, 90–1, 100–2, 160–1, 215–16

replicas, 43, 51
representation, xi, 4
　as imprisonment, 2
　self, 1, 5, 12, 82
researchers, 90, 145
resistance, 133–9, 174, 186
resources, 83
　government, 94
　management of, 100, 102, 170
　natural, 68, 141–2, 207
　virtually unlimited, 134
respect, 31, 34, 35, 43, 129, 138–9, 176
　learning of, 106, 113, 195–6
　losing, 192
　mutual, 196, 211, 213
　for others, 211–13
　protocols of, 70
　self-, 144
　for stories, 50
responsibility, 106, 208
revenge, 201–2
revival, 11, 14, 79, 132, 150, 157
　cultural, 10, 11, 144, 175–6, 180, 182, 185, 203, 217:
　　proposals for, 89, 219;
　　workshops of, 86, 162, 175
　religious, 34, 175
Rigano, John, 17
rites of passage, 128
ritual, 71–2, 73, 90, 116, 138, 212
　greeting, 73, 117
Roberts, Freda, 22, 48
Roberts, Mike, 16
Rodney, Pakon, Bong, 186
Rossen, Jack, 174
Rotorua, 16, 30, 193
　Maori Arts and Crafts Institute, 73, 117
Royal Commission on Aboriginal Peoples, 115
Royal Scottish Museum, 14, 24, 187, 190
Russia
　Beslen, 201

sacred
　knowledge, 66, 151–2
　land, 33, 119, 211
　materials, 129, 211
　objects, 14, 31, 35, 43, 49, 50, 96
Sahlins, Marshall, 4
Salish, 183
　Coast, 71, 178–9, 183; stories, 71–2, 183
　language, 71, 111, 179
salmon, x, 71, 218
　drying racks, 140–1
Sami, 184
Samoa, 25, 64
Sanborn, Andrea, 22, 95–6
Saskatchewan, 50, 121–2
　Indian: Cultural Centre, 50, 96; Nations, 121
　Wanuskewin, 74
Saskatoon, 50, 74, 96, 128, 149
　Treaty Awareness Speakers Bureau, 128
Saulteau, 35
Sawkins, Phil, 26
Scarangella, Linda, 18, 21
schools, 11, 57, 68, 78, 133, 145, 182
　curriculum, 125, 128, 129, 158–9, 163
　dropouts, 94
　immersion, 97, 106, 110–16, 123, 147, 180; preschool, 111, 148
　offering language, 111–12
　residential, 87–9, 106–10, 176, 185: abuse in, 212; Christian, 105, 110; escape from, 106–7, 143; museum displays about, 110; recommendations for closure of, 89, 108; reunion of "survivors," 89; "reverse," 176
　speakers to, 92
　trips, 168–9, 173
　teachers, 89, 108, 111, 126; respect for, 106
　tribal, 112

Index

science, 30, 31, 50, 113, 161, 209
    camp, 113
Scotland, 57, 147, 177, 180, 187, 190
    dancing, 179, 183
    people, 179, 183
Scott, Pauline, 23
Scow, Leonard, 72
sculpture, 32, 75, 150
sea, 100–01, 133, 157, 160
sealskin, 164, 209
sealing, 169
Seattle, 22, 30
    Burke Museum, 23, 37, 53
self-governance, 11, 70
self-representation, 43, 44–7, 81–103, 215
Seneca, 173
    Ganondagan historical site, 173
    National Museum, 47, 78, 173
Service, Robert, 69
settlers, 29, 57, 65, 125–6, 172
Shamsul, A.B., 16
SHARE, 174–5
sharing, 101, 103, 145, 185–6, 193, 194–8, 200–02, 214
Shelton, Anthony, 21, 188–9
Shimizu, Katsunobu, 26
Shirley, Jamal, 23
shops, 62, 64, 77, 78, 95, 138, 203, 218–19
    craft, 175
    gift, 99, 101, 151–2, 167, 189
    and stalls, 76
Shore, Crispin and Fiona, 16
Simpson, Sally, 16
Singapore, 125
singing, 64–5, 143, 145, 146, 179, 183
    and songs, 69, 96, 102, 116, 123, 128
Sioux, 33, 47, 145, 175, 211
    languages, 33, 36, 96
    "look," 62
    see also Lakota
Sivan, Athi, 16

Six Nations, 9, 117, 148, 208, 212–14
    Band Council, 19, 203–4, 205
    of the Grand River, 9, 74, 89, 173
    member(s), 20, 43, 74, 146, 205
    Powwow, 76, 185
    rationale for alliance, 41–2, 97, 213–14
    reserve, 18, 19, 25, 74, 109, 121, 173, 176, 204
    schools, 112; Emily C. General, 141–3
    Tourism, 75, 148
    Writers, 76, 129, 146, 185
    see also Haudenosaunee
Skelton, Judy, 26
Skutnabb-Kangas, Tove, 112, 200
Smith, Linda Tuhiwai, 3
Smith, Wendy, 25
Smithsonian Institution, 31, 46
smudging, 34, 72
snowshoes, 89
social
    scientists, 3
    work courses, 120
South America, 191–2, 207, 209
South Dakota, 197, 211
    Cheyenne River, 175
    state museum, 33
    Wall, 47
South Korea, 182
South Pacific, 14, 48, 85–7, 133–5
souvenirs, 59, 75, 131–2, 136
Sowdluapik, Sakiasie, 170–1
S'pa<u>k</u>wús Slúlum (Eagle Song Dancers), 183
spelling, ix
Spencer, Baldwyn, 38–**9**
spirituality, 34, 43, 72, 120, 121, 138–9, 153, 210–13
    Native, 127
    revitalizing, 175–6
Squamish, 21, 71, 157, 183–4
stereotypes, 8, 40, 52, 129
    formation of, 60–3

Stonehenge, 161
Storyeum, 25, 71–2
story(ies), 41, 58, 69, 98, 108, 116, 131, 177, 219
    re-telling, 47, 158, 185
    passing on, 159, 176
    safeguarding, 96, 206
    sharing, 147, 152, 185–6
    telling, 33, 36, 40, 49, 52, 64–5, 71, 75, 102, 116, 117, 123, 149, 151, 163, 193: through dance, 144–5; own, 91, 143
Strand, Diane, 22, 162, 184
student(s), x, xi, 138, 144, 174, 193, 198
demonstrations, 10
summer, 58, 91, 171, 219
suicide, 94
Sullivan, Ann, 16, 157
summer solstice, 121, 141, 161
Surman, Peter, 15–16
survival, 11–12, 95, 109, 160, 161
    lack of, 107
Survival International, 181, 209
sweat lodges, 34
Sweden, 52, 191
Sweetgrass First Nations Language Council, 20, 116
    annual conference, 105–6, 112, 114–15, 146, 175, 200
Symons, T.H.B. Fellowship, 18

TNT, the Northern Thunder, 148–9
Tagé Cho Hudän, 156, 216
Tahiti, 64
Taiwan, 184, 219
    Aboriginal people, 184
Takaya, 25, 71–2
Tandanya National Aboriginal Cultural Institute, 25, 150–2
Tanzania, 17, 28, 67–8, 111, 123–4, 135–7, 191, 208
    Arts Council, 136
    Bagamoyo, 144

National Museum of, 44; Ethnic Days Programme, 44–5
taonga, 138–9, 153
Task Force on Museums and First Peoples, 20, 50–4
Tasmania, 151–3, 156
tax, 173, 197
technological achievements, 3, 6, 134, 154
fonoteca, 84
Indigenous, 64–5, 126–7, 161; display of, 90
mediateque, 134
Tegler, Jim, 23
Tekahonwén:sere Diabo, Melvin, 114
television, 143, 163, 208
    broadcasting training programme, 147
terminology, ix
    anthropological, 12
terra nullis, 8, 11, 157, 176
Teshi, Sigiko, 219
Texas
    San Antonio, 182
theater, 65, 102, 118, 132, 143–51, 218–20
theft, 10, 11, 49, 51
theory, 3, 10
Thomas, Dennis, 25, 71–2
Thomas, Jake, 117, 119
Thomas, Sam and Lorna Thomas Hill, 214
Thomas, Yvonne, 117
timber industry, 160
Tinga Tinga, Edward Said, 136–7
tipis, 33, 35, 58, 73–4, 128
    shaped ceremonial room, 121
Tlingit
    Heritage Centre, 22, 48, 141
    objects in Haida museum, 101
Tokyo, x, 10, 188
tools, 57, 125, 165, 166
Toledo, Francisco, 84–5
Tonga, 64–5

240　Index

Toronto, 30, 62, 108, 149, 182
　Centre for Aboriginal Media, 148
　Centre for Indigenous Theatre, 149
　First Nations House, 121
　Harbourfront, 148
　Native Canadian Centre, 128
　Native Theatre School, 149
　Sky Dome, 75, 146, 193
Torres Straits Islanders, 151
tours, 17, 20, 21, 23, 24, 34, 37, 38, 57, 75
　educational, 66, 125
　walking, 124
tourism
　Aboriginal, 56–80, 95–6, 100, 193–4; management, 22, 123
　associations, 70
　cost of, 64, 67
　cultural, 17, 22, 60, 64, 67–8
　international, 193–4
　literature, 74
　power of good, 63
　profits from, 60, 63–7
　as support, 95–6, 100, 137, 169
　world, 59; conference on, 59
tourists, 9, 44, 48, 136, 138, 153, 173, 202, 216
　doubts about, 100
　trap, 218
trade, 7, 9, 33, 40, 100, 101, 108, 158
training, 51, 86, 117, 144
　courses, 22, 58, 90, 102–3, 127, 149, 182
　programs, 95, 119, 147
travelers, 196
　'purist', 59
　wariness of, 58–60
traveling shows, 61–2, 168, 187
Travis, 34, 211
treasure(s),
　box of, 47, 95
　house, 48, 96
treaties, 36, 83, 143
　broken, 47, 215

Trent University, 119
Tr'ondëk Hwëch'in
　Cultural Centre, 22, 48, 69
　First People, 37, 69, 140–1, 159
Trudeau, Pierre, 69
Tsimshian people, 175, 183
Tsleilwaututh First Nation, 71–2
"Turtle Island," 193
　Tourism Company, 77

Uganda, 137
Uilta, 184
Ukoti, Emmanuel John, 136
U'Mista Cultural Centre, 22, 37, 46, 95–6, 110, 161, 188
United Kingdom, 109, 114, 161, 187
　Surrey Institute of Art and Design, 194–5
United Nations
　High Commission for Human Rights, 181
　Standing Committee on Indigenous Peoples, 181
United States, 7, 20, 47, 110, 138, 150, 161
　Canada border, 9, 20, 34, 97, 173, 214
　'dime novels', 61
　government, 62, 127
　National Wildlife Federation, 175
　Plains, 15, 57
University of British Columbia, ix, 157: First Nations House of Learning, 120, 139; Museum of Anthropology, 21, 36–7, 188–9; Reciprocal Research Network, 188
University of the South Pacific, 16, 135
University of Western Ontario, 105, 108

Vancouver, 21, 22, 25, 36, 71, 157, 179, 185, 188, 218
　Capilano Park, 70, 99
　Chinese community, 21

Index

Grouse Mountain, 22, 70, 178, 183; Corporation, 71
Island, 22, 37, 43, 95–6, 108: Campbell River Museum, 37; Nimmo Bay, 95
Stanley Park, 70
VanEvery, L.M., 185
Vanuatu, 16, 147, 186, 207
  Ambrym, 186
  Kastom, 86
  Lolihor Youth Awareness Team, 186
  national museum, 48, 66, 85–7; *Tabu* room, 86
  Port Vila, 48–9, 66, 135
Victoria, 30
  Island, 77
  Pacific People's Partnership, 186
  Royal British Columbia Museum, 37, 53
'villages', x, 4, 44, 58–9, 117, 218–20
  Aboriginal Experiences, 77, 194
  Ekasup Cultural Village, 66, 73, 85
  Kahnawake tourist, 62
  'Ksan Historical Village, 48
  Polynesian, 64–5
  Sentosa Asian Village, 125
visions, 34
voices, 33
  Aboriginal, 38, 188–9
  contemporary, 33, 37
  of people, 182: displayed, 39, 168–9, 187, 189–90; in 'story sticks', 32, 34

Waarusha people, 67–8
Wabie, Bernadette, 20, 92, 126, 129
wampum, 117, 121, 215
  two-row, 40–1, 43, 143, 213, 215
war, 8, 10, 44, 89, 100, 133, 180, 213
Warry, Wayne, 18
Washington
  DC, 30, 182, 189–90; Museum of American History

State, 22; Neah Bay, 161
  University of, 23, 53
weapons, 7, 162, 213, 216
Weasel Head, Frank, 49, 187
weaving, 37, 66, 117, 120, 138–9, 153, 187–8
  meaning of, 153
websites, 67, 129–30, 135, 180, 190
Wellington, 16, 111, 143, 193
Wells, Katherine, 25, 152
Wenzel, George, 23
West, Rick, 26
Western
  world, 2, 185–6, 206, 208
whaling, 161, 169, 170, 209
Whetung Ojibwa Centre, 77
Whiteduck, Gilbert, 21, 98
Whitehorse, 22, 162
Wier, Janis, 18
'wilderness', 157, 159, 162
  camps, 70
Wilfred Laurier University, 127
Wilkinson, Jane, 24, 187
Williams, Inawinytji, 131, 149
Winnipeg, 24, 36, 50, 147, 185
  Thunderbird House, 128
wisdom, 201–2, 205, 210, 216
Wogin, Gill, 20
Wood, Felicity, 26
Woodland Cultural Centre, 8–10, 20, 52, 74, 75, 82, 129, 144, 203
  board members of, 90, 92, 108
  educational; program, 125–7
  events, 25, 145, 153–4, 182, 213
  gallery, 90
  gift shop, 19
  history of, 87–93, 107, 110
  and language, 105
  library and resource centre, 19, 87–**8**, 90–2
  mobile unit, 91
  museum, 20, 39–43, 90–1, 117
  performing arts centre plan, 148–9
  rationale for, 87–92

Woodland Cultural—*continued*
  and tourism, 60–3
  visits, 192–3
World
  Council of Indigenous Peoples, 181
  Fairs, 7, 9, 60
  Heritage: Indigenous Peoples
    Council of Experts, 181;
    UNESCO sites of, 57, 160
  Indigenous Peoples Conference
    on Education, 122
Wounded Knee
  Museum of, 47
  site of massacre, 197
'wrapping', 6
  as power, 7, 215
writers, 129, 185–6, 196

Wu, Joy, 16
Wurundjeri people, 38

Xai:sla, 21, 37

Yellowknife
  Prince of Wales Northern
    Heritage Centre, 190
Yoneda, Yoshihara, 25
Yukon, 22, 48, 68–70, 140, 158,
    162, 165
  River, 69, 141
  Teslin, 22, 48, 141

Zapotec, 15, 84, 85
  Shan-Dany museum, 45
Zeme, Kara Dawne, 23